The Story of Modern International Justice, 1993-2025

David J. Scheffer · Mark S. Ellis

The Story of Modern International Justice, 1993-2025

Springer

David J. Scheffer
Council on Foreign Relations (CFR)
Washington, DC, USA

Mark S. Ellis
International Bar Association
London, UK

ISBN 978-3-032-33242-4 ISBN 978-3-032-33243-1 (eBook)
https://doi.org/10.1007/978-3-032-33243-1

This work was supported by International Bar Association.

This Springer imprint is published by the registered company Springer Nature Switzerland AG
The registered company address is: Gewerbestrasse 11, 6330 Cham, Switzerland

This book is dedicated to those members of the International Bar Association who have dedicated their professional lives to the pursuit of international justice before the modern atrocity crimes tribunals and the international and regional courts that in our time have enforced fundamental human rights and international criminal law

Foreword

The final decades of my professional life as a lawyer, prosecutor, and judge coincide with the 32 years during which modern international justice rose: 1993–2025. The many tribunals that were created and the permanent courts that were strengthened during this period were all engaged with powerful cases that generated significant bodies of jurisprudence. Indeed, their story is only beginning to be told. Co-authors David J. Scheffer and Mark S. Ellis, whom I have known for decades, bore witness to this phenomenon and indeed have made their own substantial contributions to the pursuit of international criminal justice and international human rights during their dynamic careers.

The Story of Modern International Justice, 1993–2025 is timely and essential for a foundational understanding of what transpired during the post-Cold War era in an impressive number of judicial bodies: International Court of Justice, International Tribunals for the former Yugoslavia and Rwanda, Special Court for Sierra Leone, Extraordinary Chambers in the Courts of Cambodia, Special Tribunal for Lebanon, Extraordinary African Chambers, International Criminal Court, European Court of Human Rights, Inter-American Court of Human Rights, and African Court of Human and Peoples' Rights. Never before in the history of humankind have so many leading perpetrators of atrocity crimes and governments responsible for gross violations of human rights been held to account and international justice upheld and fortified. At the same time, we must recognize that genocide, crimes against humanity, war crimes, aggression, and violations of fundamental human rights and United Nations Charter prohibitions on the use of force, have continued, unacceptably, to the present day. But there has been a reckoning in recent decades, and justice and the rule of law have been served in international and regional courtrooms. That story is told in this book, not only with clarity, but also with the very words used by judges in rendering theirs. Scheffer and Ellis also rightly devote an entire chapter to the role of defense counsel, who have been and remain indispensable to the litigation of every case before all the tribunals and courts discussed by the authors. As a prosecutor, this was always a particular area of focus for me. International criminal tribunals are not judged by convictions alone; they must adhere to international standards of fair trials, which include an adequately resourced defense.

Now, with the birth of the Special Tribunal for the Crime of Aggression against Ukraine, we anticipate the historic work it will accomplish in the years ahead. And we await the verdicts of the Kosovo Specialist Chambers.

When I served as the first Chief Prosecutor of the International Criminal Tribunals for the former Yugoslavia and for Rwanda, the challenges were daunting both in following the tradition of the Nuremberg Trials and in carving out a novel structure of international criminal justice. I wondered at times how the future would unfold, not only on my watch but in the experiences of my successors. After reading this book and looking back at three decades of hard work by prosecutors, plaintiffs' lawyers, defense counsel, civil counsel, registrars, and judges and the mountain of jurisprudence that locks in principles of international justice in perpetuity, I see no downside to what has transpired. Mistakes occurred along the way, of course, but the achievements overshadow the setbacks and critiques, however properly reasoned, that we who have worked in the trenches fully recognize. The foundation for international justice has been built, and there must never be any turning back.

Richard Goldstone

Richard Goldstone formerly served at the Chief Prosecutor of the International Criminal Tribunals for the former Yugoslavia and Rwanda, Judge of the Supreme Court of South Africa and of the Constitutional Court of South Africa, Chair of the Commission of Inquiry Regarding the Prevention of Public Violence and Intimidation in South Africa, and Chair of the International Commission on Kosovo. He received the 2009 MacArthur Award for International Justice and is author of *For humanity: reflections of a war crimes investigator* (Yale University Press, 2000).

Acknowledgements

the global voice of
the legal profession

The authors warmly acknowledge the International Bar Association (IBA) for its indispensable support in making this book possible. The IBA is the world's largest organization of international legal practitioners, bar associations and law societies. The IBA's present membership is comprised of more than 80,000 individual international lawyers from most of the world's leading law firms and some 170 countries. The IBA was established in 1947. Based on the founding principles of the United Nations, its aim is to protect and advance the rule of law globally. The IBA was born out of the conviction that an organization of legal practitioners could contribute to global stability and peace through the administration of justice. The IBA views this book as an important expression of its mission, particularly in the book's focus on enforcing the rule of law through the international and regional courts and tribunals of the modern era. Many members of the IBA have been part of that judicial endeavor and they take great pride in what has been accomplished while knowing that more always needs to be done in pursuit of international justice. The IBA's Special Project Fund allocated funding to this project so that the authors could undertake the research and writing required of it. Without this funding, completing this book would not have been achieved.

The authors would like to thank Alexander Sarchet, Ryan Byrne, Matteo Reed, Ashley Sebastian, Matthew Fox, Chelsea Wright, and Kai Macauley for their skilled research and editing assistance, and Talia Dove for her valuable administrative support. The library of the Sandra Day O'Connor College of Law of Arizona State University provided access to literary resources. The authors also express their appreciation to Laura Hofmann and Julia Bieler of Springer Nature Switzerland AG for their editing and tireless cooperation in publishing the book.

Finally, Mark Ellis wants to thank his son, Andrew, for his love and support. David Scheffer expresses his deep gratitude to the International Bar Association, family, friends, and colleagues who have supported his work on this book. He also wishes to thank the Francqui Foundation in Belgium and the opportunity it afforded him to be the International Francqui Professor of 2022 at KU Leuven under the initiative and collaboration of Professor Stephan Parmentier. Scheffer's lectures in Belgium under that professorship informed the beginnings of this book.

Competing Interests The authors have no competing interests to declare that are relevant to the content of this manuscript.

Contents

About the Authors

David J. Scheffer is Professor of Practice in the School of Politics and Global Studies at Arizona State University and a Senior Fellow at the Council on Foreign Relations focusing on international law and international criminal justice. He was the Mayer Brown/Robert A. Helman Professor of Law at Northwestern University Pritzker School of Law (2006–2020) and is Director Emeritus of the Center for International Human Rights. Scheffer was the first U.S. Ambassador at Large for War Crimes Issues (1997–2001) and negotiated the creation of five war crimes tribunals. He was the U.N. Secretary-General's Special Expert for U.N. Assistance to the Khmer Rouge Trials (2012–2018) and was Senior Adviser and Counsel to Dr. Madeleine Albright during her tenure as the U.S. Permanent Representative to the United Nations, when he also represented the U.S. Mission to the United Nations on the National Security Council's Deputies Committee (1993–1997). Scheffer was Vice President of the American Society of International Law (2020–2022) and the International Francqui Professor at KU Leuven in 2022. He co-authored, with Mark S. Ellis, *The UN Charter: Five Pillars for Humankind* (Springer, 2025). He also authored the award-winning *All the Missing Souls: A Personal History of the War Crimes Tribun*als (Princeton, 2012) and *The Sit Room: In the Theater of War and Peace* (Oxford, 2019). Among his honors, he received the American Bar Association's *2024 Eleanor Roosevelt Prize for Global Human Rights Advancement* and the *Berlin Prize* of the American Academy in Berlin in 2013. Scheffer is a graduate of Harvard, Oxford, and Georgetown Universities and is a member of the New York, District of Columbia and Supreme Court Bars.

Mark S. Ellis is the Executive Director of the International Bar Association. Previously, he directed the American Bar Association's Central European and Eurasian Law Initiative. He served as Legal Advisor to the Independent International Commission on Kosovo and was appointed by the OSCE to advise on creating Serbia's War Crimes Tribunal. Ellis was actively involved with the ICTY *Tadić* case and with the Iraqi High Tribunal and acted as legal consultant to the defense team in the *Nuon Chea* case at the Extraordinary Chambers in the Courts of Cambodia. He previously served as Chair of the ICTY Advisory Panel and the U.N.-created Advisory

Panel in Matters Relating to Defence Counsel of the International Residual Mechanism for Criminal Tribunals. Ellis is presently an adjunct Professor at Florida State University College of Law. Twice a Fulbright Scholar at the Economic Institute in Zagreb, Croatia, he earned his J.D. and B.S. (Economics) degrees from Florida State University and his Ph.D. in Law from King's College, London. He has published extensively on international humanitarian law, war crimes tribunals, and the development of the rule of law. Among his honors, Ellis was awarded the *Ukraine Order of Merit* in 2026. He is the recipient of the American Bar Association's *World Order Under Law Award*, Florida State University's *Distinguished Alumni Award*, and the *International Impact Award* from King's College London. In 2024, Ellis was made a *Fellow* of Kings College. Scheffer and Ellis are co-authors of *The UN Charter: Five Pillars for Humankind* (Springer 2025).

Chapter 1
Introduction: Path-Breaking Courts and Cases

During the last three decades, international justice arrived as a permanent feature of world affairs and international law. By "international justice" is meant holding accountable individual perpetrators of atrocity crimes (genocide, crimes against humanity, war crimes, aggression)[1] and judging the responsibility of nations for the use of armed force, the protection of human life and human rights, and the prevention of atrocities. The judicial bodies responsible for the advancement of international justice, particularly from 1993 to the present day, include the International Court of Justice, an impressive number of special atrocity crimes tribunals, and three permanent regional courts of human rights. The litigation before these courts, representing the highest ideals of the rule of law in the global community, reveals remarkable advancements in international justice within a relatively short space of time. No other book conveys this story of progress holistically but succinctly for a general audience of readers. Granted, critiques of the modern era of jurisprudence abound and merit recognition.[2] But we aim to share with a global audience the judgments of international courts and tribunals that have inspired the rise of modern international justice in our lifetimes.

The transformative events in world affairs of recent years have challenged the integrity of international organizations, international law (or the "rules-based international order"), and international criminal and human rights law eliciting critiques that span the spectrum of political ideology and legal theory. One solid truth is that there are gale force winds jeopardizing and shaping the future of the world order. Despite such disruption, we strongly believe it is essential to maintain a healthy perspective of what in fact has transpired during recent decades in the realm of international justice and that continues to fortify the rule of law globally. There are standing judicial judgments and ongoing litigation within institutions of high

[1] Scheffer (2012), pp. 428-437; Hola, Nyseth Nzitatira, and Weerdesteijun (eds) (2022).

[2] Drumbl (2007); Fraser (2008); Schabas (2012); Kurze and Lamont (eds) (2019); Hillebrecht (2021); Ibsen (2023); Kurze, Peterka-Benton, and Rubin (2024).

D. J. Scheffer and M. S. Ellis, *The Story of Modern International Justice, 1993-2025*,
https://doi.org/10.1007/978-3-032-33243-1_1

integrity that will, in our view, outlive contemporary challenges by authoritarian and nationalist leaders and governments.

Our intent in this book is to supplement the contemporary phenomenon of demoralizing and negativist perspectives of international law and the courts that adjudicate its meaning and relevance in the modern world with a brief book that narrates the significant achievements and advances in international justice of recent years. Often the impressive record of jurisprudence developed by and pending before the international and regional courts and tribunals is sidelined as the focus turns to both populist and scholarly skepticism and cynicism of international norms and institutions. We want to cast into high profile what has transpired and is currently underway in the name of international justice so that the rush by some political leaders to abandon the principles and institutions of international law is tempered by the truth of what has been accomplished. It is always easier to demolish rather than to build and preserve, but we choose the latter path.

We focus on thirteen courts, some of permanent character, others of temporary or residual tenure, and one recently created. The five fully operational permanent courts are the International Court of Justice (The Hague),[3] the International Criminal Court (The Hague),[4] the European Court of Human Rights (Strasbourg),[5] the Inter-American Court of Human Rights (San José),[6] and the African Court on Human and Peoples' Rights (Arusha).[7]

Seven other courts, which no longer exist except in residual form, have been of either *ad hoc* character (authorized by the U.N. Security Council under U.N. Charter Chapter VII enforcement power) or hybrid character (created by special legal arrangements). They included the *ad hoc* International Criminal Tribunals for the former Yugoslavia (The Hague)[8] and Rwanda (Arusha)[9] and the hybrid bodies of the Special Court for Sierra Leone (Freetown),[10] Extraordinary Chambers in the Courts of Cambodia (Phnom Penh),[11] Special Tribunal for Lebanon (The Hague),[12] and Extraordinary African Chambers (Dakar).[13] Still functional is the temporary *ad hoc* International Residual Mechanism for Criminal Tribunals (The Hague),[14] having been established by the U.N. Security Council in 2010 to complete the remaining

[3] International Court of Justice (2026).

[4] International Criminal Court (2026).

[5] European Court of Human Rights (2026).

[6] Inter-American Court of Human Rights (2026).

[7] African Court on Human and People's Rights (2026).

[8] United Nations International Criminal Tribunal for the former Yugoslavia (2017).

[9] United Nations International Criminal Tribunal for Rwanda (2015).

[10] Residual Special Court for Sierra Leone (2026).

[11] The Extraordinary Chambers in the Courts of Cambodia (2026).

[12] Refworld (2026).

[13] Williams (2013).

[14] United Nations International Residual Mechanism for Criminal Tribunals (2026).

work of the International Criminal Tribunals for the former Yugoslavia and Rwanda once their respective mandates finally ended in 2017 and 2015.[15]

The newest court, namely the Special Tribunal for the Crime of Aggression against Ukraine (The Hague), was established in 2025 by agreement between the Council of Europe and Ukraine.[16] The Special Tribunal's investigative and prosecutorial work lies ahead, but already its mere existence reaffirms the vibrancy of the legal principles at stake where the situation pertains to the crime of aggression. The Appendix at the end of this book provides data on the disposition of cases before all of the criminal tribunals examined in the following pages.

In this book we will focus on key cases before each of these courts as emblematic of the defense and advancement of major principles of international law and, in particular, principles of international criminal law. At the International Court of Justice, the cases we have selected address the crime of genocide, the legality of the use of force, application of the *erga omnes* principle, climate change, and the legality of the threat or use of nuclear weapons. With respect to the atrocity crimes tribunals that were built and have held criminal trials during the last thirty years, an enormous amount of their jurisprudence created, clarified and strengthened rules on the crime of genocide, crimes against humanity, war crimes, international terrorism, and torture as well as general principles of law about superior responsibility, complicity, superior orders, criteria of gravity of crimes, defending the rights of the accused, head of state immunity, amnesties, complementarity with domestic prosecutions, jurisdiction, and what constitutes the greatest responsibility for the commission of atrocity crimes. The newly-established Special Tribunal for the Crime of Aggression against Ukraine will pioneer how the crime of aggression should be investigated and then how and against whom it will be prosecuted (with respect to the Russia-Ukraine War), thus creating precedents that doubtless will inform the International Criminal Court as other aggression situations and cases begin to appear on its docket in the future.

The three permanent regional human rights courts in Europe, Latin America, and Africa have been exceptionally active in recent decades and delivered landmark rulings on a wide range of legal principles protecting the human rights of individuals or concerning social issues. Several excellent treatises examining the corpus of their jurisprudence have been recently published.[17] The European Court of Human Rights has ruled, for example, on the right to life, the prohibition of torture, the prohibition of slavery and forced labor, the right to liberty and security, the right to a fair trial, the prohibition of punishment without law, the right to respect for private and family life, the freedom of religion and of expression, the prohibition of discrimination, the protection of property, the prohibition of collective expulsions, and the violation of human rights by an aggressive force. We explore four of these cases.

Major judgments of the Inter-American Court of Human Rights have included the rights of indigenous peoples, the right to health and vulnerable groups, freedom

[15] United Nations Security Council (2010).

[16] Council of Europe (2026).

[17] See Burgorgue-Larsen (2024); Stone Sweet and Sandholtz (2024); Almutawa and Magliveras (eds) (2025).

of expression and information, amnesty laws and impunity, and the responsibility of business to respect human rights. The Inter-American Court's judgments have had a profound impact on codifying human rights protections in the national legislation of Latin American countries and on state practice to protect vulnerable populations and ensure accountability. We examine four such cases and one historic advisory opinion on climate change.

At the African Court on Human and Peoples' Rights, the most significant judicial rulings have centered on fair trials and impunity, electoral rights, socio-economic rights, abolition of the death penalty, authoritarianism in government, and holding states accountable for failing to prevent, investigate, and prosecute human rights violations, including when vulnerable groups of persons are victimized. We focus on three of the African cases.

The critical role of defense counsel in the litigation before the judicial bodies highlighted in this book is a factor that we also emphasize, as the legal proceedings and the jurisprudence simply would not be possible without the strong and effective participation of lawyers dedicated to due process and fair trials for all of the parties represented in the courtroom.

With its global reach, the International Bar Association (IBA) has been at the forefront of what transpired before these courts during the last three decades. In researching this book, we have consulted closely with expert members of the IBA who have worked on cases before these judicial bodies and/or are leading scholars of the jurisprudence. The IBA War Crimes Committee has been a reservoir of knowledge and experience informing the research and drafting of this book.

The information and insights that we describe in this book only scratch the surface of a large body of law and practice advancing international justice in our lifetimes. Our approach to this task is less commentary and more direct quotation and reference to the jurisprudence as written by judges. In a book of this length, we can only provide nuggets from the judgments, but we have endeavored to select instructive passages that demonstrate the accelerated growth of international law. We are confident that many of the major achievements shine through on these pages and that readers will recognize the trajectory of international justice not only in recent years but also aimed for the future. In our view, these fortified principles of the rule of law will withstand the turbulence of a disrupted world.

References

African Court on Human and Peoples' Rights (2026) African Court on Human and Peoples' Rights. https://www.african-court.org/afchpr/. Accessed 8 May 2026

Almutawa A, Magliveras KD (eds) (2025) A comparison of the European, inter-American, African and Arab human rights courts: Institutional aspects. TMC Asser Press, The Hague

Burgorgue-Larsen L (2024) The 3 regional human rights courts in context: justice that cannot be taken for granted. Oxford University Press, Oxford

Council of Europe (2026) Special Tribunal for the Crime of Aggression against Ukraine. https://www.coe.int/en/web/special-tribunal-ukraine/home. Accessed 8 May 2026

Drumbl MA (2007) Atrocity, punishment, and international law. Cambridge University Press, Cambridge

European Court of Human Rights (2026) European Court of Human Rights. https://www.echr.coe.int/. Accessed 8 May 2026

The Extraordinary Chambers in the Courts of Cambodia (2026) The Extraordinary Chambers in the Courts of Cambodia. https://www.eccc.gov.kh/en. Accessed 8 May 2026

Fraser N (2008) Scales of justice: Reimagining political space in a globalizing world. Polity Press, Cambridge

Hillebrecht C (2021) Saving the international justice regime: Beyond backlash against international courts. Cambridge University Press, Cambridge

Hola B, Nyseth Nzitatira H, Weerdesteijun M (eds) (2022) The Oxford handbook of atrocity crimes. Oxford University Press, New York

Ibsen MF (2023) A critical theory of global justice: The Frankfurt School and world affairs. Oxford University Press, Oxford

Kurze A, Lamont CK (eds) (2019) New critical spaces in transitional justice: Gender, art, and memory. Indiana University Press, Bloomington

Kurze A, Peterka-Benton D, Rubin G (2024) International justice: A critical and comprehensive introduction. Kendall Hunt Publishing, Dubuque

Inter-American Court of Human Rights (2026) Inter-American Court of Human Rights. https://www.corteidh.or.cr/index.cfm?lang=en. Accessed 8 May 2026

International Court of Justice (2026) International Court of Justice. https://www.icj-cij.org/home. Accessed 8 May 2026

International Criminal Court (2026) International Criminal Court. https://www.icc-cpi.int/. Accessed 8 May 2026

Refworld (2026) Special Tribunal for Lebanon. https://www.refworld.org/document-sources/special-tribunal-lebanon. Accessed 8 May 2026

Residual Special Court for Sierra Leone (2026) Residual Special Court for Sierra Leone. https://rscsl.org/. Accessed 8 May 2026

Schabas W (2012) Unimaginable atrocities: Justice, politics, and rights at the war crimes tribunals. Oxford University Press, Oxford

Scheffer D (2012) All the missing souls: A personal history of the war crimes tribunals. Princeton University Press, Princeton

Stone Sweet A, Sandholtz W (2024) The law and politics of international human rights courts: The dilemma of effectiveness. Oxford University Press, Oxford

United Nations International Criminal Tribunal for Rwanda (2015) United Nations International Criminal Tribunal for Rwanda. https://unictr.irmct.org/. Accessed 8 May 2026

United Nations International Criminal Tribunal for the former Yugoslavia (2017) United Nations International Criminal Tribunal for the former Yugoslavia. https://www.icty.org/. Accessed 8 May 2026

United Nations International Residual Mechanism for Criminal Tribunals (2026) United Nations International Residual Mechanism for Criminal Tribunals. https://www.irmct.org/en. Accessed 8 May 2026

United Nations Security Council (2010) Resolution 1966 (2010), adopted by the Security Council at its 6463rd meeting, on 22 December 2010. United Nations Security Council. Available via United Nations Digital Library. https://digitallibrary.un.org/record/695418. Accessed 8 May 2026

Williams S (2013) J Intl Crim Justice 11(5):1139–1160. https://doi.org/10.1093/jicj/mqt060

Chapter 2
The International Court of Justice: State Responsibility on Trial

The most prominent global court is the International Court of Justice (ICJ), which is the judicial arm of the United Nations. Its governing statute is an integral part of the United Nations Charter,[1] its judges are elected by the General Assembly and the Security Council, and its operations are funded by the United Nations. The ICJ is the world's premier "state responsibility" court, meaning that its authority and jurisprudence only address the responsibility of a state and its government to comply with international law. The ICJ exercises no jurisdiction over individuals (including any criminal charges against persons) or corporate entities. Since it commenced its operations and case work in 1946, the ICJ has delivered major rulings and advisory opinions concerning the obligations of countries under international law. Admittedly, the ICJ can only scratch the surface of international justice in its limited number of rulings and advisory opinions. But those cases it adjudicates are of profound importance in understanding and guiding state conduct and rendering judgment on its legal legitimacy.

In this chapter we look at significant ICJ rulings and advisory opinions since 1993 with respect to the crime of genocide, the rise of *erga omnes partes* jurisdiction, the use of military force, the obligations of states in respect of climate change, and the threat or use of nuclear weapons.

2.1 Crime of Genocide

The Balkans War of 1991–1995[2] generated two ICJ cases centered on whether the crime of genocide had been committed by the Serbian government as a state entity, as distinct from an individual being charged with genocide and prosecuted, for example,

[1] Scheffer and Ellis (2025); United Nations (2026).

[2] Silber and Little (1995); Magaš and Žanić (2001); Scheffer (2019).

D. J. Scheffer and M. S. Ellis, *The Story of Modern International Justice, 1993-2025*,
https://doi.org/10.1007/978-3-032-33243-1_2

by the International Criminal Tribunal for the former Yugoslavia (ICTY) or for Rwanda (ICTR) that we examine in Chap. 3 of this book. ICJ judgments were handed down in 2007 with respect to *Bosnia and Herzegovina v. the Federal Republic of Yugoslavia* (FRY) when the FRY consisted of both Serbia and Montenegro,[3] and in 2015 with respect to *Croatia v. Serbi*a (after most of the territory of the FRY had transitioned to being only the nation of Serbia).[4] For our purposes here, it might help to think of the defendant, or respondent, in each of the cases as the ethnic Serbian government governing from its capital city of Belgrade.

Before these two cases were adjudicated by the ICJ, no country had ever been charged in a court of law for commission of the crime of genocide. The territory of the former Yugoslavia had been covered at all times by the Convention on the Prevention and Punishment of the Crime of Genocide (the "Genocide Convention") that the United Nations had completed in 1948 and presented for ratification or accession by all nations.[5] Article IX of the Genocide Convention provides that any dispute "relating to the responsibility of a State for genocide or for any of the other acts enumerated in article III [conspiracy, incitement, attempt, complicity], shall be submitted to the International Court of Justice at the request of any of the parties to the dispute."[6]

The ICJ examined two alleged situations of genocide in the *Bosnia* case and two alleged situations of genocide in the *Croatia* case and found that genocide occurred (albeit not attributable to the government in Belgrade, aside from the failure to prevent and punish under the Genocide Convention) in only one of these four situations, namely the Srebrenica (Bosnia) genocide of July 1995. The first allegation of genocide in the *Bosnia* case dated to 1992, when Bosnian Serb forces overwhelmed the Bosnian Muslim civilian populations in six municipalities of northern Bosnia and forced them to flee under murderous and injurious conditions that, it was alleged before the ICJ, mirrored the crime of genocide. While the ICJ found that acts of genocide in the six municipalities indeed had occurred, the necessary mental element of specific intent by the government in Belgrade to orchestrate or assist such acts in order to destroy in whole or in part a protected group under the Genocide Convention was not shown.

The second situation in the *Bosnia* case occurred in the vicinity of Srebrenica, Bosnia, in July 1995, when about 8000 Bosnian Muslim men and boys were massacred by Bosnian Serb forces.[7] Examining ICTY jurisprudence, the ICJ affirmed that acts of genocide had occurred at Srebrenica and that Bosnian Serb officials had possessed the requisite specific intent to commit genocide with the use of Bosnian Serb forces. But the Court found no evidence proving that the government in Belgrade either possessed such specific intent or that the Yugoslav Army (of the Federal Republic of Yugoslavia) directly participated in the Srebrenica genocide.

[3] International Court of Justice (2026b).

[4] International Court of Justice (2026c).

[5] Office of the United Nations High Commissioner for Human Rights (2026b).

[6] Id., art. IX.

[7] See Rohde (2012).

The third situation occurred in Croatia between 1991 and 1995 when the Yugoslav Army and Serbian militia overwhelmed and controlled a number of Croatian regions and committed acts of genocide during their occupation of Croatian territory.[8] Nonetheless, in *Croatia v. Serbia* the Court failed to find any specific intent by the government in Belgrade to commit genocide when such actions were undertaken in Croatia. In that same case, Serbia counter-claimed against Croatia regarding "Operation Storm" that had occurred in August 1995 when the Croatian army routed the Serbian forces and governing authorities from the occupied Croatian territory, a counter-offensive that helped speed the end of the Balkans War by Fall 1995.[9] But again, while the Court found that acts of genocide had occurred during Operation Storm, it did not find any specific intent on the part of the Croatian Government to commit the crime of genocide.

With respect to the Srebrenica genocide, the ICJ nonetheless concluded that the FRY Government, which had influence over the Bosnian Serb forces, was responsible for failing to prevent the genocide and for failing to punish (diligently track, arrest, and prosecute) Ratko Mladić, one of the Bosnian Serb military leaders long charged by the ICTY for orchestrating the Srebrenica genocide and presumed to have found sanctuary across the border in Serbia. No such similar finding of failure to prevent or punish was identified for any of the other situations presented to the ICJ: the Bosnian Serb assaults on six Bosnian municipalities in 1992, the foreign military occupation of part of Croatia from 1991 to 1995, or Operation Storm conducted by Croatian forces in August 1995.

In the development of modern international criminal law, the ICJ judgments in the *Bosnia* and *Croatia* cases stand out as significantly confirming (1) the criteria that determines the crime of genocide, and (2) the responsibility of a government to prevent, refrain from committing, and punish the crime of genocide. With respect to the criteria, the ICJ in the *Bosnia* case relied heavily on the jurisprudence of the ICTY but importantly clarified at the ICJ's level of state responsibility that the specific intent to destroy all or part of a protected group (ethnic, racial, religious, or national) must be a discriminatory intent to destroy that particular group "as such."

The ICJ validated what the ICTY had found seven years earlier in that "when persecution escalates to the extreme form of willful and deliberate acts designed to destroy a group or part of a group, it can be held that such persecution amounts to genocide."[10] The ICJ continued, "the specific intent is also to be distinguished from other reasons or motives the perpetrator may have. Great care must be taken in finding in the facts a sufficiently clear manifestation of that intent."[11] And "the targeted group must in law be defined positively, and thus not negatively as [for example] the 'non-Serb' population."[12] As for intending to destroy "part" of a protected group, the ICJ found that "the intent must be to destroy at least a substantial part of the particular

---

[8] See Nazor (2016).

[9] Gugo (2016).

[10] United Nations International Criminal Tribunal for the former Yugoslavia (2000), para. 636.

[11] International Court of Justice (2007), paras. 188–189.

[12] Id., paras. 196.

group. That is demanded by the very nature of the crime of genocide: since the object and purpose of the [Genocide] Convention as a whole is to prevent the intentional destruction of groups, the part targeted must be significant enough to have an impact on the group as a whole."[13]

In the *Croatia* case, the ICJ further clarified several key criteria for the crime of genocide. First, the ICJ held that, "Since it is the group, in whole or in part, which is the object of genocidal intent, the Court is of the view that it is difficult to establish such intent on the basis of isolated acts. It considers that, in the absence of direct proof, there must be evidence of acts on a scale that establishes an intent not only to target certain individuals because of their membership to a particular group, but also to destroy the group itself in whole or in part."[14]

Second, the ICJ held that specific genocidal intent could be "established indirectly by inference." On its face, this appears perfectly reasonable as often a government's intent may not be recorded explicitly in written documents or even uttered in oral statements. The availability of determining a specific intent proven by actions that establish the inference of a genocidal intent is vital to enforcement of the crime, whether it be in a criminal trial against an individual or an ICJ proceeding against a government. But with respect to the 1992 assault on the six municipalities in Bosnia, the Srebrenica massacres of July 1995, and the operations against the Croatians by Yugoslav Army and Serb forces in 1991–1995, the ICJ could not satisfy with respect to the Serbian government one critical requirement for the crime of genocide: The conduct must, as the *Bosnia* judgment held, "be such that it could only point to the existence of such [genocidal] intent" and, with fresh reasoning in the *Croatia* case, the ICJ clarified that "in order to infer the existence of *dolus specialis* [specific intent] from a pattern of conduct, it is necessary and sufficient that this is the *only* inference that could reasonably be drawn from the acts in question."[15] (Emphasis added) Granted, with the Srebrenica massacres the ICJ found specific intent to commit genocide but only as it already had been proven by the ICTY with respect to individuals, such as General Radislav Krstić, and not, as claimed before the ICJ and within its jurisdiction to determine, by the government in Belgrade.

Third, the ICJ expounded on criteria for the various acts of the crime of genocide that reach beyond killing members of the protected group. These criteria often are overlooked in the popular conception of what constitutes genocide, such as mass killings, but they are increasingly focused upon in contemporary situations, such as ongoing litigation before the ICJ pertaining to the Rohingya,[16] Ukrainians,[17] and Palestinians.[18] Where the act causes "serious bodily or mental harm to members of the group," the ICJ wrote that usage of "serious" means the act "must be such as to

[13] Id., para. 198.

[14] International Court of Justice (2015), para. 139.

[15] Id., para. 148.

[16] International Court of Justice (2026e).

[17] International Court of Justice (2026a).

[18] International Court of Justice (2026d).

contribute to the physical or biological destruction of the group, in whole or in part."[19] That is a high bar to meet. But it was scaled for both killings and serious bodily or mental harm as acts of genocide in all of the situations examined by the ICJ in both of the cases. Lacking, however, and thus dispositive of the final judgments, was any finding of specific intent on the part of the government in Belgrade to perpetrate such acts.

But a less severe standard was set for "deliberately inflicting on the group conditions of life calculated to bring about its physical destruction." There, the ICJ held that such an act "covers methods of physical destruction, other than killing, whereby the perpetrator ultimately seeks the death of the members of the group. Such methods of destruction include notably deprivation of food, medical care, shelter or clothing, as well as lack of hygiene, systematic expulsion from homes, or exhaustion as a result of excessive work or physical exertion (*Brdanin*, IT-99-36-T, Trial Chamber, Judgment of 1 September 2004, para. 691) ..."[20] Importantly, the ICJ clarified that the commonly used term of "ethnic cleansing" since the Balkans War era can constitute the crime of genocide "provided such action is carried out with the necessary specific intent (*dolus specialis*), that is to say with a view to the destruction of the group, as distinct from its removal from the region..."[21] If "forced displacements took place in such circumstances that they were calculated to bring about the physical destruction of the group," then the crime of genocide would merit review.[22] Absent that specific intent to commit genocide, the ethnic cleansing likely would constitute a crime against humanity—a man-made humanitarian catastrophe meriting prosecution but not genocide.

Another important ruling on the categories of genocidal acts set forth in Article II of the Genocide Convention was the ICJ's conclusion in the *Croatia* case that rape and other acts of sexual violence "are capable of constituting the *actus reus* of genocide within the meaning of Article II(d) of the Genocide Convention [Imposing measures intended to prevent births within the group], provided that they are of a kind which prevent births within the group. In order for that to be the case, it is necessary that the circumstances of the commission of those acts, and their consequences, are such that the capacity of members of the group to procreate is affected."[23] The ICJ cautioned that "the systematic nature of such acts has to be considered in determining whether they are capable of constituting the *actus reus* of genocide within the meaning of Article II(d) of the [Genocide] Convention."[24]

Finally, the ICJ delivered a significant finding in the *Croatia* case that interpreted the Genocide Convention as prohibiting States from actually committing the crime of genocide, and not only preventing its commission and punishing its individual perpetrators as stated in the Genocide Convention. This was a common sense reading

[19] International Court of Justice (2015), paras. 157–160.

[20] Id., para. 161.

[21] Id., para. 162.

[22] Id., para. 163.

[23] Id., para. 166.

[24] Id.

of the prevention language in the Genocide Convention, but the ICJ explained it publicly in its ruling, and thus the point would not be lost on governments that might think that the obligation to prevent genocide under the Convention has nothing to do with the illegality of actually committing genocide. The ICJ ruled:

> [I]n the view of the Court, taking into account the established purpose of the [Genocide] Convention, the effect of Article I is to prohibit States from themselves committing genocide. Such a prohibition follows, first, from the fact that the Article categorizes genocide as "a crime under international law": by agreeing to such a categorization, the States parties must logically be undertaking not to commit the act so described. Secondly, it follows from the expressly stated obligation to prevent the commission of acts of genocide. That obligation requires the States parties, *inter alia*, to employ the means at their disposal…to prevent persons or groups not directly under their authority from committing an act of genocide or any of the other acts mentioned in Article III. It would be paradoxical if States were thus under an obligation to prevent, so far as within their power, commission of genocide by persons over whom they have a certain influence, but were not forbidden to commit such acts through their own organs, or persons over whom they have such firm control that their conduct is attributable to the State concerned under international law. In short, the obligation to prevent genocide necessarily implies the prohibition of the commission of genocide.[25]

The ICJ's interpretation of the Genocide Convention to prohibit the State from committing the crime of genocide resonated with subsequent genocide cases before the ICJ, namely *The Gambia v. Myanmar*, *Ukraine v. Russian Federation* ("Allegations of Genocide"), and *South Africa v. Israel*, which remained pending for final judgment as of this writing. In each of these cases, the claimant State has argued that the respondent State actually committed genocide as well as failing to prevent and punish the crime.

2.2 *Erga Omnes Partes* Standing

In recent years, three ICJ cases concerning atrocity crimes (genocide and mass torture)[26] have significantly advanced a relatively dynamic principle of international law known in legal circles by its Latin term, *erga omnes partes*.[27] Normally, in State responsibility litigation before international or regional courts, the plaintiff State lodging the claim against another State is required to demonstrate tangible injury inflicted on it by the defendant State. But there is an exception in international law—*erga omnes partes*—whereby no such injury needs to be shown if the right or obligation at issue is granted and owed to all States, regardless of proximity to or impact of injury under the circumstances of the case. This is particularly evident where the two or more States belong to a treaty embodying the right or obligation with prominent universal character. Such a treaty would be described as having *erga omnes partes* protection for the right or obligation at stake. An international treaty that prohibits

---

[25] International Court of Justice (2007), para. 166.

[26] See International Court of Justice (2026d, 2026e, 2026h).

[27] See generally Kammerhofer (2024).

genocide or torture exemplifies the point. Upholding under the authority of a treaty commitment a people's right to self-determination, which is a *jus cogens* norm under international law, also would qualify for application of *erga omnes partes.*

The *erga omnes partes* principle was prominently deliberated by the ICJ in *The Gambia v. Myanmar* with a procedural ruling delivered in 2020 that granted standing to the West African nation of The Gambia to pursue a genocide case against Myanmar for alleged acts of genocide against its Rohingya minority population in 2017. Beginning in August of that year, thousands of Rohingya were massacred by the Myanmar military and an estimated 700,000 were forcibly routed onto adjoining Bangladesh territory to live precariously in squalid conditions in camps to the present day.[28] Both countries are party to the Genocide Convention, which under Article IX requires disputes under the treaty ultimately to be adjudicated by the ICJ.[29] The Gambia and its people suffered no injury as a consequence of the Rohingya situation and are located seven thousand miles from the impacted region. But the ICJ ruled that The Gambia had standing to uphold the common interest of all States parties under the Genocide Convention to prevent, suppress, and punish genocide:

> All the States parties to the Genocide Convention... have a common interest to ensure the prevention, suppression[,] and punishment of genocide, by committing themselves to fulfilling the obligations contained in the Convention.... [S]uch a common interest implies that the obligations in question are owed by any to all the other States parties to the relevant convention; they are obligations *erga omnes partes*, in the sense that each State party has an interest in compliance with them in any given case.[30]
>
> The Court continued: "It follows that any State party to the Genocide Convention may invoke the responsibility of another State party, including through the institution of proceedings before the Court, with a view to determining the alleged failure to comply with its obligations *erga omnes partes* under the Convention and to bringing that failure to an end."[31]

Earlier, in July 2012, the ICJ had applied the *erga omnes partes* principle to Belgium's claim against Senegal under the Convention Against Torture and Other Cruel, Inhuman or Degrading Treatment or Punishment ("Torture Convention"), under which both countries are States Parties. The Court ruled in *Questions Relating to the Obligation to Prosecute or Extradite (Belgium v. Senegal)*[32] that even though Belgium had declared a special interest in bringing Hassan Habré, the former president of Chad who at that time resided in Senegal, to justice, Belgium need not prove any such special interest. Rather, simply by being a State Party of the Torture Convention, Belgium had standing to bring Senegal to account for failing to fulfil its obligation under the Torture Convention to prosecute Habré for the crime of torture.

Given the *erga omnes* character of the prohibition of the crime of torture under customary international law, when that prohibition then is codified in the Torture Convention, each State Party of that international treaty may invoke the *erga omnes*

[28] See United States Holocaust Memorial Museum (2026).

[29] Office of the United Nations High Commissioner for Human Rights (2026b), art. IX.

[30] International Court of Justice (2022a), para. 107.

[31] Id., para. 112.

[32] International Court of Justice (2026h).

partes principle to hold any other State Party of the Torture Convention to account for performance of that State Party's responsibilities under the treaty. The additional leap taken by the ICJ in *The Gambia v. Myanmar* arose from the fact that The Gambia never claimed that it had any special interest in the Rohingya or in Myanmar. The country acted upon principle under the treaty, relying solely on the *erga omnes partes* principle to gain standing, which the ICJ granted it under the Genocide Convention because that treaty embodies the *jus cogens* prohibition on the crime of genocide.

In 2024, the ICJ ruled on provisional measures in *Application of the Convention on Prevention and Punishment of the Crime of Genocide in the Gaza Strip (South Africa v. Israel)*,[33] a case that has not reached a merits judgment as of this writing. Both South Africa and Israel are States Parties to the Genocide Convention. The State of Palestine also has State Party status under the Genocide Convention. South Africa is over 4000 miles from the Gaza Strip and has no conventional interest in actions bearing upon the Gaza Strip and its people. But the ICJ stated that Israel did not challenge the standing of South Africa to bring the case. The Court recited its earlier ruling in the *Myanmar* case about the validity of *erga omnes partes* with respect to claims by States Parties under the Genocide Convention. Set forth below is the ICJ's reasoning in *South Africa v. Israel*:

> 33. The Court notes that the Respondent [Israel] did not challenge the standing of the Applicant [South Africa] in the present proceedings. It recalls that, in the case concerning the *Application of the Convention on the Prevention and Punishment of the Crime of Genocide (The Gambia v. Myanmar)* where Article IX of the Genocide Convention was also invoked, it observed that all the States parties to the Convention have a common interest to ensure the prevention, suppression and punishment of genocide, by committing themselves to fulfilling the obligations contained in the Convention. Such a common interest implies that the obligations in question are owed by any State party to all the other States parties to the relevant convention; they are obligations *erga omnes partes*, in the sense that each State party has an interest in compliance with them in any given case. The common interest in compliance with the relevant obligations under the Genocide Convention entails that any State party, without distinction, is entitled to invoke the responsibility of another State party for an alleged breach of its obligations *erga omnes partes*. Accordingly, the Court found that any State party to the Genocide Convention may invoke the responsibility of another State party, including through the institution of proceedings before the Court, with a view to determining the alleged failure to comply with its obligations *erga omnes partes* under the Convention and to bringing that failure to an end (*Application of the Convention on the Prevention and Punishment of the Crime of Genocide (The Gambia v. Myanmar), Preliminary Objections, Judgment, I.C.J. Reports 2022 (II)*, pp. 515-517, paras. 107-108 and 112).
> 34. The Court concludes, prima facie, that South Africa has standing to submit to it the dispute with Israel concerning alleged violations of obligations under the Genocide Convention.[34]

One can expect that in years to come the *erga omnes partes* principle will resonate among the States Parties of a number of significant international treaties beyond those prohibiting genocide or torture. Other treaties include the Geneva Conventions of 12 August 1949,[35] the 1977 Additional Protocols to the Geneva Conventions of 1949,

[33] International Court of Justice (2024).

[34] International Court of Justice (2024), paras. 33–34.

[35] International Committee of the Red Cross (2026).

the International Covenant on Civil and Political Rights (ICCPR),[36] the Convention on the Elimination of All Forms of Discrimination Against Women (CEDAW),[37] the Paris Agreement on climate change,[38] and such regional human rights treaties as the European Convention on Human Rights,[39] the American Convention on Human Rights,[40] and the African Charter on Human and Peoples' Rights.[41] This new era of enforcement of human rights treaties against States is only beginning.

2.3 The Use of Force

In 2005, the ICJ delivered a major judgment concerning the use of military force and related commission of atrocity crimes and human rights violations in *Armed Activities on the Territory of the Congo (Democratic Republic of the Congo v. Uganda).*[42] Showing little tolerance for Uganda's excuses for its large military presence on territory of the Democratic Republic of the Congo (the "DRC"), the ICJ proceeded to knock down practically each of Uganda's rationales and, in doing so, strengthened the U.N. Charter's provisions on both the use of force and on self-defense. Nonetheless, the Court did not venture into the broader modern context of military actions, a point emphasized by two concurring judges.

Initially, the DRC had officially consented to the presence of Uganda's military forces on its territory in northeastern DRC in order to fight rebel groups marauding over vast stretches of eastern Congo in the 1990s. But that consent was withdrawn by the government in August 1998. The ICJ demonstrated no flexibility, ruling that once a nation's consent for such engagement is withdrawn, the foreign nation's forces must be withdrawn. Uganda had not followed that edict, maintaining its forces in the DRC until 2003. Either a country consents to the presence of foreign troops on its territory as part of the country's self-defense, or, lacking such consent, the foreign country should no longer deploy or maintain its forces on that nation's territory. The Ugandan authorities should have withdrawn their troops promptly when the DRC consent was terminated in August 1998.

The ICJ found Uganda's failure to withdraw from the DRC a violation of U.N. Charter Article 2(4), the preeminent non-use of force provision of the U.N. Charter. It requires that, "All Members shall refrain in their international relations from the threat or use of force against the territorial integrity or political independence of any state, or in any other manner inconsistent with the Purposes of the United Nations." The ICJ found that Uganda had committed "a grave violation of the prohibition on

[36] Office of the United Nations High Commissioner for Human Rights (2026c).

[37] Office of the United Nations High Commissioner for Human Rights (2026a).

[38] United Nations (2015).

[39] European Court of Human Rights (2026).

[40] Organization of American States (2011).

[41] Organization of African Unity (1981).

[42] International Court of Justice (2026f).

the use of force" in deploying and continuing its deployment of its armed forces to fight on DRC territory long after the DRC had no longer consented to the presence of Ugandan troops.[43] But the ICJ fell short of labeling Uganda's action as aggression and relied instead on the U.N. Security Council's decision that the Uganda-DRC conflict constituted "a threat to peace, security and stability in the region"[44] and the Ugandan forces exacerbated that threat.

The ICJ acknowledged that the DRC continued to negotiate the withdrawal of Ugandan troops following the withdrawal of consent, but found that such negotiated terms to achieve Ugandan withdrawal did not obviate the illegality of the continued Ugandan presence on DRC territory.

Second, the ICJ denied Uganda a self-defense justification for its military activities on DRC territory. Uganda had never claimed an actual attack on Ugandan soil from any military threat, of regular soldiers or irregular militia, based in the DRC. The evidence did not show that rebels attacking Uganda had any connection with the DRC government, including being instructed or encouraged to make such attacks. Uganda never notified the U.N. Security Council, as required by U.N. Charter 51, that it had been under attack and thus meriting their own military acts of self-defense. Since the case involved the responsibility and liability of governments (DRC and Uganda), and the evidence did not establish a link between the DRC government and irregular forces that allegedly attacked targets on Ugandan territory, the ICJ did not address Uganda's right to repel such irregular forces.

In their separate opinions relating to the judgment, ICJ Judges Pieter Kooijmans (Netherlands)[45] and Bruno Simma (Germany)[46] nonetheless objected to the Court's reluctance on this count. In their view it was a simple matter of logic and practical reality that large-scale attacks by irregular forces emanating from another State's territory could be legitimately defended against provided rules of necessity and proportionality were complied with by the defending State. For that matter, the Al-Qaeda terrorist attacks on 11 September 2001 against American targets led directly back to Afghanistan and merited self-defense measures by the United States and its allies, the general application of which was approved by the U.N. Security Council.

Third, the ICJ invoked the law of military occupation but narrowly applied it only to the one DRC district—Ituri—where Ugandan military forces fully occupied and administered the territory. Even though Uganda's proxy rebel movements occupied *de facto* other DRC districts, the ICJ did not find Uganda responsible for upholding international humanitarian law and human rights standards in these other districts—only in Ituri did the Ugandan Government have that legal responsibility.[47] Judge Kooijmans criticized the majority, arguing once again a practical reality check on what was actually occurring on the ground in eastern DRC. He saw Uganda substituting its authority for that of the DRC in the districts where rebel forces aligned

[43] International Court of Justice (2005a), para. 165.

[44] Id., para. 151.

[45] International Court of Justice (2005b).

[46] International Court of Justice (2005c).

[47] International Court of Justice (2005a), para. 173.

with Ugandan interests controlled the territory. Thus in Kooijmans' view, Uganda had responsibility for human rights compliance, including under military occupation law, in the rebel-held districts.[48]

Finally, the ICJ found that during the armed conflict in eastern DRC, Uganda had not prevented members of its armed forces from looting, plundering, and exploiting DRC's natural resources. The Court noted that a nation's sovereignty over its natural resources is a principle of customary international law. Particularly in the context of a military intervention, such as Ugandan forces operating on DRC territory and without authority under international law, soldiers should be held to account for the war crime of pillage. But where rebel groups looted, pillaged, and illegally exploited natural resources, Uganda could only be held responsible for such conduct in the Ituri district where it exercised obligations as a military occupying power.

The ICJ ordered Uganda on 9 February 2022 to pay the DRC reparations totaling 325 million dollars to cover damage to the victims, for damage to property, and for damage related to natural resources. The Court established an installment plan to achieve that sum.[49]

In this case the ICJ upheld narrow and critically significant meanings of Articles 2(4) (prohibiting use of force) and 51 (right of self-defense) of the U.N. Charter but the majority of judges avoided the pragmatic interpretations presented by Judges Kooijmans and Simma on the law of self-defense and Judge Kooijmans on military occupation law. Given the increasing relevance in the modern world of anticipatory self-defense in state behavior and the continuing use of proxy forces to achieve state aims, these concurring judges' views doubtless will rise to the fore again. The large reparations award also reconfirmed, with an important precedent, that the ICJ will not shy away from transforming violations of international law into sizeable monetary damages.

2.4 Climate Change

There is no more long-term existential issue facing humankind than the ultimate consequences of global warming, otherwise known as climate change. Granted, the most imminent existential issue remains the prospect that nuclear weapons actually would be used in a highly volatile world. The ICJ addressed that perpetual omnipotent nuclear danger in the 1990's in two advisory opinions, one of which we discuss below. But here we focus on a recent historic advisory opinion, delivered by the ICJ on 23 July 2025, about *Obligations of States in Respect of Climate Change.*[50] The advisory opinion of the ICJ was unanimously requested by the U.N. General Assembly in 2023 and attracted the highest total number of states (98) and international organizations (13) participating with written submissions or only oral submissions for either a case

[48] International Court of Justice (2005b), paras. 36–64.

[49] International Court of Justice (2022b).

[50] International Court of Justice (2025a).

or an advisory opinion in the history of the Court.[51] ICJ advisory opinions do not adjudicate any contentious case between States before the ICJ; rather, an advisory opinion examines the international law that pertains to a general situation and delivers a legal opinion authored by the ICJ judges about that general situation. While the advisory opinion is designed both to clarify the international law governing the situation presented by the General Assembly and how such law should be complied with in a general sense, the ICJ's advisory opinion does not deliver a binding judgment on any Member State of the United Nations.

Nonetheless, the ICJ's non-binding advisory opinion on climate change will be an influential oracle of law influencing state behavior and future judicial judgments on climate change issues that will arise in governing circles and in national or international courts. The judges' unanimous opinion on a large range of complex and controversial environmental issues creates a systematic framework for state action and compliance in the future.

The U.N. General Assembly's request to the ICJ for this advisory opinion should be read in its entirety to understand the breadth of international law that the judges covered:

> Having particular regard to the Charter of the United Nations, the International Covenant on Civil and Political Rights, the International Covenant on Economic, Social and Cultural Rights, the United Nations Framework Convention on Climate Change, the Paris Agreement, the United Nations Convention on the Law of the Sea, the duty of due diligence, the rights recognized in the Universal Declaration of Human Rights, the principle of prevention of significant harm to the environment and the duty to protect and preserve the marine environment,
>
> (a) What are the obligations of States under international law to ensure the protection of the climate system and other parts of the environment from anthropogenic emissions of greenhouse gases for States and for present and future generations?
>
> (b) What are the legal consequences under these obligations for States where they, by their acts and omissions, have caused significant harm to the climate system and other parts of the environment, with respect to:
>
>   (i) States, including, in particular, small island developing States, which due to their geographical circumstances and level of development, are injured or specially affected by or are particularly vulnerable to the adverse effects of climate change?
>
>   (ii) Peoples and individuals of the present and future generations affected by the adverse effects of climate change?[52]

The ICJ's 113-page advisory opinion presents a cascade of principles in response to these questions that stresses repeatedly their application in strictly a "general" sense and the "legal obligations of all States," and not with respect to any particular State, dispute, or situation.[53] That said, the advisory opinion's power punch of views about international law in the performance, or lack thereof, of States confronted with the climate change phenomenon "pushed the boundaries of international law on many points."[54]

The ICJ judges concluded in their advisory opinion the following:

---

[51] United Nations General Assembly (2023).

[52] Id.

[53] International Court of Justice (2025b), pp. 2–3.

[54] Burri (2025).

1. In considering State obligations regarding climate change, treaty obligations must be paired with obligations arising under customary international law. The notion of any treaties creating a *lex specialis* of regulation superseding customary international law was flatly rejected by the judges. In short, when it comes to the environment, the entire corpus of international law applies in determining State obligations and responsibility.
2. With respect to the climate change treaties, the ICJ confirmed the obligations of the States Parties to limit their greenhouse emissions, to take the necessary measures to achieve a temperature goal of limiting global warming to 1.5 °C above pre-industrial levels, and to pursue measures to achieve relevant objectives under such treaties.[55]
3. Regarding customary international law, which binds all States, the ICJ described two general duties in these words:

   (a) States have a duty to prevent significant harm to the environment by acting with due diligence and to use all means at their disposal to prevent activities carried out within their jurisdiction or control from causing significant harm to the climate system and other parts of the environment, in accordance with their common but differentiated responsibilities and respective capabilities;
   (b) States have a duty to co-operate with each other in good faith to prevent significant harm to the climate system and other parts of the environment, which requires sustained and continuous forms of co-operation by States when taking measures to prevent such harm.[56]

4. The ICJ concluded that under the United Nations Convention on the Law of the Sea, States Parties are obligated to adopt measures to protect and preserve the marine environment, including from the adverse effects of climate change and to co-operate in good faith.[57]
5. As summarized by the ICJ, all States are obligated under international human rights law to respect and ensure the effective enjoyment of human rights by taking necessary measures to protect the climate system and other parts of the environment.[58] The ICJ confirmed a human right to a clean, healthy, and sustainable environment drawn from treaty law, the rulings of regional and national courts, and the codification of the right in the laws of more than 100 States. The ICJ pointed to the significance of U.N. General Assembly resolution 76/300 of 28 July 2022, which "*Recognizes* the right to a clean, healthy, and sustainable environment as a human right."[59] A super-majority of 161 Member States of the United Nations adopted this non-binding but pathbreaking resolution reflecting

[55] International Court of Justice (2025c).

[56] Id.

[57] Id.

[58] Id.

[59] United Nations General Assembly (2022); These two descriptive preambular paragraphs from resolution 76/300 summarize the challenge: "*Recognizing* that sustainable development, in its three dimensions (social, economic and environmental), and the protection of the environment, including ecosystems, contribute to and promote human well-being and the full enjoyment of all human rights,

that such a right exists globally under customary international law. This resolution and the ICJ advisory opinion doubtless will become potent weapons for both advocacy and action, joining environmental and human rights activists and national lawmakers who together can frame the climate change issue in terms of both the protection of the environment and the defense of human rights.

2.5 Nuclear Weapons

Delivered three decades ago, the ICJ's advisory opinion on the *Legality of the Threat or Use of Nuclear Weapons* (8 July 1996)[60] likely has faded from the collective memory of almost everyone, especially the younger generations. But its contribution to international law on the use of force, particularly when it can affect millions of individuals who would perish under the power of even a single nuclear weapon, should be explained afresh. The threats of Russian President Vladimir Putin[61] and of Deputy Chairman of the Security Council of Russia Dmitry Medvedev[62] to use nuclear weapons if NATO forces defend Ukraine in the war of aggression launched by Russia against Ukraine point to the fragility of nuclear warfare and the convenience by which it can be unleashed by strongmen leaders with braggadocio.

Nowhere in international criminal law or the law of armed conflict is the use of nuclear weapons explicitly and completely outlawed; such arsenals of radioactive mass destruction are not identified as prohibited weapons in relevant treaties, including the Geneva Conventions of 1949, Protocols I and II of 1997, and the Rome Statute of the International Criminal Court. But the U.N. General Assembly asked one simple question of the ICJ in December 1994 when seeking its advice: "Is the threat or use of nuclear weapons in any circumstance permitted under international law?"[63] The ICJ's answer in its advisory opinion resonates today (particularly when reflecting on the Ukraine-Russia war and Putin's threats) and yet may surprise those unfamiliar with the opinion three decades after its public reading at The Peace Palace in The Hague.

In its advisory opinion, the ICJ provides a theoretical framework for the lawful use of nuclear weapons that can defy one's imagination and yet permits nations to possess nuclear weapons which potentially, of course, could be used. The ICJ first explains that nuclear weapons are not exempted from the fundamental prohibition

---

for present and future generations, *Recognizing also* that, conversely, the impact of climate change, the unsustainable management and use of natural resources, the pollution of air, land and water, the unsound management of chemicals and waste, the resulting loss of biodiversity and the decline in services provided by ecosystems interfere with the enjoyment of a clean, healthy and sustainable environment and that environmental damage has negative implications, both direct and indirect, for the effective enjoyment of all human rights."

[60] International Court of Justice (1996, 2026g).

[61] Blank (2025).

[62] Teslova (2026).

[63] United Nations General Assembly (1995).

on the use of force set forth in Article 2(4) of the U.N. Charter. If a nuclear weapon is to be used, it must not violate Article 2(4)'s prohibition on use of force, and that is a difficult scenario to imagine.

However, the ICJ concluded that where the nation exercises its inherent right of individual or collective self-defense under Article 51 of the U.N. Charter, then (in theory) that right permits the use of nuclear weapons in self-defense. But it cannot be that simple as otherwise nuclear weapons would be an easily justifiable use of force to inflict catastrophic consequences, perhaps globally. The ICJ opens the door to a self-defense rationale for the use of nuclear weapons provided, first, that such use accords with the principle of proportionality that regulates use of force in self-defense, although how the use of a nuclear weapon against conventional weapons could be proportional is difficult to imagine. (If the conflict is one of nuclear weapons used against nuclear weapons—a not unlikely scenario—then their usage in split-second decision-making between adversaries would be exceptionally difficult to strategize in terms of proportionality.)

Second, the ICJ legitimized the use of a nuclear weapon only in the "extreme circumstance of self-defence, in which the very survival of a State would be at stake."[64] Even then, the ICJ further concluded that any nuclear weapon must be used—again only in self-defense—in strict accordance with two further principles of international humanitarian law: (a) The nuclear weapon must be used in such a way as to draw a distinction between combatants and non-combatants, and thus spare civilians from harm. (b) The nuclear weapon must not inflict unnecessary suffering on the combatants.[65]

The ICJ emphasized that these conditions apply equally to the threat to use nuclear weapons as well as to actual use of nuclear weapons. Thus no threat can be made unless the threatening State can be certain of the right to self-defense arising and that the prospective use of such weapons would comply with all of the relevant principles of international humanitarian law described by the Court in the advisory opinion.

In the context of nuclear warfare, the ICJ's advisory opinion thus skates on a thin surreal landscape. Indeed, the ICJ admitted, "In view of the unique characteristics of nuclear weapons…the use of such weapons in fact seems scarcely reconcilable with respect for [the requirements of law applicable in armed conflict]."[66] Nonetheless, the ICJ advisory opinion stands as an interpretation of international law on the threat or use of nuclear weapons that essentially narrows their lawfulness to an almost implausible scenario of determinations. Putin's threat to use nuclear weapons in the Russia-Ukraine War failed every condition imposed by the ICJ in its 1996 advisory opinion and should be understood accordingly as an unlawful threat.

---

[64] International Court of Justice (1996), p. 44.

[65] Id., para. 78.

[66] Id., para. 95.

References

Blank S (2025) Vladimir Putin's endless nuclear threats are a sign of Russian weakness. Atlantic Council. https://www.atlanticcouncil.org/blogs/ukrainealert/vladimir-putins-endless-nuclear-threats-are-a-sign-of-russian-weakness/. Accessed 8 May 2026

Burri T (2025) The ICJ's opinion on climate change: pushing the boundaries of international law. ASIL insights 29(13) https://asil.org/insights/volume-29-issue-13/

European Court of Human Rights (2026) European Convention on Human Rights. https://www.echr.coe.int/european-convention-on-human-rights. Accessed 8 May 2026

Gugo A (2016) In the eye of the storm: political, diplomatic and military struggle for Croatian independence. Self-published

International Committee of the Red Cross (2026) The Geneva Conventions of 12 August 1949. https://elearning.icrc.org/healthcareindanger-legal-framework/en/media/attachements/chapter-1/gva-conv.pdf. Accessed 8 May 2026

International Court of Justice (1996) Legality of the threat or use of nuclear weapons, advisory opinion. International Court of Justice. Accessible via ICJ Reports. https://www.icj-cij.org/sites/default/files/case-related/95/095-19960708-ADV-01-00-EN.pdf. Accessed 8 May 2026

International Court of Justice (2005a) Armed activities on the territory of The Congo (Democratic Republic of the Congo v. Uganda), judgment. International court of justice. Accessible via ICJ Reports. https://www.icj-cij.org/sites/default/files/case-related/116/116-20051219-JUD-01-00-EN.pdf. Accessed 8 May 2026

International Court of Justice (2005b) Armed activities on the territory of The Congo (Democratic Republic of the Congo v. Uganda), separate opinion of judge Kooijmans. International Court of Justice. Accessible via ICJ Reports. https://www.icj-cij.org/sites/default/files/case-related/116/116-20051219-JUD-01-03-EN.pdf. Accessed 8 May 2026

International Court of Justice (2005c) Armed activities on the territory of The Congo (Democratic Republic of the Congo v. Uganda), separate opinion of judge Simma. International Court of Justice. Accessible via ICJ Reports. https://www.icj-cij.org/sites/default/files/case-related/116/116-20051219-JUD-01-05-EN.pdf. Accessed 8 May 2026

International Court of Justice (2007) Application on the convention on the prevention and punishment of the crime of genocide (Bosnia and Herzegovina v. Serbia and Montenegro), judgment. International Court of Justice. Accessible via ICJ Reports. https://www.icj-cij.org/sites/default/files/case-related/91/091-20070226-JUD-01-00-EN.pdf. Accessed 8 May 2026

International Court of Justice (2015) Application on the convention on the prevention and punishment of the crime of genocide (Croatia v. Serbia and Montenegro), judgment. International court of justice. Accessible via ICJ Reports. https://www.icj-cij.org/sites/default/files/case-related/118/118-20150203-JUD-01-00-EN.pdf. Accessed 8 May 2026

International Court of Justice (2022a) Application on the convention on the prevention and punishment of the crime of genocide (The Gambia v. Myanmar), preliminary objections, judgment. International court of justice. Accessible via ICJ Reports. https://www.icj-cij.org/sites/default/files/case-related/178/178-20220722-jud-01-00-en.pdf. Accessed 8 May 2026

International Court of Justice (2022b) Armed activities on the territory of The Congo (Democratic Republic of the Congo v. Uganda), reparations, judgment. International Court of Justice. Accessible via ICJ Reports. https://www.icj-cij.org/sites/default/files/case-related/116/116-20220209-jud-01-00-en.pdf. Accessed 8 May 2026

International Court of Justice (2024) Application of the convention on the prevention and punishment of the crime of genocide in the Gaza strip (South Africa v. Israel), provisional measures, order of 26 January 2024. International Court of Justice. Accessible via ICJ Reports. https://www.icj-cij.org/sites/default/files/case-related/192/192-20240126-ord-01-00-en.pdf. Accessed 8 May 2026

International Court of Justice (2025a) Obligations of states in respect of climate change, advisory opinion. International Court of Justice. Accessible via ICJ Reports. https://www.icj-cij.org/sites/default/files/case-related/187/187-20250723-adv-01-00-en.pdf. Accessed 8 May 2026

International Court of Justice (2025b) Obligations of states in respect of climate change, summary of the advisory opinion of 23 July 2025. https://www.icj-cij.org/sites/default/files/case-related/187/187-20250723-sum-01-00-en.pdf. Accessed 8 May 2026

International Court of Justice (2025c) Obligations of states in respect of climate change, press release: The Court gives its advisory opinion and responds to the questions posed by the General Assembly. https://www.icj-cij.org/sites/default/files/case-related/187/187-20250723-pre-01-00-en.pdf. Accessed 8 May 2026

International Court of Justice (2026a) Allegations of Genocide under the Convention on the Prevention and Punishment of the Crime of Genocide (Ukraine v. Russian Federation). https://www.icj-cij.org/case/182. Accessed 8 May 2026

International Court of Justice (2026b) Application of the Convention on the Prevention and Punishment of the Crime of Genocide (Bosnia and Herzegovina v. Serbia and Montenegro). https://www.icj-cij.org/case/91. Accessed 8 May 2026

International Court of Justice (2026c) Application of the Convention on the Prevention and Punishment of the Crime of Genocide (Croatia v. Serbia). https://www.icj-cij.org/case/118. Accessed 8 May 2026

International Court of Justice (2026d) Application of the Convention on the Prevention and Punishment of the Crime of Genocide in the Gaza Strip (South Africa v. Israel). https://www.icj-cij.org/case/192. Accessed 8 May 2026

International Court of Justice (2026e) Application of the Convention on the Prevention and Punishment of the Crime of Genocide (The Gambia v. Myanmar: 11 states intervening). https://www.icj-cij.org/case/178. Accessed 8 May 2026

International Court of Justice (2026f) Armed activities on the territory of the Congo (Democratic Republic of the Congo v. Uganda). https://www.icj-cij.org/case/116. Accessed 8 May 2026

International Court of Justice (2026g) Legality of the threat or use of nuclear weapons. https://www.icj-cij.org/case/95. Accessed 8 May 2026

International Court of Justice (2026h) Questions relating to the obligation to prosecute or extradite (Belgium v. Senegal). https://www.icj-cij.org/case/144. Accessed 8 May 2026

Kammerhofer J (2024) Obligations erga omnes. In: the max Planck encyclopedia of public international law. Max Planck Institute for Comparative Public law and International law. Accessible via Oxford Public International Law. https://opil.ouplaw.com/display/10.1093/law:epil/9780199231690/law-9780199231690-e1400. Accessed 8 May 2026

Magaš B, Žanić I (2001) The war in Croatia and Bosnia-Herzegovina, 1991–1995. Routledge, Abingdon

Nazor A (2016) The Croatian war of independence: Serbia's war of conquest against Croatia and the defeat of Serbian imperialism 1991–1995. Self-published

Office of the United Nations High Commissioner for Human Rights (2026a) Convention on the elimination of all forms of discrimination against women, New York, 18 December 1979. https://www.ohchr.org/en/instruments-mechanisms/instruments/convention-elimination-all-forms-discrimination-against-women. Accessed 8 May 2026

Office of the United Nations High Commissioner for Human Rights (2026b) Convention on the Prevention and Punishment of the Crime of Genocide. https://www.ohchr.org/en/instruments-mechanisms/instruments/convention-prevention-and-punishment-crime-genocide. Accessed 8 May 2026

Office of the United Nations High Commissioner for Human Rights (2026c) International Covenant on Civil and Political Rights. https://www.ohchr.org/en/instruments-mechanisms/instruments/international-covenant-civil-and-political-rights. Accessed 8 May 2026

Organization of African Unity (1981) African Charter on Human and Peoples' Rights. https://au.int/sites/default/files/treaties/36390-treaty-0011_-_african_charter_on_human_and_peoples_rights_e.pdf. Accessed 8 May 2026

Organization of American States (2011) American Convention on Human Rights "Pact of San Jose, Costa Rica" (B-32). https://www.oas.org/dil/treaties_b-32_american_convention_on_human_rights.pdf. Accessed 8 May 2026

Rohde D (2012) Endgame: the betrayal and fall of Srebrenica, Europe's worst massacre since world war II, 2nd edn. Penguin Books, New York

Scheffer D (2019) The sit room: in the theater of war and peace. Oxford University Press, Oxford

Scheffer DJ, Ellis MS (2025) The UN charter: five pillars for humankind. Springer, Cham

Silber L, Little A (1995) The death of Yugoslavia. Penguin Books, London

Teslova E (2026) Russia's Medvedev warns of nuclear response if west gives up Ukraine nuclear weapons. Anadolu Ajansı. https://www.aa.com.tr/en/asia-pacific/russias-medvedev-warns-of-nuclear-response-if-west-gives-ukraine-nuclear-weapons/3838998. Accessed 8 May 2026

United Nations (2015) Paris Agreement. United Nations. Accessible via United Nations Treaty Collection. https://treaties.un.org/doc/Treaties/2016/02/20160215%2006-03%20PM/Ch_XXVII-7-d.pdf. Accessed 8 May 2026

United Nations (2026) United Nations Charter (full text). https://www.un.org/en/about-us/un-charter/full-text. Accessed 8 May 2026

United Nations General Assembly (1995) General and complete disarmament. United Nations General Assembly. Accessible via UNDOCS. https://docs.un.org/en/a/res/49/75. Accessed 8 May 2026

United Nations General Assembly (2022) The human right to a clean, healthy and sustainable environment. United Nations General Assembly. Accessible via UNDOCS. https://docs.un.org/en/A/RES/76/300. Accessed 8 May 2026

United Nations General Assembly (2023) Request for an advisory opinion of the International Court of Justice on the obligations of states in respect of climate change. United Nations General Assembly. Accessible via UNDOCS. https://docs.un.org/en/A/RES/77/276. Accessed 8 May 2026

United Nations International Criminal Tribunal for the former Yugoslavia (2000) Judgment in the case of Kupreškić et al. (IT-95-16). United Nations International Criminal Tribunal for the former Yugoslavia. https://www.icty.org/x/cases/kupreskic/tjug/en/kup-tj000114e.pdf. Accessed 8 May 2026

United States Holocaust Memorial Museum (2026) Burma. https://www.ushmm.org/genocide-prevention/countries/burma. Accessed 8 May 2026

Chapter 3
Three *Ad Hoc* International Criminal Tribunals: Individual Accountability for Atrocity Crimes

The modern atrocity crimes tribunals that have been carved into the international criminal justice landscape since the early 1990s began with the U.N. Security Council using its enforcement powers under Chap. 7 of the U.N. Charter to create two *ad hoc* international criminal tribunals: the International Criminal Tribunal for the former Yugoslavia (ICTY) in 1993 that would investigate and prosecute atrocity crimes arising from the Balkans War of 1991-1995 and the Kosovo War of 1999, and the International Criminal Tribunal for Rwanda (ICTR) in 1994 to investigate and prosecute the Rwandan genocide of that year.[1] Then, in 2010, the UN Security Council created the International Residual Mechanism for Criminal Tribunals (IRMCT) to handle any lingering case work and trials of remaining indicted individuals and incarceration of all convicted individuals that would follow the closings of the ICTY and ICTR.

The historical records of these three *ad hoc* tribunals as well as the hybrid and permanent criminal tribunals created after 1994 and explored in Chaps. 3 and 4 of this book are voluminous. They will occupy untold digital space and acres of archival floors for the long reach of the future. Given the magnitude of the achievements of the *ad hoc* tribunals, we share some of the more prominent ones in this chapter through the prism of significant cases and judgements that have advanced the march of international criminal justice during turbulent years of armed conflicts and internal upheavals that impacted the lives of millions of innocent civilians. The work of these *ad hoc* tribunals and the other modern atrocity crimes tribunals described in this book constitutes a historic achievement in the rule of law—indeed in the rule of international criminal law—and will remain deeply embedded in customary and treaty law long after the fluctuations of political leadership in today's democratic or authoritarian governments have steered humanity towards either progressive or regressive governance.

---

[1] Schabas (2012); Scheffer (2012); Matheson and Scheffer (2016).

D. J. Scheffer and M. S. Ellis, *The Story of Modern International Justice, 1993-2025*,
https://doi.org/10.1007/978-3-032-33243-1_3

3.1 International Criminal Tribunal for the former Yugoslavia and the International Residual Mechanism for Criminal Tribunals

The scores of final judgements delivered by the ICTY and IRMCT in connection with the Balkans War of 1991-1995 and the subsequent Kosovo War of 1999 render a historical record and a body of international justice that far exceed what can be related here. We choose four major cases at the ICTY to examine, two of which migrated to the IRMCT after the formal closure of the ICTY in 2017. The *Tadić* and *Furundzija* cases present a body of rulings emblematic of the pathbreaking jurisprudence of the ICTY, while the *Mladić* and *Karadžić* judgements show how skillful judges adjudicated vast troves of evidence of atrocity crimes spanning several years and arrived at reasoned conclusions about the content, scope, and enforcement of international criminal law. While the *Milošević* case would have produced a blockbuster judgement if the defendant, Slobodan Milošević as the President of Serbia during the Balkans War and of the Federal Republic of Yugoslavia during the Kosovo war, had survived to see the end of his trial, that opportunity did not arise with his inopportune death in 2006.[2] Other top leaders were tried and convicted by the ICTY, including in the *Mladić* and *Karadžić* cases where the highest Bosnian Serb officials were prosecuted for committing atrocity crimes during the Balkans War. Their stories and others of lesser rank are set forth below.

3.1.1 Prosecutor v. Tadić

Indictment for war crimes and crimes against humanity: 13 February 1995 (amended twice thereafter)

Arrested in Germany: 12 February 1994

Trial began: 7 May 1996

Trial Chamber judgement: 7 May 1997

Appeals Chamber judgement: 16 July 1999

Duško Tadić was a Bosnian Serb soldier and the first individual convicted by the ICTY (absent a guilty plea).[3] He actively participated as a low-level leader in the ethnic cleansing of non-Serbs (Bosnian Muslims and Croats) from several north Bosnian towns during April and May 1992 and engaged in abusive (gross unhealthy conditions) and violent detention (beatings, sexual assaults, torture and executions) of non-Serbs in the Omarska, Keraterm and Trnopolje camps. Tadić's trial was heralded

[2] See United Nations International Criminal Tribunal for the former Yugoslavia (2006b).

[3] Lamb (2009); United Nations International Criminal Tribunal for the former Yugoslavia (2026c).

by some as "The Trial of the Century" when it began in The Hague in 1997.[4] That claim might have been overreaching, but the case gave rise to profoundly important legal issues that the judges had to resolve as the young court dove into its growing caseload. Defense counsel, discussed in Chap. 8, played key roles in bringing these issues to the fore.

3.1.1.1 Security Council's Authority to Establish International Criminal Tribunals

The ICTY was established pursuant to resolutions adopted by the U.N. Security Council on 22 February and 25 May 1993[5] under Chap. 7 enforcement authority of the U.N. Charter. The ICTY would be a subsidiary organ of the Security Council and all Member States of the United Nations would be required to cooperate with it. Never before had the idea of the Security Council creating a criminal court with mandatory powers over Members States and their peoples been considered as part of the Council's enforcement arsenal under the U.N. Charter. Yet it was a non-military measure seized upon under the U.N. Charter's Article 41 authority, which sets forth the clear concept of "measures not involving the use of armed force to give effect to its decisions, and it may call upon the Members of the United Nations to apply such measures."

Defense counsel challenged the legal authority of the Security Council to create the ICTY, describing the novel initiative as *ultra vires* of the Council's power. The Appeals Chamber of the ICTY disagreed in *Tadić*, drawing upon Chap. 7 of the U.N. Charter, the Council's power to create subsidiary organs with judicial powers, and Article 41's non-military measures option. The appeals judges also concluded that the ICTY has competence to determine its own jurisdiction under law, which defense counsel had attempted to deny it. Further, the Appeals Chamber determined that the ICTY's authority superseded that of domestic courts without violating the rights of the accused or of state sovereignty.[6]

These rulings were unprecedented and profoundly important, not only for the power of the ICTY to adjudicate cases with full authority, but also as justification for the Security Council's subsequent creation of the ICTR in November 1994 as a criminal tribunal to adjudicate the 1994 genocide in Rwanda.[7] Since then, for largely political and economic reasons, the Security Council has not invoked its Chap. 7 power to create another international criminal tribunal (other than the IRMCT) to adjudicate atrocity crimes. But the precedents are well entrenched now and can readily be invoked to establish such a subsidiary body under a new situation of

---

[4] Scharf and Epps (1996); Zaid (1997).

[5] United Nations Security Council (1993a, 1993b).

[6] United Nations International Criminal Tribunal for the former Yugoslavia (1995), paras. 28–64.

[7] United Nations Security Council (1994).

atrocity crimes, particularly if that situation falls outside of the jurisdiction of the International Criminal Court and if Security Council members can reach the political agreement to do so.

3.1.1.2 Atrocity Crimes in Non-international Conflicts

The ICTY Appeals Chamber clarified in *Tadić* what constitutes an "armed conflict" with respect to an international armed conflict or an internal conflict and the range of application of international humanitarian law in either type of armed conflict. In particular, the judges looked to both common Article 3 of the Geneva Conventions and customary international law to identify the range of war crimes and crimes against humanity that could be prosecuted in connection with internal, or non-international, armed conflicts.[8] This set the stage for categorizing which sets of atrocity crimes could be prosecuted (depending on the characterization of the armed conflict) in relevant subsequent cases before the modern atrocity crimes tribunals.[9]

3.1.1.3 Overall Control Test for State Responsibility

In *Nicaragua v. United States* (1986), the International Court of Justice had earlier viewed the issue of state responsibility, notably that of the United States, for what constitutes the proper test for state control of private individuals engaged in an armed conflict to be one judged under a narrow test of "effective control," which requires "continuing practical guidance to the effective control of situations of armed conflict such as is there alleged to exist."[10] In contrast, the ICTY Appeals Chamber wrote of a broader "overall control" test that should be applied with respect to a state's relationship with a relatively well-organized group engaged in armed conflict. The Bosnian Serb army was such an armed non-state group and the Federal Republic of Yugoslavia at the time, with its capital in Belgrade, was such a national government. To trigger state responsibility, the group as a whole had to be under the "overall control" of the State.[11] The test did not require production of specific orders or detailed planning by the state of the group's military operations. Rather, overall control could include training, financing, equipping, or providing organizational support to the group and some role for the state in orchestrating the group's military operations.[12] The ICJ later disagreed with the Appeals Chamber's assessment of what is required to demonstrate state control of an armed group like the Bosnian Serb army.[13] The two courts'

[8] United Nations International Criminal Tribunal for the former Yugoslavia (1999), para. 70.

[9] Id., paras. 80–84, 137, 142.

[10] International Court of Justice (1984), para. 99.

[11] United Nations International Criminal Tribunal for the former Yugoslavia (1999), para. 120.

[12] Id., paras. 121–137.

[13] International Court of Justice (2007), paras. 393–394. "393. However, so to equate persons or entities with State organs when they do not have that status under internal law must be exceptional,

joust over the meaning of "control" presented competing analyses that remain open to debate.

3.1.1.4 Criteria for Crimes against Humanity

The ICTY Appeals Chamber laid down a critical standard for prosecuting crimes against humanity, namely that neither customary international law nor Article 5 (crimes against humanity) of the ICTY Statute requires any showing of discriminatory intent to commit crimes against humanity other than for the crime of persecution.[14] The fundamental requirements in *Tadić* were acts in the context of an international or internal armed conflict directed against any civilian population involving the commission of at least one of the enumerated crimes against humanity in Article 5, which are murder, extermination, enslavement, deportation, imprisonment, torture, rape, persecutions on political, racial and religious groups, and other inhumane acts.

While the crimes against humanity committed during the Balkans War essentially all occurred within the context of that armed conflict, the condition persisted as a convenience of logical reasoning that the ICTY did not seek to explicitly override. So the judges confirmed the "armed conflict" requirement in Article 5 of the ICTY Statute, which served the purpose of safely mirroring the same requirement in the London Charter of the International Military Tribunal of Nuremberg five decades earlier.[15] The ICTY in *Tadić* simply noted that the requirement of an armed conflict is no longer required by international customary law.[16] The armed conflict requirement thereafter never appeared in any of the other governing statutes of the modern atrocity crimes tribunals.

A ruling by the Appeals Chamber in a subsequent case eliminated the Trial Chamber's requirement in *Tadić* that crimes against humanity be part of a plan or policy.[17] And in *Kunarac*,[18] the Appeals Chamber determined that the ICTY Statute's wording on crimes against humanity should be interpreted to require a "widespread or systematic attack" against a civilian population. Taken together, this evolution of ICTY jurisprudence on crimes against humanity, which appeared boldly in *Tadić*,

---

for it requires proof of a particularly great degree of State control over them, a relationship which the Court's Judgment [in *Nicaragua v. United States of America*] quoted above expressly described as 'complete dependence'. It remains to be determined in the present case whether, at the time in question, the persons or entities that committed the acts of genocide at Srebrenica had such ties with the FRY that they can be deemed to have been completely dependent on it; it is only if this condition is met that they can be equated with organs of the Respondent for the purposes of its international responsibility. 394. The Court can only answer this question in the negative. At the relevant time, July 1995, neither the Republika Srpska nor the VRS could be regarded as mere instruments through which the FRY was acting, and as lacking any real autonomy." Id.

[14] United Nations International Criminal Tribunal for the former Yugoslavia (1999), paras. 287–292.

[15] Yale Law School Lillian Goldman Law Library (2008).

[16] United Nations International Criminal Tribunal for the former Yugoslavia (1995), para. 30.

[17] United Nations International Criminal Tribunal for the former Yugoslavia (2004), para. 120.

[18] United Nations International Criminal Tribunal for the former Yugoslavia (2002a), para. 85.

securely propelled this category of atrocity crimes to the forefront of prosecutions in the modern atrocity crimes tribunals.

3.1.1.5 Joint Criminal Enterprise

Finally, the Appeals Chamber in the *Tadić* judgement created the "joint criminal enterprise" mode of liability that was then applied repeatedly in later judgments of the modern atrocity crimes tribunals, although the International Criminal Court chose to develop a different modality to reflect an individual's liability in a group context. In *Tadić*, the Appeals Chamber held that even though Dusko Tadić had not personally killed five men in the Bosnian town of Jaskici, his participation in implementing a common criminal plan resulting in such killings triggered his personal liability. The common plan had been acted upon physically alongside others and Tadić was part of the brain trust of the plan.[19] The Appeals Chamber held that "the notion of common purpose design as a form of accomplice liability is firmly established in customary international law."[20] The judges then described three types of joint criminal enterprise, each with three common characteristics (*actus reus*) but also reflecting a different mental, or *mens rea*, requirement.[21] Tadić was found guilty of one of these three modes of joint criminal enterprise freshly defined by the judges.[22]

3.1.2 Prosecutor v. Furundžija

(Trial Chamber Judgement of 1998).[23]

Indictment for war crimes: 10 November 1995 (thereafter amended)

[19] United Nations International Criminal Tribunal for the former Yugoslavia (1999), paras. 186–190.

[20] Id., para. 220.

[21] Id., paras. 227–228. "228. By contrast, the *mens rea* element differs according to the category of common design under consideration. With regard to the first category, what is required is the intent to perpetrate a certain crime (this being the shared intent on the part of all co-perpetrators). With regard to the second category (which, as noted above, is really a variant of the first, personal knowledge of the system of ill-treatment is required (whether proved by express testimony or a matter of reasonable inference from the accused's position of authority), as well as the intent to further this common concerted system of ill-treatment. With regard to the third category, what is required is the intention to participate in and further the criminal activity or the criminal purpose of a group and to contribute to the joint criminal enterprise or in any event to the commission of a crime by the group. In addition, responsibility for a crime other than the one agreed upon in the common plan arises only if, under the circumstances of the case, i) it was *foreseeable* that such a crime might be perpetrated by one or other members of the group and (ii) the accused *willingly took that risk*." Id., para. 228.

[22] Id., paras. 231–233.

[23] United Nations International Criminal Tribunal for the former Yugoslavia (1998).

Arrested by multinational Stabilisation Force (SFOR): 18 December 1997

Trial began: 8 June 1998

Trial Chamber Judgement: 10 December 1998

Appeals Chamber Judgement: 21 July 2000

Anto Furundžija, a Bosnian Croat, commanded a special unit of the Croatian Defense Council in Bosnia and Herzegovina known as the "Jokers." He was a combatant who had participated in the violent ethnic cleansing of Muslims from the Bosnian village of Ahmici in April 1993. But he was indicted and convicted for actions taken at the Jokers headquarters in the adjacent village of Nadiocia a month later (and just before the ICTY was operationally launched by U.N. Security Council Resolution 827 in May 1993). These acts—all war crimes—included torture and outrages upon personal dignity, including rape. Furundžija conducted the questioning of a naked Muslim woman while another Jokers officer sadistically abused and raped her with particular cruelty in public view, actions permitted by Furundžija who watched it all. A male witness was also drawn into Furundzija's interrogation, beaten along with the woman, forced to witness the sexual abuse of his friend, the woman, and who also experienced severe physical and mental suffering.

The Trial Chamber of the ICTY delivered three major rulings, all confirmed by the Appeals Chamber, that set the basis for future judgments on torture and rape.

3.1.2.1 The *Jus Cogens* Status of Torture

At the time of the *Furundžija* judgement in 1998, the adjudication of the crime of torture at an international level had never been undertaken. But the Trial Chamber filled that gap in jurisprudence with a simple conclusion: The prohibition of torture has achieved the status of a *jus cogens* norm of international law. The Trial Chamber ruled: "Because of the importance of the values it protects, this principle has evolved into a peremptory norm or *jus cogens*, that is, a norm that enjoys a higher rank in the international hierarchy than treaty law and even 'ordinary' customary rules. The most conspicuous consequence of this higher rank is that the principle at issue cannot be derogated from by States through international treaties or local or special customs or even general customary rules not endowed with the same normative force."[24] The Trial Chamber continued, "Clearly, the *jus cogens* nature of the prohibition against torture articulates the notion that the prohibition has now become one of the most fundamental standards of the international community. Furthermore, this prohibition is designed to produce a deterrent effect, in that it signals to all members of the international community and the individuals over whom they wield authority that the prohibition of torture is an absolute value from which nobody must deviate."[25]

[24] Id., para. 153.

[25] Id., para. 154.

Finally, "[I]n spite of possible national authorization by legislative or judicial bodies to violate the principle banning torture, individuals remain bound to comply with that principle. As the International Military Tribunal at Nuremberg put it: 'individuals have international duties which transcend the national obligations of obedience imposed by the individual State'."[26]

Today these words may seem self-evident regarding the crime of torture, but they were a welcome and unprecedented judicial pronouncement in 1998. Nonetheless, the systemic torture that occurred in connection with the wars in Afghanistan and Iraq only a few years later stood in sharp contrast to the ICTY's jurisprudence which should have been viewed as a red flag to prevent such illegal conduct. In the international courts, however, nothing has occurred to modify the ICTY's interpretation of international law on torture.

3.1.2.2 Definition of Torture

Amplifying beyond the definition of torture in the Convention against Torture and Other Cruel, Inhuman or Degrading Treatment or Punishment,[27] the Trial Chamber found "that the elements of torture in an armed conflict require that torture: (i) consists of the infliction, by act or omission, of severe pain or suffering, whether physical or mental; in addition (ii) this act or omission must be intentional; (iii) it must aim at obtaining information or a confession, or at punishing, intimidating, humiliating or coercing the victim or a third person, or at discriminating, on any ground, against the victim or a third person; (iv) it must be linked to an armed conflict; (v) at least one of the persons involved in the torture process must be a public official or must at any rate act in a non-private capacity, e.g. as a de facto organ of a State or any other authority-wielding entity."[28] The last element was rescinded by the ICTY in the *Kunarac* Trial Judgement on 22 February 2001.[29] The *Furundžija* Trial Chamber further reflected "that among the possible purposes of torture one must also include that of humiliating the victim. This proposition is warranted by the general spirit of international humanitarian law: the primary purpose of this body of law is to safeguard human dignity....[There is] a momentum towards addressing, through legal process, the use of rape in the course of detention and interrogation as a means of torture and, therefore, as a violation of international law. Rape is resorted to either by the interrogator himself or by other persons associated with the interrogation of a detainee, as a means of punishing, intimidating, coercing or humiliating the victim, or obtaining information, or a confession, from the victim or a third person. In human rights law, in such situations the rape may amount to torture...".[30]

[26] Id., para. 155.

[27] Office of the United Nations High Commissioner for Human Rights (2026a).

[28] United Nations International Criminal Tribunal for the former Yugoslavia (1998), para. 162.

[29] United Nations International Criminal Tribunal for the former Yugoslavia (2001), paras. 488–496.

[30] United Nations International Criminal Tribunal for the former Yugoslavia (1998), paras. 162–163.

3.1.2.3 Definition of Rape in International Criminal Law

Lacking a well-accepted definition for rape in international criminal law, the Trial Chamber addressed that deficiency. It discerned a trend "in the national legislation of a number of States of broadening the definition of rape so that it now embraces acts that were previously classified as comparatively less serious offences, that is sexual or indecent assault. This trend shows that at the national level States tend to take a stricter attitude towards serious forms of sexual assault: the stigma of rape now attaches to a growing category of sexual offences, provided of course they meet certain requirements chiefly that of forced physical penetration."[31] The Trial Chamber then defined the elements of rape under international criminal law for the first time in stark detail.[32] In a later case, *Prosecutor v. Kunarac*, the ICTY clarified that lack of consent rather than coercion is an essential element of the crime of rape.[33]

3.1.3 Prosecutor v. Galic

(Trial Chamber Judgement of 2003).[34]

Indicted: 28 March 1998 and 26 March 1999

Arrested: 20 December 1999

Trial began: 3 December 2001

Trial Chamber Judgement: 5 December 2003

Appeals Chamber Judgement: 30 December 2006 (life imprisonment)

Major General Stanislav Galic was Commander of the Sarajevo Romaija Corps (SRK) of the Bosnian Serb Army which laid siege to Sarajevo, the capital of Bosnia and Herzegovina, from November 1992 to August 1994. That siege dominated world headlines for its deadly impact on the civilian population of Sarajevo. The ICTY offered vivid details in the testimony of witnesses and victims and its various documents, including the Trial Chamber and Appeals Chamber judgements and in information provided about the case. The latter reads in part:

> The [Trial] Chamber found that the evidence demonstrated beyond reasonable doubt that Sarajevo civilians were indeed made the objects of deliberate attacks by SRK forces. The [Trial] Chamber heard from local witnesses who had experienced multiple attacks in their neighbourhoods. They were attacked while attending funerals, while in ambulances, trams, and buses, and while cycling. They were attacked while tending gardens, or shopping in markets, or clearing rubbish in the city. Children were targeted while playing or walking in the streets. These attacks were mostly carried out in daylight. They were not in response

[31] Id., para. 179.

[32] Id., para. 185.

[33] United Nations International Criminal Tribunal for the former Yugoslavia (2001), paras. 453–460.

[34] United Nations International Criminal Tribunal for the former Yugoslavia (2003).

> to any military threat. The attackers could for the most part easily tell that their victims were engaged in everyday civilian activities. The topography of Sarajevo, with its ridges and high-rise buildings, provided vantage-points for SRK personnel to target civilians in the city. Certain locations in Sarajevo became notorious sniping spots. For example, several witnesses testified that the main thoroughfare in Sarajevo was known as "Sniper Alley". Although civilians adapted to some extent to the frequent attacks, by closing schools, by living at night and hiding during the day, by moving around Sarajevo as little as possible, and by setting up steel containers to shield against sniper fire, they were still not safe. They were still seen and targeted. There was little effective protection against shelling….
> The exact number of civilian casualties from the sniping and shelling attacks is not known. What is known is that hundreds of civilians were killed and thousands were injured in incidents over the two-year period covered by the indictment. A fraction of these, but no more than a fraction, may have been accidents. Because, to the majority, it was clear from the evidence that civilians were deliberately attacked by the SRK in a large number of incidents over a long period of time, they were persuaded that the attacks were not isolated incidents but amounted to a widespread or systematic campaign. In addition to supporting the existence of a campaign, the evidence as understood by the majority revealed that the campaign against civilians was intended primarily to terrorise the civilian population. It had no discernible significance in military terms. The frequency of attacks may have fluctuated from day to day, but they always underscored the fact that no civilian of Sarajevo was safe anywhere.[35]

3.1.3.1 Crime of Terror against the Civilian Population as a War Crime

The charge of terrorism as a war crime during the siege of Sarajevo trial was powerfully presented by the prosecution in the *Galic* case; the Trial Chamber judgement reflected the strength of those arguments. These excerpts of numbered paragraphs from the Trial Chamber judgement demonstrate the importance of this pathbreaking case:

> 66. The charge, as such, of terror against the civilian population is one that until now has not been considered in a Tribunal judgement, although evidence of terrorization of civilians has been factored into convictions on other charges.[36] This is also the first time an international tribunal has pronounced on the matter.[37]
> 133. [T]he crime of terror against the civilian population in the form charged in the Indictment is constituted of the elements common to offences falling under Article 3 of the [ICTY] Statute, as well as of the following specific elements:
>
> 1. Acts of violence directed against the civilian population or individual civilians not taking direct part in hostilities causing death or serious injury to body or health within the civilian population.
> 2. The offender wilfully made the civilian population or individual civilians not taking direct part in hostilities the object of those acts of violence.
> 3. The above offence was committed with the primary purpose of spreading terror among the civilian population.[38]

---

35 Communications Service of the International Criminal Tribunal for the former Yugoslavia (2026), pp. 3–4.

36 See United Nations International Criminal Tribunal for the former Yugoslavia (2002b), fn. 114.

37 United Nations International Criminal Tribunal for the former Yugoslavia (2002a), para. 66; see United Nations International Criminal Tribunal for the former Yugoslavia (2002b), fn. 115.

38 United Nations International Criminal Tribunal for the former Yugoslavia (2002a), para. 133.

> 134. The Majority [of the Trial Chamber judges] rejects the Parties' submissions that actual infliction of terror is an element of the crime of terror. The plain wording of Article 51(2) [of the 1977 Protocol I of the Geneva Conventions of 12 August 1949, and Relating to the Protection of Victims of International Armed Conflicts], as well as *the travaux preparatoires* of the Diplomatic Conference 1974-1977 [which negotiated Protocols I and II of the Geneva Conventions of 12 August 1949] exclude this from the definition of the offence. Since actual infliction of terror is not a constitutive legal element of the crime of terror, there is also no requirement to prove a causal connection between the unlawful acts of violence and the production of terror, as suggested by the Parties.[39]
>
> 135. With respect to the "acts of violence," these do not include legitimate attacks against combatants but only unlawful attacks against civilians.[40]
>
> 136. "Primary purpose" signifies the *mens rea* of the crime of terror. It is to be understood as excluding *dolus eventualis* or recklessness from the intentional state specific to terror. Thus the Prosecution is required to prove not only that the Accused accepted the likelihood that terror would result from the illegal acts—or, in other words, that he was aware of the possibility that terror would result—but that that was the result which he specifically intended. The crime of terror is a specific intent crime.[41]
>
> 137. The meaning of "civilian population" was given in the section discussing the crime of attack on civilians. The Majority accepts the Prosecution's rendering of "terror" as "extreme fear." The *travaux preparatoires* of the Diplomatic Conference do not suggest a different meaning.[42]
>
> 138. The Majority is of the view that an offence constituted of acts of violence wilfully directed against the civilian population or individual civilians causing death or serious injury to body or health within the civilian population with the primary purpose of spreading terror among the civilian population—namely the crime of terror as a violation of the laws or customs of war—formed part of the law to which the Accused and his subordinates were subject to during the Indictment period. The Accused knew or should have known that this was so. Terror as a crime within international humanitarian law was made effective in this case by treaty law. The Tribunal has jurisdiction *ratione materiae* by way of Article 3 of the Statute. Whether the crime of terror also has a foundation in customary law is not a question which the Majority is required to answer.[43]

The ICTY Appeals Chamber, however, was prepared to consider whether the crime of terror had a foundation in customary law at the time of the Balkans War, and found that it did. In his courtroom reading of the summary of the Appeals Chamber judgement on 30 November 2006, Judge Fausto Pocar set forth guidelines for the criminalization of the prohibition of terror against the civilian population based on customary international law:

> With regard to *the prohibition of terror against the civilian population in customary international law*, the Appeals Chamber confirms the Trial Chamber's finding that the prohibition of terror, as contained in the second sentences of both Article 51(2) of Additional Protocol I and Article 13(2) of Additional Protocol II, amounts to "a specific prohibition within the general (customary) prohibition of attacks on civilians". The principles underlying the prohibition of attacks on civilians, namely the principles of distinction and protection, have

[39] Id., para. 134.

[40] Id., para. 135.

[41] Id., para. 136.

[42] Id., para. 137.

[43] Id., para. 138.

> a long-standing history in international humanitarian law, incontrovertibly form the basic foundation of international humanitarian law and constitute intransgressible principles of international customary law. As the Appeals Chamber has held in previous decisions, the conventional prohibition on attack on civilians contained in Articles 51 of Additional Protocol I and 13 of Additional Protocol II constitutes customary international law.
> With regard to *the criminalisation of the prohibition of terror against the civilian population*, the Appeals Chamber finds, by majority, Judge Schomburg dissenting, that customary international law imposed individual criminal liability for violations of the prohibition of terror against the civilian population as enshrined in Article 51(2) of Additional Protocol I and Article 13(2) of Additional Protocol II, from at least the period relevant to the Indictment.
> I will now turn to *the elements of the crime of acts or threats of violence the primary purpose of which is to spread terror among the civilian population.* Having found that the prohibition on terror against the civilian population in the Additional Protocols was declaratory of customary international law, the Appeals Chamber bases its analysis of the elements of the crime under consideration under Count 1 of the Indictment on the definition found therein: "Acts or threats of violence the primary purpose of which is to spread terror among the civilian population." On that basis, the Appeals Chamber finds the following:
> With regard to the *actus reus*, the Appeals Chamber finds that the crime of acts or threats of violence the primary purpose of which is to spread terror among the civilian population can comprise attacks or threats of attacks against the civilian population. Those acts or threats shall not however be limited to direct attacks against civilians or threats thereof but may include indiscriminate or disproportionate attacks or threats thereof. The nature of the acts or threats of violence directed against the civilian population can vary; the primary concern is that those acts or threats of violence be committed with the specific intent to spread terror among the civilian population. Further, the crime of acts or threats of violence the primary purpose of which is to spread terror among the civilian population is not a case in which an explosive device was planted outside of an ongoing military attack. Rather, and following the language of the Indictment, the crime under consideration concerns cases of "extensive trauma and psychological damage" being caused by "attacks [which] were designed to keep the inhabitants in a constant state of terror". Such extensive trauma and psychological damage form part of the acts or threats of violence.
> With regard to the *mens rea* and result requirement, the Appeals Chamber, relying on the plain language of Article 51(2) of Additional Protocol I, on its object and purpose and on the *travaux préparatoires* to Additional Protocol I, finds that actual terrorisation of the civilian population is not an element of the crime. The *mens rea* of the crime of acts or threats of violence the primary purpose of which is to spread terror among the civilian population is composed of the specific intent to spread terror among the civilian population. Further, the Appeals Chamber finds that a plain reading of Article 51(2) suggests that the purpose of the unlawful acts or threats to commit such unlawful acts need not be the only purpose of the acts or threats of violence. The fact that other purposes may have coexisted simultaneously with the purpose of spreading terror among the civilian population would not disprove this charge, provided that the intent to spread terror among the civilian population was principal among the aims. Such intent can be inferred from the circumstances of the acts or threats, that is from their nature, manner, timing and duration.[44]

The *Galic* Appeals Chamber judgement took the historic step of confirming the *war crime* of spreading terror among the civilian population and affirming that it is part of customary international law. The next step in the modern tribunals would be confirming the crime of international terrorism under international law, and that would occur in an interlocutory decision of the Special Tribunal for Lebanon in 2011, which is explained in the next chapter of this book.

[44] United Nations International Criminal Tribunal for the former Yugoslavia (2006a), pp. 4–5.

3.1.4 Prosecutor v. Radovan Karadžić; Prosecutor v. Ratko Mladić

Prosecutor v. Karadžić.[45]

Indicted: 25 July 1995; operational indictment dated 19 October 2009
Arrested in Belgrade: 21 July 2008
Trial began: 26 October 2009
Trial Chamber Judgement: 24 March 2016
Appeals Chamber (IRMCT) Judgement: 20 March 2019

Prosecutor v. Mladić.[46]

Indicted: 25 July 1995; operational indictment dated 16 December 2011
Arrested in Serbia: 26 May 2011
Trial began: 16 May 2012
Trial Chamber Judgement: 22 November 2017
Appeals Chamber (IRMCT) Judgement: 8 June 2021

Aside from Serbian leader Slobodan *Milošević*, who died near the end of his trial at the ICTY, the prosecutions and convictions of two other prominent defendants in the Balkans War for atrocity crimes committed between 1992 and 1995 demonstrated that leaders who orchestrate mass atrocity crimes sometimes can be brought to justice regardless of their positions of power, their domestic base of support and campaigns of disinformation, or their efforts to avoid capture and trial before international judges. Granted, there are political and military leaders who will, until their dying days, escape the reach of international justice for their assaults on humankind. That is the inevitable reality of enforcing any system of criminal law for any category of crimes, whether investigations and trials are held at the local, national, or international level. But the *Karadžić* and *Mladić* cases before the ICTY Trial Chambers, followed at the appeals level before the IRMCT, represent historic judicial precedents for accountability at the highest levels.

Karadžić and Mladić were found guilty and sentenced to life imprisonment for committing genocide, a vast array of crimes against humanity, and numerous violations of the laws or customs war (war crimes) in Bosnia and Herzegovina during the Balkans War. They worked in tandem, Karadžić as the President and Supreme Commander of the armed forces of Republika Srpska and Mladić as the Commander of the Main Staff of the Army of Republika Srpska. Here we focus on two major results in the judgements rendered by the ICTY Trial Chamber and the IRMCT Appeals Chamber in both cases:

---

[45] United Nations International Criminal Tribunal for the former Yugoslavia (2026a).

[46] United Nations International Criminal Tribunal for the former Yugoslavia (2026b).

3.1.4.1 Joint Criminal Enterprises

The novel formulation of the joint criminal enterprise (JCE) mode of liability in the *Tadić* case became the predominant finding of each defendant's participation in unlawful conduct in the *Karadžić* and *Mladić* judgements. Four theaters of combat were identified where the two leaders collaborated to commit atrocity crimes. The "overarching" JCE was to permanently remove Bosnian Muslims and Bosnian Croats from territory claimed by the Bosnian Serbs and to do so by committing atrocity crimes in municipalities throughout Bosnia and Herzegovina. This became known as the ethnic cleansing campaign that proved so effective and fueled the Balkans war. The second JCE established and conducted a campaign of sniping and shelling against the civilian population of Sarajevo in order to spread terror among the civilians. The siege of Sarajevo by Bosnian Serb forces seized headlines for years and required prolonged planning and organization that the JCE facilitated under the leadership of Karadžić and Mladić. The third JCE involved taking United Nations personnel hostage in May and June 1995 in order to compel NATO to refrain from launching air strikes against Bosnian Serb military targets. The fourth JCE involved the genocidal plan to eliminate Bosnian Muslims from Srebrenica that was implemented in July 1995 by killing men and boys and forcibly removing women, young children, and the elderly from the area.

With the affirmation of each of these joint criminal enterprises by the ICTY Trial Chamber and then by the IRMCT Appeals Chamber, the latter ruling on Karadžić in 2019 and then Mladić in 2021, the JCE mode of liability became firmly entrenched in international criminal law alongside the common purpose mode of participation developed in parallel by the International Criminal Court.[47]

3.1.4.2 Criteria for the Crime of Genocide

The indictments against Karadžić and Mladić each charged the crime of genocide for Bosnian Serb assaults on six municipalities in northern Bosnia and Herzegovina in 1992 as well as the Bosnian Serb massacres of Bosnian Muslims near Srebrenica in July 1995. The assaults on the municipalities in 1992 were massive ethnic cleansing operations that resulted in convictions for crimes against humanity. The ICTY also determined that killing members of a protected group (of national, racial, ethnic, or religious character) and causing serious bodily or mental harm to members of a protected group were acts of genocide that occurred during these operations. However, the majority of the judges did not find that either Karadžić or Mladić possessed in 1992 the specific intent to destroy all or a substantial part of a protected group and thus, lacking such specific intent, the crime of genocide had not been

[47] United Nations International Criminal Tribunal for the former Yugoslavia (2016), paras. 556–570; United Nations International Criminal Tribunal for the former Yugoslavia (2017), paras. 3556–5163; United Nations International Criminal Tribunal for the former Yugoslavia (2019), paras. 358–437; United Nations International Criminal Tribunal for the former Yugoslavia (2021), paras. 150–275.

proven. There must exist both an act of genocide *and* the specific mental intent, when committing such act of genocide, to destroy in whole or in part a protected group.

The Appeals judges applied reasoning first articulated by the International Court of Justice in *Bosnia and Herzegovina v. the Federal Republic of Yugoslavia* (2007) and in *Croatia v. Serbia* (2015): "Karadzic was found not guilty of genocide in relation to Count 1 of the Indictment [concerning the six Bosnian municipalities in 1992]…The Trial Chamber reviewed the pattern of crimes committed in each of the Count 1 Municipalities and found that the evidence did not establish, as the only reasonable inference, the existence of the intent to destroy the Bosnian Muslim and/or Bosnian Croat groups in these municipalities. Rather, it considered that another reasonable inference was the intent to 'ensure the removal' of the targeted groups from the Count 1 Municipalities."[48] The reasonable inference identified by the Appeals Chamber was ethnic cleansing and thus the culpability of the defendant to commit a crime against humanity, but not genocide.

The particular charge of genocide covering the 1992 operations against the populations of six Bosnian municipalities led to a novel prosecution strategy of sequencing commission of the crime of genocide as the act that resulted in ethnic cleansing of the municipalities. The *Karadžić* Appeals Chamber judgement of 2016 described the Prosecution's strategy—to prove that acts of genocide resulted in ethnic cleansing—as follows:

> The Prosecution argues that the Trial Chamber failed to consider that the objective of permanent removal can be accomplished through genocide and, thereby, did not sufficiently assess whether Karadžić and the Overarching JCE members [who included Mladić] possessed genocidal intent and used acts of genocide to achieve the joint criminal enterprise's objective of permanent removal…[T]he record did not support, as the only reasonable inference, the finding of genocidal intent with respect to the crimes committed in the Count 1 Municipalities…[T]he Prosecution's contention ignores the Trial Chamber's extensive assessment of evidence, which the Prosecution argues would suggest that the objective of permanent removal could be achieved through acts of genocide…[T]he Appeals Chamber finds, Judge de Prada dissenting, that the Prosecution fails to demonstrate that the Trial Chamber erroneously concluded that the objective of permanent removal precluded a finding of genocidal intent…Absent direct evidence of genocidal intent, the 'scale of the atrocities committed' is one of several factors relevant to determining genocidal intent and the fact that more members of a targeted group could have been, for example, killed, but were not, may indicate a lack of the dolus specialis required to prove such intent.[49]

This exercise in fine-tuning the elements of the crime of genocide emphasizes that the evidence of the perpetrator's actions must clearly demonstrate, to qualify as the crime of genocide, both the act of genocide and the specific intent to destroy all or a substantial part of a protected group, and, importantly, that such evidence of genocide must be the *only* reasonable interpretation of what happened and why it happened. In the *Karadžić* and *Mladić* cases, what happened in 1992 in northern

[48] United Nations International Residual Mechanism for Criminal Tribunals (2019), paras. 712, 714.

[49] Id., para. 143.

Bosnia and Herzegovina never reached the level of the crime of genocide because the requisite level of specific intent to commit genocide could not be established. The Prosecution's novel strategy of casting the assaults on the six municipalities initially as genocide that led to ethnic cleansing, which is a crime against humanity, presented a legal rationale that, if the evidence in a future situation so demonstrates, would be another pathbreaking development in international criminal law.

3.2 International Criminal Tribunal for Rwanda

The cascade of genocidal acts that overwhelmed the citizens of Rwanda from the beginning of April 1994 through June of that year gave rise relatively quickly to the U.N. Security Council creating in November 1994 its second *ad hoc* tribunal, namely the International Criminal Tribunal for Rwanda (ICTR). Most of the many cases that were tried by the ICTR were centered on prosecution of the crime of genocide. But crimes of humanity and war crimes also were charged and prosecuted through to conviction. We present two cases where these sets of crimes were under scrutiny, the first involving the leader of a common Rwandan settlement swept into the genocide ravaging practically the entire country, and the second is about Rwandan media titans who incited atrocity crimes. The judgements in each case modernized the law governing genocide and the law governing crimes against humanity and set the stage for further prosecutions.

3.2.1 Prosecutor v. Jean-Paul Akayesu[50]

Indicted: 13 February 1996

Arrested in Zambia: 10 October 1995

Trial began: 9 January 1997

Trial Chamber Judgement: 2 September 1998

Appeals Chamber Judgement: 1 June 2001

A notorious Hutu local leader who fueled the genocide of 1994, Jean-Paul Akayesu, was the *bourgmestre* (mayor) of a commune, Taba, in the Gitarama prefecture (now province) of central Rwanda. The ICTR prosecuted and convicted him for genocide, crimes against humanity, and war crimes. Akayesu's trial was the first held at the ICTR and it resulted in significant interpretations of international criminal law by the ICTR judges of the Trial Chamber and Appeals Chamber.

[50] United Nations International Criminal Tribunal for Rwanda (1998, 2001).

3.2.1.1 Ethnic Identity

The Trial Chamber confronted a seemingly complex problem of identifying the ethnic character of the Tutsi minority that was the target of the genocide, which ultimately took an estimated 800,000 civilian lives. The Hutu majority of the population shared the same language and culture as the Tutsis. The division between the two groups, however, was largely artificial and the consequence of Belgian colonial rule in the past and divisions codified in the Rwandan constitution and laws. Significantly, the Trial Chamber determined that the ethnic divide existed because of the subjective perception of ethnic distinction that was held by the Hutu perpetrators of their Tutsi victims. The holding broke through what could have been a barrier to identifying ethnic diversity along strictly biological or cultural characteristics.

3.2.1.2 Rape and Sexual Violence as Genocide

The *Akayesu* Trial Chamber judgement held, for the first time in any tribunal judgement, that rape and sexual violence can be an act of genocide. There was evidence, determined the Trial Chamber, that rape had been used against the Tutsi ethnic group for the purpose of destroying it. More precisely, mass rape can serve to destroy, physically and psychologically, the victims and families of a protected group (such as the Tutsis of Rwanda) in a manner that constitutes genocide. The historic ruling of the Trial Chamber significantly widened the scope of conduct that could qualify as an act of genocide. The following extract from the Trial Chamber judgement describes this broader dimension to the crime of genocide:

> [R]egard[ing]...rape and sexual violence, the Chamber wishes to underscore the fact that in its opinion, they constitute genocide in the same way as any other act as long as they were committed with the specific intent to destroy, in whole or in part, a particular group, targeted as such. Indeed, rape and sexual violence certainly constitute infliction of serious bodily and mental harm on the victims and are even, according to the Chamber, one of the worst ways [to] inflict harm on the victim as he or she suffers both bodily and mental harm. In light of all the evidence before it, the Chamber is satisfied that the acts of rape and sexual violence...were committed solely against Tutsi women, many of whom were subjected to the worst public humiliation, mutilated, and raped several times, often in public, in the Bureau Communal premises or in other public places, and often by more than one assailant. These rapes resulted in physical and psychological destruction of Tutsi women, their families and their communities. Sexual violence was an integral part of the process of destruction, specifically targeting Tutsi women and specifically to their destruction and to the destruction of the Tutsi group as a whole.
>
> The rape of Tutsi women was systematic and was perpetrated against all Tutsi women and solely against them...This sexualized representation of ethnic identity graphically illustrates that [T]utsi women were subjected to sexual violence because they were Tutsi. Sexual violence was a step in the process of destruction of the [T]utsi group—destruction of the spirit, of the will to live, and of life itself....
>
> [I]t appears clearly to the Chamber that the acts of rape and sexual violence, as other acts of serious bodily and mental harm committed against the Tutsi, reflected the determination to make Tutsi women suffer and to mutilate them even before killing them, the intent being to destroy the Tutsi group while inflicting acute suffering on its members in the process...

> The Chamber is further satisfied beyond reasonable doubt that these various acts were committed by Akayesu with the specific intent to destroy the Tutsi group, as such....[H]ence, the Chamber finds Akayesu individually criminally responsible for genocide.[51]

3.2.1.3 Incitement to Commit Crimes against Humanity or War Crimes

The Statute of the ICTR explicitly requires that any incitement to commit genocide must be "public and direct" in order to trigger an individual's criminal responsibility.[52] The Genocide Convention also contains this requirement.[53] But for the first time the Appeals Chamber clarified that the requirement underpinning incitement to genocide does *not* translate into one required for incitement of crimes of humanity and war crimes. Inciting the latter two categories of atrocity crimes need be neither direct nor public in character; in other words, incitement of crimes against humanity or of war crimes can be implemented indirectly or privately.[54]

3.2.1.4 Most Crimes against Humanity Need Not Be Committed with Discriminatory Intent

In the *Tadić* case before the ICTY, the Appeals Chamber found that the commission of a crime against humanity does not require a finding that the defendant exercised discriminatory intent except when the crime against humanity being prosecuted is persecution. The Appeals Chamber in *Akayesu* confirmed this significant point of law, namely that crimes against humanity "continue to be governed in the usual manner by customary international law, namely that discrimination is not a requirement for the various crimes against humanity, except where persecution is concerned."[55] This was particularly important to confirm because the Statute of the ICTR was uniquely drafted at the insistence of the new Rwandan Government in 1994, following the genocide, to require evidence of a particular discriminatory intent in its provision on crimes against humanity ("...a widespread or systematic attack against any civilian population on national, political, ethnic, racial or religious grounds...").[56] The Appeals Chamber in *Akayesu* clarified that despite such narrow wording in the ICTR Statute, under customary international law the ambit of crimes against humanity is very wide and lacking any need by the prosecution to prove a discriminatory intent other than where the crime of persecution is being charged. The objective requirements for crimes against humanity, best set forth in the Rome

---

[51] United Nations International Criminal Tribunal for Rwanda (1998), pp. 731–734.

[52] Office of the United Nations High Commissioner for Human Rights (2026c), art. 2(3)(c).

[53] Office of the United Nations High Commissioner for Human Rights (2026b), art. III(c).

[54] United Nations International Criminal Tribunal for Rwanda (2001), paras. 470–483.

[55] Id., para. 466.

[56] See Office of the United Nations High Commissioner for Human Rights (2026c), art. 3.

Statute of the International Criminal Court,[57] focus not on any discriminatory intent but rather on the widespread or systematic character of an attack on a civilian population regardless of the purpose or intent behind the attack and provided that the perpetrator had knowledge of the widespread or systematic attack directed against the civilian population.

3.2.2 Prosecutor v. Nahimana, Barayagwiza, and Ngeze (Media Case)

Indicted: Nahimana on 15 November 1999; Barayagwiza on 14 April 2000; Ngeze on 10 November 1999

Arrested: Nahimana in Cameroon on 27 March 1996; Barayagwiza in Cameroon on or about 26 March 1996; Ngeze in Kenya on 18 July 1997

Joint Trial began: 23 October 2000

Trial Chamber Judgement: 3 December 2003

Appeals Chamber Judgement: 28 November 2007

The *Media* case, in[58] which three defendants who had been businessmen holding influential positions in Rwanda's media realm of radio and print in 1994, was one of the most important cases litigated before the ICTR. The case put to the test how acts to disseminate incendiary information to the public at times and in ways to incite or otherwise propagate genocide or crimes against humanity could be enforced by an international criminal tribunal. Two of the defendants, Julius Streicher and Hans Fritzsche, prosecuted before the International Military Tribunal at Nuremberg in 1945 and 1946 were propagandists charged with using the media to stoke antisemitism and resulting violence against Jews.[59] Streicher was convicted and hanged. Fritzsche was acquitted. Their prosecutions set a precedent for such media-focused conduct as crimes against humanity. Decades later the ICTR's *Media* case was the first trial in the modern atrocity crimes tribunals to hold propagandists, who were intertwined with the business aims of *Radio Mille Collines* or the *Kangura* newspaper, to account for atrocity crimes and to demonstrate how their manipulation of the media achieved unlawful aims.

Defendant Ferdinand Nahimana was the Director of ORINFOR, the Rwandan Office of Information from 1990 to 1992, and then he and others set up a company known as *Radio television libre des mille collines, S.A.*, (*Radio Mille Collines*) which would play a central role in inciting commission of the atrocity crimes in Rwanda in

[57] See International Criminal Court (2013), arts. 7–7(1)(k); International Criminal Court (2024), art. 7.

[58] For list of trial and appeals judgments documents, see United Nations International Criminal Tribunal for Rwanda (2026).

[59] International Military Tribunal (1946).

1994. Jean-Bosco Barayagwiza helped organize the founding of *Radio Mille Collines* and he was Director of Political Affairs in the Ministry of Foreign Affairs. Hassan Ngeze founded *Kangura* and became its editor-in-chief.

Drawing significant precedents from the *Media* case to demonstrate the evolution and enforceability of international criminal law at first can appear challenging. Many of the convictions rendered by the Trial Chamber on various charges did not survive review in the Appeals Chamber. They were reversed and in the end the sentences of each of the defendants were reduced by the Appeals Chamber. But some of the reversals of the Trial Chamber convictions turned on the insufficiency, in the view of the Appeals Chamber, of the evidence to support the charges. Many of the Trial Chamber convictions were upheld by the Appeals Chamber and the underlying interpretations of international criminal law by the Trial Chamber prevailed and strengthened numerous principles.

3.2.2.1 Temporal Jurisdiction

The governing Statute of the ICTR established a temporal jurisdiction of one calendar year, namely the 365 days of 1994. This time period had been the subject of intense negotiations in the talks leading to the creation of the ICTR in late 1994.[60] The Trial Chamber, however, used evidence of actions arising *prior* to 1994 to support its convictions for the crimes of conspiracy and direct and public incitement to commit genocide, which had occurred in 1994. The Appeals Chamber considered "that the drafters of the Statute indicated that the Tribunal could only exercise its jurisdiction to sentence an accused if all the facts that must be established to find him guilty existed in 1994. Such an interpretation is consistent with the principle of strict interpretation of the provisions conferring jurisdiction on an international tribunal and with the principle of strict interpretation in criminal law. The Appeals Chamber finds that the Trial Chamber erred by basing some of the findings of guilt of the Appellants on criminal conduct prior to 1 January 1994. Moreover, the Appeals Chamber considers that even if the continuous criminal conduct began prior to 1 January 1994 and continued during that year, a finding of guilt can only be based on that part of the criminal conduct which occurred in 1994."[61] This ruling resulted in discarding evidence of the media stoking genocidal fever in the Hutu population of Rwanda prior to 1994—which would be a common sensical understanding of how incitement works its will with a population over often long periods of time—and emphasizing that the precise parameters of temporal jurisdiction is a critical factor in determining the jurisdictional reach of a modern atrocity crimes tribunal. That point would be important guidance for how other tribunals need to heed the statutory temporal jurisdiction and whether it is stated generally or very precisely. Such determination in each case included the ICTY's open-ended temporal jurisdiction that began "since 1991" (meaning any time during the calendar year 1991) without a stated end date

[60] Scheffer (2012), pp. 80–84.

[61] United Nations International Criminal Tribunal for Rwanda (2007), p. 7.

but found to extend through the Kosovo War of 1999; the Special Court of Sierra Leone's open-ended temporal jurisdiction that began on November 30, 1996; and the explicitly limited temporal jurisdiction of the Extraordinary Chambers in the Courts of Cambodia spanning the dates of 17 April 1975 to 6 January 1979. The temporal jurisdiction of the Special Tribunal of Lebanon extended from 1 October 2004 to 12 December 2005. The International Criminal Court was established and operational as of 1 July 2002, but the temporal jurisdiction for each State Party of the Rome Statute of the ICC commences 60 days after the effective date of ratification of or accession to the Rome Statute for that State.[62] Once the start date of temporal jurisdiction for the new State Party is established, then the ICC's temporal jurisdiction is perpetual for that State Party and its conduct.

3.2.2.2 Genocide: Direct and Public Incitement

The Trial Chamber in the *Media* case found that broadcasts by RTLM contributed significantly to the commission of acts of genocide, but the Appeals Chamber limited that finding to broadcasts made after the first day of the genocide, namely 6 April 1994. The Trial Chamber convicted each of the defendants on charges of direct and public incitement to commit genocide, thus setting a precedent for how this can be achieved based upon manipulation of the media. The Appeals Chamber modified some of the convictions based upon temporal jurisdiction determinations but upheld the basic premise of criminal responsibility for incitement to genocide through the media. Importantly, the Appeals Chamber focused on the distinction between hate speech and direct incitement to commit genocide. The appeals judges ruled that the act of "direct and public incitement to commit genocide" cannot be used to hold a defendant liable for hate speeches that do not directly incite genocide. They found

> that given that not every hate speech constitutes incitement to genocide, case-law on incitement to hatred, discrimination and violence is not immediately applicable in determining what would characterize direct incitement to commit genocide. However, the Appeals Chamber considers that in the present case, the Trial Chamber simply discussed certain general principles of interpretation and accountability for media-based speech. Therefore, the Trial Chamber did not erroneously modify the constituent elements of the crime of direct and public incitement to commit genocide in the context of the mass media.[63]

The Appeals Chamber set forth two guidelines for determining direct and public incitement to commit genocide, finding "an approach whereby incitement to commit genocide is considered direct only when it is explicit and whereby the Judge can in no circumstance consider the contextual elements in determining if a speech constitutes direct incitement to genocide is too restrictive." The first guideline established the

---

[62] Any nation, whether as a State Party to the Rome Statute or as a non-party State, can exercise a right under Article 12(3) of the Rome Statute to explicitly accept the jurisdiction of the International Criminal Court for a situation preceding any date that nation becomes a State Party, but only for a situation occurring after 1 July 2002.

[63] United Nations International Criminal Tribunal for Rwanda (2007), P. 12–13.

possibility "that it was open to the Trial Chamber to find that a speech which was not an explicit call to commit genocide or which could appear ambiguous at first sight nevertheless amounted to direct incitement to commit genocide in a particular context." The second guideline rejected

> the argument that the Trial Chamber held that a speech which does not contain any direct call to commit genocide can nevertheless constitute the actus reus of direct and public incitement to commit genocide if the author of the speech had a criminal intent. The Appeals Chamber also considers that the Trial Chamber could have taken into account the fact that genocide had taken place and considered that as one of the indicia in this case showing that, in a given context, the speech had been perceived as an incitement to commit genocide. In the opinion of the Appeals Chamber, the Trial Chamber did not commit an error in holding that it was necessary to consider the potential impact of words in their particular context in order to determine whether those words constitute direct and public incitement to commit genocide.[64]

The Appeals Chamber further clarified that incitement to commit genocide does not continue until the completion of the intended acts of genocide. "On the contrary direct and public incitement is completed as soon as the words in question are uttered, broadcast or published."[65] The Appeals Chamber then undertook a very detailed analysis of all relevant RTLM broadcasts and published articles of *Kangura* to determine which constituted incitement to commit genocide and which did not do so. Certain broadcasts and certain articles were found to meet the legal standard of incitement to commit genocide.

3.2.2.3 Crimes against Humanity: Hate Speech as Persecution

The Appeals Chamber in the *Media* case confirmed that the RTLM broadcasts after 6 April 1994 constituted acts of persecution that contributed substantially to the extermination of Tutsi and thus a crime against humanity. On this basis the Trial Chamber conviction of Nahimana was upheld. The Appeals Chamber was

> of the view that a hate speech targeting a population on ethnic grounds or on any other discriminatory grounds violate[s] the right for the respect of the human dignity of [a] member of the group, and constitute[s] 'factual discrimination' even though hate speech cannot on its own amount to a violation of the right to life, freedom and physical integrity. As to whether hate speech can be considered as being of the same gravity as other crimes against humanity, the Appeals Chamber is of the opinion that it is not necessary to determine here whether ordinary hate speeches which do not incite violence among members of an ethnic group are in themselves of a gravity equivalent to other crimes against humanity, In the present case, the Appeals Chamber concludes that the hate speeches were accompanied by calls for genocide against the Tutsi ethnic group and that all those speeches were part of a massive campaign for persecution directed against the Tutsi population of Rwanda, this campaign being also characterized by acts of violence and destruction of property. When considered together, in their context, the RTLM speeches in question were, in the opinion of the Appeals Chamber, of equivalent gravity as the other crimes against humanity. The Appeals Chamber

[64] Id., p. 13.

[65] Id.

> therefore concludes that the hate speeches and the speeches that called for violence against the Tutsi made after 6 April 1994 are in themselves acts of persecution.[66]

The Appeals Chamber found that the RTLM broadcasts made after 6 April 1994, which had substantially contributed to the killing of Tutsi, not only instigated the commission of acts of genocide but also of acts of persecution, and Nahimana was convicted under superior responsibility principles for such unlawful broadcasts.

3.2.2.4 Judicial Notice of Genocide

The situations in which atrocity crimes occur are typically widespread in their geographical reach, continuous for months or years, colossal in their size, thousands of casualties (both dead and wounded), and destruction of property, and thus seemingly obvious to the naked eye. Given the proliferation of atrocity crimes cases underpinning the jurisprudence of the criminal tribunals in the modern era, this tool of historical accuracy and indisputable evidence has enabled more timely and efficient prosecution of such cases. The reliance on judicial notice of atrocity crimes situations became a hallmark of the ICTR in particular with regard to the genocide of 1994 in Rwanda, but milestones on judicial notice also were reached in other tribunals, thus greatly reducing the burden of proof required for prosecution of such large-scale atrocities.[67]

The core meaning of "judicial notice" is that a court or tribunal hearing a case can accept designated facts as proven without hearing evidence about them, which can be extremely time-consuming and repetitive of testimony and findings about widespread atrocities proven during prior cases. The conclusive judicial notice ultimately embraced by the ICTR was that genocide occurred in Rwanda between April and July 1994. The case that brought the Appeals Chamber of the ICTR to render that judgement, and thus establish taking judicial notice of the 1994 genocide for all subsequent litigation before the tribunal, was *Prosecutor v. Edouard Karemera, Mathieu Ngirumpatse, and Joseph Nzirorera* (ICTR-98-44-AR73(C))[68] and in particular one of its preliminary rulings, *Prosecutor's Interlocutory Appeal on Judicial Notice*, 16 June 2006.[69] The ICTR reported on that ruling about taking judicial notice in the following press release:

> The Appeals Chamber of the International Criminal Tribunal for Rwanda on 16 June 2006 ruled that the Trial Chambers must take judicial notice of the following facts:
>
> 1) The existence of Twa, Tutsi and Hutu as protected groups falling under the Genocide Convention;
> 2) The following state of affairs existed in Rwanda between 6 April 1994 to 17 July 1994: there were throughout Rwanda widespread or systematic attacks against a civilian population based on Tutsi ethnic identification. During the attacks, some Rwandan

[66] Id., pp. 17–18.

[67] See generally Stewart (2009).

[68] United Nations International Residual Mechanism for Criminal Tribunals (2026).

[69] United Nations International Criminal Tribunal for Rwanda (2006b); see La Haye et al. (2009).

citizens killed or caused serious bodily or mental harm to person [s] perceived to be Tutsi. As a result of the attacks, there were a large number of deaths of persons of Tutsi ethnic identity;

3) Between 6 April 1994 and 17 July 1994 there was genocide in Rwanda against Tutsi ethnic group.

This landmark decision was delivered by the Appeals Chamber on Prosecutor's Appeal on Judicial Notice, dated 16 June 2006, in the trial of *Prosecutor v. Karemera, Ngirumpatse and Nzirorera*, ICTR-98-44-AR73 (C). The decision will have an immediate impact on the trial proceedings in the *Karemera et al* case, and will be felt in all of the current and pending trials before the Trial Chambers of the ICTR. Judicial notice of the above matters means that they are to be taken as established beyond any dispute and not requiring any proof.

This is one of the most significant rulings of the Tribunal, given the consequences in terms of putting the occurrence of the genocide beyond legal dispute. It can be recalled that until now the OTP [Office of the Prosecutor] has had to in each case lead evidence and prove the occurrence of the genocide. This will no longer be necessary.

In the view of the OTP the ruling should now silence the 'rejectionist' camp which has been disputing the occurrence of genocide. By relieving the OTP of a substantial burden of proof the ruling has the potential to shorten the cases as each will essentially focus on the personal involvement of the accused person in genocide.[70]

In its decision, the Appeals Chamber agreed "with the Prosecution: the fact that genocide occurred in Rwanda in 1994 should have been recognized by the Trial Chamber as a fact of common knowledge. Genocide consists of certain acts, including killing, undertaken with the intent to destroy, in whole or in part, a national, ethnical, racial or religious group, as such. There is no reasonable basis for anyone to dispute that, during 1994, there was a campaign of mass killing intended to destroy, in whole or at least in very large part, Rwanda's Tutsi population, which (as judicially noticed by the Trial Chamber) was a protected group. That campaign was, to a terrible degree, successful; although exact numbers may never be known, the great majority of Tutsis were murdered, and many others were raped or otherwise harmed. These basic facts were broadly known even at the time of the Tribunal's establishment; indeed, reports indicating that genocide occurred in Rwanda were a key impetus for its establishment, as reflected in the Security Council resolution establishing it and even the name of the Tribunal. During its early history, it was valuable for the purpose of the historical record for the Trial Chambers to gather evidence documenting the overall course of the genocide and to enter findings of fact on the basis of that evidence. Trial and Appeals Judgements thereby produced (while varying as to the responsibility of particular accused) have unanimously and decisively confirmed the occurrence of genocide in Rwanda, which has also been documented by countless books, scholarly articles, media reports, U.N. reports and resolutions, national court decisions, and government and NGO reports. At this stage, the Tribunal need not demand further documentation. The fact of the Rwandan genocide is a part of world history, a fact as certain as any other, a classic instance of a "fact of common knowledge."[71] (Internal citations omitted.)

---

[70] United Nations International Residual Mechanism for Criminal Tribunals External Relations and Communication Outreach Unit (2006).

[71] United Nations International Criminal Tribunal for Rwanda (2006b), para. 35.

The ICTR Appeals Chamber further explained that "common knowledge" means "'those facts which are not subject to reasonable dispute including, common or universally known facts, such as general facts of history, generally known geographical facts and the laws of nature.'" The tribunal must be able to "'determine also that the matter is reasonably indisputable.'"[72]

On reconsideration of the 16 June 2006 ruling, which had been appealed by the defendants, the Appeals Chamber explained:

> There is a significant difference between the taking of judicial notice of the fact of genocide and the determination that an accused is individually criminally responsible for the crime of genocide. The former gives a factual context to the allegations of the crime of genocide. The latter requires a finding of whether the elements of the crime of genocide, such as *actus reus* and *mens rea*, exist in order to ascertain whether an accused is responsible for the crime. Consequently, the taking of judicial notice of genocide does not, in itself, go to the alleged conduct or acts of the Applicants as charged in the indictment.[73] (Internal citation omitted.)

The Appeals Chamber carefully distinguished in its Reconsideration of the Decision on Judicial Notice between the meaning and finality of judicial notice and the continuing requirement at trial to meet the burden of proof against the individual defendant:

> The Appeals Chamber recalls and emphasizes its statement in the Decision on Judicial Notice that
>
>> the practice of judicial notice must not be allowed to circumvent the presumption of innocence and the defendant's right to a fair trial, including his right to confront his accusers. Thus, it would plainly be improper for facts judicially noticed to be the "basis for proving the Appellant's criminal responsibility" (in the sense of being *sufficient* to establish that responsibility), and it is always necessary for Trial Chambers to take careful consideration of the presumption of innocence and the procedural rights of the accused.[74]
>
> The Appeals Chamber also reiterates that judicially noticed facts do not relieve the Prosecution of its burden of proof.[75]

The Appeals Chamber reconfirmed its finding in the Decision on Judicial Notice that the armed conflict in Rwanda in 1994 was of a non-international character and that it should remain standing as such and be seen as being on judicial notice:

> The Appeals Chamber recalls that in the Decision on Judicial Notice, it relied on its findings in the *Semanza* Appeal Judgment where it held that the existence of a non-international armed conflict is a notorious fact not subject to a reasonable dispute. [Decision on Judicial Notice, para. 29, referring to *Prosecutor v. Semanza*, Case No. ICTR-97-20-A, Judgement, 20 May 2005, para. 192 (footnotes omitted) ("*Semanza* Appeal Judgment").] The fact that there may have been evidence in other cases before the Tribunal which alluded to the conflict being of an international character and that some reports and publications may express a similar view does not demonstrate a clear error in holding that it is a fact of common knowledge

[72] Stewart (2009), p. 398; see United Nations International Criminal Tribunal for Rwanda (2006b), paras. 22, 30, 42.

[73] United Nations International Criminal Tribunal for Rwanda (2006a), para. 16.

[74] United Nations International Criminal Tribunal for Rwanda (2006b), para. 47.

[75] United Nations International Criminal Tribunal for Rwanda (2006a), para. 26, (2006b), para. 37.

> that the conflict in Rwanda was of a non-international character. Furthermore, the Appeals Chamber has already indicated above that whether a fact is one of common knowledge is a legal question, the answer to which does not turn on the evidence introduced in a particular case.[76]

There emerged numerous ICTR judgements confirming judicial notice of facts of common knowledge, and the judicial tactic also appeared in cases being litigated before the ICTY and the Special Court for Sierra Leone. In several cases, the ICTY confirmed judicial notice of "adjudicated facts" that had been arrived at in prior judgements of the ICTY.[77]

References

Communications Service of the International Criminal Tribunal for the former Yugoslavia (2026) (IT-98-29) Stanislav Galić case information sheet. International Criminal Tribunal for the former Yugoslavia. https://www.icty.org/x/cases/galic/cis/en/cis_galic_en.pdf. Accessed 8 May 2026

International Court of Justice (1984) Military and paramilitary activities in and against Nicaragua (Nicaragua v. United States of America), jurisdiction and admissibility, judgment. International Court of Justice. Accessible via ICJ Reports. https://www.icj-cij.org/sites/default/files/case-related/70/070-19841126-JUD-01-00-EN.pdf. Accessed 8 May 2026

International Court of Justice (2007) Application on the Convention on the Prevention and Punishment of the Crime of Genocide (Bosnia and Herzegovina v. Serbia and Montenegro), judgment. International Court of Justice. Accessible via ICJ Reports. https://www.icj-cij.org/sites/default/files/case-related/91/091-20070226-JUD-01-00-EN.pdf. Accessed 8 May 2026

International Criminal Court (2013) Elements of crimes. International Criminal Court. https://www.icc-cpi.int/sites/default/files/Publications/Elements-of-Crimes.pdf. Accessed 8 May 2026

International Criminal Court (2024) Rome statute of the international criminal court. International Criminal Court.. https://www.icc-cpi.int/sites/default/files/2024-05/Rome-Statute-eng.pdf. Accessed 8 May 2026

International Military Tribunal (1946) Nuremberg judgment against major war criminals. International Military Tribunal. Accessible via Legal Tools Database. https://www.legal-tools.org/doc/45f18e/. Accessed 8 May 2026

La Haye E, de Bertodano S, Deshaies M (2009) Karemera. In: Cassese A (ed) The Oxford companion to international criminal justice. Oxford University Press, New York, pp 752–753

Lamb S (2009) Tadić Case. In: The Max Planck encyclopedia of public international law. Max Planck Institute for Comparative Public Law and International Law. Accessible via Oxford Public International Law. https://opil.ouplaw.com/display/10.1093/law:epil/9780199231690/law-9780199231690-e215. Accessed 8 May 2026

Matheson MJ, Scheffer D (2016) Am J of Intl Law 110(2):173–190. https://doi.org/10.5305/amerjintelaw.110.2.0173

Office of the United Nations High Commissioner for Human Rights (2026a) Convention against torture and other cruel, inhuman or degrading treatment or punishment. Office of the United Nations High Commissioner for Human Rights. https://www.ohchr.org/en/instruments-mechanisms/instruments/convention-against-torture-and-other-cruel-inhuman-or-degrading. Accessed 8 May 2026

[76] United Nations International Criminal Tribunal for Rwanda (2006a), para. 11.

[77] See Stewart (2009), pp. 398–399.

Office of the United Nations High Commissioner for Human Rights (2026b) Convention on the prevention and punishment of the crime of genocide. Office of the United Nations High Commissioner for Human Rights. https://www.ohchr.org/en/instruments-mechanisms/instruments/convention-prevention-and-punishment-crime-genocide. Accessed 8 May 2026

Office of the United Nations High Commissioner for Human Rights (2026c) Statute of the international criminal tribunal for the prosecution of persons responsible for genocide and other serious violations of international humanitarian law committed in the territory of Rwanda and Rwandan citizens responsible for genocide and other such violations committed in the territory of neighbouring states, between 1 January 1994 and 31 December 1994. Office of the United Nations High Commissioner for Human Rights. https://www.ohchr.org/en/instruments-mechanisms/instruments/statute-international-criminal-tribunal-prosecution-persons. Accessed 8 May 2026

Schabas W (2012) The UN international criminal tribunals: the former Yugoslavia. Cambridge University Press, New York, Rwanda and Sierra Leone

Scharf M, Epps V (1996) The international trial of the century: a cross-fire exchange on the first case before the Yugoslavia war crimes tribunal. Cornell Intl Law J 29(3):635–663

Scheffer D (2012) All the missing souls: a personal history of the war crimes tribunals. Princeton University Press, Princeton

Stewart J (2009) Judicial notice. In: Cassese A (ed) The Oxford companion to international criminal justice. Oxford University Press, New York, pp 397–399

United Nations International Criminal Tribunal for Rwanda (1998) Judgement in the case of Akayesu. United Nations International Criminal Tribunal for Rwanda. https://ucr.irmct.org/LegalRef/CMSDocStore/Public/English/Judgement/NotIndexable/ICTR-96-04/MSC44787R0000619822.PDF. Accessed 8 May 2026

United Nations International Criminal Tribunal for Rwanda (2001) Appeals judgement in the case of Akayesu. United Nations International Criminal Tribunal for Rwanda. https://www.un.org/en/preventgenocide/rwanda/pdf/AKAYESU%20-%20APPEAL%20JUDGEMENT.pdf. Accessed 8 May 2026

United Nations International Criminal Tribunal for Rwanda (2006a) Decision on motions for reconsideration. United Nations International Criminal Tribunal for Rwanda. https://ucr.irmct.org/LegalRef/CMSDocStore/Public/English/Decision/NotIndexable/ICTR-98-44/MSC22564R0000552134.PDF. Accessed 8 May 2026

United Nations International Criminal Tribunal for Rwanda (2006b) Decision on prosecutor's interlocutory appeal of decision on judicial notice. United Nations International Criminal Tribunal for Rwanda. https://ucr.irmct.org/LegalRef/CMSDocStore/Public/English/Decision/NotIndexable/ICTR-98-44/MSC22557R0000550490.PDF. Accessed 8 May 2026

United Nations International Criminal Tribunal for Rwanda (2007) Summary of judgement in the case of Nahimana et al. (ICT-99-52-a). United Nations International Criminal Tribunal for Rwanda. https://ucr.irmct.org/LegalRef/CMSDocStore/Public/English/Judgement/NotIndexable/ICTR-99-52/MSC34871R0000555176.PDF. Accessed 8 May 2026

United Nations International Criminal Tribunal for Rwanda (2026) Selected documents, [media] - Nahimana, Ferdinand - Barayagwiza, Jean Bosco - Ngeze, Hassan (ICTR-99-52). United Nations International Criminal Tribunal for Rwanda. https://ucr.irmct.org/scasedocs/case/ICTR-99-52. Accessed 8 May 2026

United Nations International Criminal Tribunal for the former Yugoslavia (1995) Decision on the defence motion for interlocutory appeal on jurisdiction. United Nations International Criminal Tribunal for the former Yugoslavia. https://www.icty.org/x/cases/tadic/acdec/en/51002.htm. Accessed 8 May 2026

United Nations International Criminal Tribunal for the former Yugoslavia (1998) Appeals judgement in the case of Furundžija. United Nations International Criminal Tribunal for the former Yugoslavia. https://www.icty.org/x/cases/furundzija/tjug/en/. Accessed 8 May 2026

United Nations International Criminal Tribunal for the former Yugoslavia (1999) Appeals judgement in the case of Tadić (IT-94-1-a). United Nations International Criminal Tribunal for the former

Yugoslavia. https://www.refworld.org/jurisprudence/caselaw/icty/1999/40180. Accessed 8 May 2026

United Nations International Criminal Tribunal for the former Yugoslavia (2001) Judgement in the case of Kunarac et al. United Nations International Criminal Tribunal for the former Yugoslavia. https://www.icty.org/x/cases/kunarac/tjug/en/kun-tj010222e.pdf. Accessed 8 May 2026

United Nations International Criminal Tribunal for the former Yugoslavia (2002a) Appeals judgement in the case of Kunarac et al. United Nations International Criminal Tribunal for the former Yugoslavia. https://www.icty.org/x/cases/kunarac/acjug/en/. Accessed 8 May 2026

United Nations International Criminal Tribunal for the former Yugoslavia (2002b) Judgement and opinion in the case of Galić. United Nations International Criminal Tribunal for the former Yugoslavia. https://www.icty.org/x/cases/galic/tjug/en/. Accessed 8 May 2026

United Nations International Criminal Tribunal for the former Yugoslavia (2004) Appeals judgement in the case of Blaškić (IT-95-14-a). United Nations International Criminal Tribunal for the former Yugoslavia. https://www.icty.org/x/cases/blaskic/acjug/en/. Accessed 8 May 2026

United Nations International Criminal Tribunal for the former Yugoslavia (2006a) Prosecutor v. Stanislav Galić, summary of appeals judgement. United Nations International Criminal Tribunal for the former Yugoslavia. https://www.icty.org/x/cases/galic/acjug/en/061130_Galic_summary_en.pdf. Accessed 8 May 2026

United Nations International Criminal Tribunal for the former Yugoslavia (2006b) Tribunal welcomes final independent Dutch inquest results concerning death of Slobodan Milošević. United Nations International Criminal Tribunal for the former Yugoslavia. https://www.icty.org/en/press/tribunal-welcomes-final-independent-dutch-inquest-results-concerning-death-slobodan-milosevic. Accessed 8 May 2026

United Nations International Criminal Tribunal for the former Yugoslavia (2016) Prosecutor v. Radovan Karadžić, public redacted version of judgement issued on 24 march 2016. United Nations International Criminal Tribunal for the former Yugoslavia. https://www.icty.org/x/cases/karadzic/tjug/en/160324_judgement.pdf. Accessed 8 May 2026

United Nations International Criminal Tribunal for the former Yugoslavia (2017) Prosecutor v. Ratko Mladić, public with confidential annex judgment. United Nations International Criminal Tribunal for the former Yugoslavia. https://ucr.irmct.org/LegalRef/CMSDocStore/Public/English/Judgement/NotIndexable/IT-09-92/JUD275R0000516227.pdf. Accessed 8 May 2026

United Nations International Criminal Tribunal for the former Yugoslavia (2019) Prosecutor v. Radovan Karadžić, public redacted judgement. United Nations International Criminal Tribunal for the former Yugoslavia. https://cld.irmct.org/assets/filings/2019.03.20-Karadzic-Appeal-Judgement.pdf. Accessed 8 May 2026

United Nations International Criminal Tribunal for the former Yugoslavia (2021) Prosecutor v. Ratko Mladić, public redacted judgement. United Nations International Criminal Tribunal for the former Yugoslavia. https://ucr.irmct.org/LegalRef/CMSDocStore/Public/English/Judgement/NotIndexable/MICT-13-56-A/JUD285R0000638396.pdf. Accessed 8 May 2026

United Nations International Criminal Tribunal for the former Yugoslavia (2026a) Karadžić (IT-95-5/18). United Nations International Criminal Tribunal for the former Yugoslavia. https://www.icty.org/en/case/karadzic. Accessed 8 May 2026

United Nations International Criminal Tribunal for the former Yugoslavia (2026b) Mladić (IT-09-92). United Nations International Criminal Tribunal for the former Yugoslavia. https://www.icty.org/en/case/mladic. Accessed 8 May 2026

United Nations International Criminal Tribunal for the former Yugoslavia (2026c) Tadić (IT-94-1). United Nations International Criminal Tribunal for the former Yugoslavia. https://www.icty.org/en/case/tadic. Accessed 8 May 2026

United Nations International Residual Mechanism for Criminal Tribunals (2019) Appeals judgement in the case of Karadžić (MICT-13-55-a), public redacted. United Nations International Criminal Tribunal for the former Yugoslavia. https://ucr.irmct.org/LegalRef/CMSDocStore/Public/English/Judgement/NotIndexable/MICT-13-55-A/JUD283R0000522215.pdf. Accessed 8 May 2026

United Nations International Residual Mechanism for Criminal Tribunals (2026) Karemera et al. (ICTR-98-44). United Nations International Criminal Tribunal for the former Yugoslavia. https://unictr.irmct.org/en/cases/ictr-98-44. Accessed 8 May 2026

United Nations International Residual Mechanism for Criminal Tribunals External Relations and Communication Outreach Unit (2006) ICTR appeals chamber takes judicial notice of genocide in Rwanda. United Nations International Residual Mechanism for Criminal Tribunals External Relations and Communication Outreach Unit. https://unictr.irmct.org/en/news/ictr-appeals-chamber-takes-judicial-notice-genocide-rwanda. Accessed 8 May 2026

United Nations Security Council (1993a) Resolution 808 (1993), adopted by the security council at its 3175th meeting, on 22 February 1993. United Nations Security Council. Available via United Nations Digital Library. https://digitallibrary.un.org/record/243008. Accessed 8 May 2026

United Nations Security Council (1993b) Resolution 827 (1993), adopted by the security council at its 3217th meeting, on 25 may 1993. United Nations Security Council. Available via United Nations Digital Library. https://digitallibrary.un.org/record/166567. Accessed 8 May 2026

United Nations Security Council (1994) Resolution 955 (1994), adopted by the security council at its 3453rd meeting, on 8 November 1994. United Nations Security Council. Available via United Nations Digital Library. https://digitallibrary.un.org/record/198038. Accessed 8 May 2026

Yale Law School Lillian Goldman Law Library (2008) Constitution of the International Military Tribunal. In: The Avalon project. Yale Law School Lillian Goldman Law Library. Accessible via the Avalon Project. https://avalon.law.yale.edu/imt/imtconst.asp. Accessed 8 May 2026

Zaid MS (1997) Trial of the century? Assessing the case of Dusko Tadic before the international criminal tribunal for the former Yugoslavia. J of Intl and Comparative Law 3(2):589–596. https://nsuworks.nova.edu/ilsajournal/vol3/iss2/14

Chapter 4
Four Hybrid Criminal Tribunals: Individual Accountability for Atrocity Crimes

The courts that we describe as "hybrid criminal tribunals" have not been enforcement mechanisms of the U.N. Security Council (as have been the *ad hoc* international tribunals) but appeared on the world scene during the last quarter century as essentially joint venture courts established by treaty between a national government and either the United Nations or a regional organization (such as the African Union or Council of Europe). These courts were not constituted embodying the enforcement authority of the Security Council under Chap. 7 of the U.N. Charter and which by its resolutions had earlier vested the International Criminal Tribunals for the former Yugoslavia (ICTY) and Rwanda (ICTR) with the legal authority to request of Member States of the United Nations that they cooperate with the ICTY and ICTR.

In contrast, the hybrid criminal tribunals exercised essentially a localized mandate of jurisdiction with respect to their defined territorial reach (territorial jurisdiction), the range of individuals described in the tribunal's governing statute (personal jurisdiction), the types of crimes (international and national) listed in the tribunal statute (subject matter jurisdiction), and the period of time within which the crimes must have been committed (temporal jurisdiction). No nation other than the one entering into the agreement with the United Nations exercised obligatory duties. These requirements all pointed to creation of a hybrid tribunal to deal with a specific situation of criminal conduct in a particular region during a specific period of time by a particular group of potential indictees or, in one tribunal, by only a single individual, and with the mandatory cooperation of the treaty party but only the voluntary cooperation of other States.

There are four such tribunals examined in this chapter: The Special Court for Sierra Leone, the Extraordinary Chambers in the Courts of Cambodia, the Special Tribunal for Lebanon, and the Extraordinary African Chambers. Having largely achieved their mandates, none of these tribunals continue to operate except for residual purposes. We describe major cases in each such hybrid criminal tribunal and their impact on international justice.

D. J. Scheffer and M. S. Ellis, *The Story of Modern International Justice, 1993-2025*,
https://doi.org/10.1007/978-3-032-33243-1_4

We note two additional hybrid criminal tribunals: Still very active in The Hague is the Kosovo Specialist Chambers, which was created in 2015 under the legal authority of the European Union and the Government of Kosovo[1] to investigate and prosecute designated crimes committed in Kosovo against citizens of Kosovo or the Federal Republic of Yugoslavia during 1998, 1999, and 2000. While the ICTY focused under its mandate on both the Balkans War of 1991–1995 and the Kosovo War of 1999, the Kosovo Specialist Chambers has been dealing with crimes in Kosovo not investigated or prosecuted by the ICTY. Given that its most significant jurisprudence remains to be delivered as of this writing, we have not focused on this hybrid criminal court in the book. However, the Kosovo Specialist Chambers remains emblematic of the innovative and significant tribunal-building era of the last three decades, and its future rulings doubtless will contribute to the growth of international justice in coming years.

The youngest hybrid court, the Special Tribunal for the Crime of Aggression against Ukraine,[2] remains a work in progress and lacks any jurisprudence as of this writing. Given the heightened attention to international accountability arising from the Russia-Ukraine War in recent years, we consider it important, in Chap. 6, to set the stage for this particular Special Tribunal and the judicial work it is undertaking.

4.1 Special Court for Sierra Leone

During the final years of the civil war that ravaged Sierra Leone during the 1990's, negotiations initiated by the United States and involving Sierra Leone, the United Nations, the United Kingdom and other governments led to the creation of the Special Court for Sierra Leone (SCSL) in 2002 under a treaty between the Government of Sierra Leone and the United Nations (at the direction of the U.N. Security Council and negotiated by the U.N. Secretary-General but *not* as a tribunal created under the enforcement authority of Chap. 7 of the U.N. Charter).[3] The jurisdiction (personal, subject-matter, territorial, and temporal) of the SCSL limited its scope of investigation and prosecution to "persons who bear the greatest responsibility for serious violations of international humanitarian law and Sierra Leonean law committed in the territory of Sierra Leone since 30 November 1996, including those leaders who, in committing such crimes, have threatened the establishment of and implementation of the peace process in Sierra Leone."[4] Given this narrow scope of jurisdiction, 23

[1] See Kosovo Specialist Chambers and Specialist Prosecutor's Office (2026).

[2] Special Tribunal for the Crime of Aggression against Ukraine (2026); Wenaweser and Alavi (2026).

[3] Special Court for Sierra Leone (2002a); for the history of the negotiations leading to creation of the SCSL, see Scheffer (2012), pp. 296–340; for the prosecutions undertaken by the SCSL, see Crane (2019); see Jalloh (2011).

[4] Special Court for Sierra Leone (2002b), art. 1(1); Article 1(2) and Article 1(3) of the Statute provided an exception: "2. Any transgressions by peacekeepers and related personnel present in Sierra Leone pursuant to the Status of Mission Agreement in force between the United Nations

individuals were indicted and ten of those indictees actually stood trial before the SCSL. The significant jurisprudence arising from two major cases, one prosecuted against Charles Taylor and the second against three Sierra Leone leaders, follows.

4.1.1 *Prosecutor v. Charles Ghankay Taylor*[5]

Indictment for war crimes and crimes against humanity: 7 March 2003 (amended 16 March 2006)

Arrested in Nigeria: 29 March 2006

Trial began: 4 June 2007

Trial Chamber judgment: 26 April 2012

Appeals Chamber judgment: 26 September 2013

The trial of Charles Ghankay Taylor, the former President of Liberia, was a watershed moment for international justice. It marked the first time since the Nuremberg trials that a former head of state was convicted by an international tribunal for war crimes and crimes against humanity. Taylor was not prosecuted for his actions in his own country's civil war, but for his pivotal role in orchestrating and sustaining the decade-long conflict in neighbouring Sierra Leone.

Charles Taylor was a Liberian warlord turned political leader who rose to prominence during the First Liberian Civil War (1989–1997), leading the National Patriotic Front of Liberia (NPFL) in an insurgency against the government of Samuel Doe.[6] The conflict was marked by widespread atrocities against civilians, including killings, forced displacement, and the use of child soldiers.[7] Following years of conflict, Taylor consolidated power and was elected President of Liberia in 1997.[8] During his presidency (1997–2003), he became a central regional actor in West Africa and played a decisive role in the neighboring Sierra Leonean civil war.[9]

As the primary patron of the Revolutionary United Front (RUF), Taylor armed, trained, and directed the insurgency in exchange for diamonds plundered from

---

and the Government of Sierra Leone or agreements between Sierra Leone and other governments or regional organizations, or, in the absence of such agreement, provided that the peacekeeping operations were undertaken with the consent of the Government of Sierra Leone, shall be within the primary jurisdiction of the sending State. 3. In the event the sending State is unwilling or unable genuinely to carry out an investigation or prosecution, the Court may, if authorized by the Security Council on the proposal of any State, exercise jurisdiction over such persons." The authority under Article 1(3) was never activated.

[5] Special Court for Sierra Leone (2026b).

[6] Encyclopaedia Britannica (2026).

[7] Human Rights Watch (2007).

[8] Special Court for Sierra Leone (2011), para. 2.

[9] Human Rights Watch (2007).

Sierra Leone's mines. Evidence later established that he provided arms, ammunition, communications equipment, operational support, and political backing to the Revolutionary United Front. Both the RUF and the Armed Forces Revolutionary Council (AFRC), were responsible for systematic campaigns of violence against civilians, including murder, mutilation, rape, sexual slavery, forced labor, and the recruitment and use of child soldiers.[10]

By 2003, with rebellion from a group calling itself Liberians United for Reconciliation and Democracy (LURD) closing in on Monrovia and a 17-count indictment from the newly created SCSL hanging over him, Taylor stepped down as president and accepted an offer of asylum in Nigeria as part of a peace deal to end the Second Liberian Civil War (1999–2003).[11]

Framed by Chief Prosecutor David Crane, the indictment against Taylor was issued by the SCSL on 7 March 2003, while he was still President of Liberia. He was the second sitting head of state indicted by an international criminal tribunal (the first being Slobodan Milošević of Yugoslavia) and charged with bearing the greatest responsibility for war crimes, crimes against humanity, and other serious violations of international humanitarian law committed in Sierra Leone. After resigning in August 2003, Taylor lived for three years in Calabar, Nigeria, seemingly beyond the reach of the law.

However, sustained international pressure, particularly from the United States, civil society groups, the United Nations, and the newly elected Liberian President Ellen Johnson Sirleaf, eventually compelled Nigeria to act.[12] Sirleaf's request to Nigeria for Taylor's extradition was granted on 25 March 2006, whereby Nigeria agreed to release Taylor to stand trial in the SCSL.[13]

In March 2006, as Nigerian authorities moved to surrender him, Taylor attempted to flee but was apprehended at the Cameroonian border with suitcases full of cash.[14] He was then transferred to the SCSL, first in Freetown and later to The Hague for security reasons, to stand trial, which opened on 4 June 2007. In an amended indictment, Taylor was charged with eleven counts of war crimes, including aiding and abetting RUF atrocities against civilians, which left thousands dead or mutilated, with unknown numbers of people abducted and tortured. He was also accused of assisting the RUF in the recruitment of child soldiers, and other crimes including murder, sexual violence, pillage, and terrorism. The judgment was issued five years later on 26 April 2012. Taylor was found guilty on all eleven counts of war crimes and crimes against humanity. He is currently serving a 50-year sentence in a high-security prison in the UK.[15]

---

[10] Special Court for Sierra Leone (2011), paras. 163–167.

[11] Jalloh (2015).

[12] BBC News (2009).

[13] Special Court for Sierra Leone (2007).

[14] Human Rights Watch (2012).

[15] Reisman (2015).

Taylor was the first former head of state convicted by an international tribunal since Nuremberg.[16] The judgment handed down by the SCSL set profound precedents on head-of-state immunity, the definition of aiding and abetting liability for distant leaders, and the accountability for the use of child soldiers and resource-fueled conflicts.

4.1.1.1 Head-of-State Immunity

Taylor's defense argued that as a former head of state, and an incumbent one at the time of his arrest, he was entitled to sovereign immunity from prosecution. Similarly, they argued that the 2003 attempt to have him arrested in Ghana under the SCSL's indictment was a breach of the principle of sovereign equality. The SCSL swiftly dismissed both arguments.

In its *Decision on Immunity from Jurisdiction*, the Appeals Chamber held that Charles Taylor, although the incumbent President of Liberia at the time the indictment was issued, enjoyed no immunity from prosecution before the Court.[17] The Appeals Chamber affirmed that the principle of head of state immunity, which may apply in the context of national courts, does not and cannot apply before an international criminal tribunal that has a sound international legal basis.[18] The Court reasoned that the rule of personal immunity, which protects serving heads of state before foreign domestic courts, did not bar proceedings before an international criminal tribunal.[19] The Statute of the Court (Article 6(2)) explicitly established this *ex ante*, stating clearly that, "The official position of any accused person, whether as Head of State or Government or as a responsible Government official, shall not relieve such person of criminal responsibility nor mitigate punishment."[20] Though significant, this ruling was not novel. It followed the precedents set by the ICTY in the *Milošević* case and the *Yerodia* case in the International Court of Justice. However, its application to a former head of state who had been surrendered by another country (in this case, Nigeria[21]) reinforced a fundamental principle of modern international law: functional immunity is no shield against prosecution for international crimes before a duly constituted international court.

As Professor Charles Jalloh has pointed out, a key practical lesson for the international criminal justice system that this aspect of the judgment made clear is that "the indictment of a sitting president for international crimes may sometimes loosen his grip on power, thereby enabling his subsequent prosecution."[22] The case stands as a pillar in the fight against impunity, showing, as one human rights organization

[16] Bryant (2012).

[17] Special Court for Sierra Leone (2004a); Special Court for Sierra Lone (2004b).

[18] Special Court for Sierra Leone (2004b), para. 52.

[19] Id., paras. 53–54.

[20] Special Court for Sierra Leone (2002b).

[21] Durotoye (2015).

[22] Jalloh (2015), p. 230.

put it, that “even a ‘big man’ must face justice.”[23] It sends a clear message to other leaders across the world who might profit from war in a neighboring country at the expense of civilian lives.

4.1.1.2 Aiding and Abetting

The prosecution’s greatest legal challenge was to establish Taylor’s criminal responsibility for crimes committed in Sierra Leone by RUF forces while he was in Liberia. This was at the time a legal endeavor that had not previously been undertaken in the international criminal law context. Prosecutors initially hinged their case primarily on what Professor Jalloh called two “expansive and controversial modes”[24] of criminal liability in international criminal law—joint criminal enterprise (JCE) and command responsibility. However, the Trial Chamber acquitted him on these grounds, finding insufficient evidence that he exercised effective command and control over RUF forces or shared their primary intent to terrorize the civilians of Sierra Leone.[25] Instead, the Trial Chamber convicted him of aiding and abetting crimes in Sierra Leone, a mode of liability with a lower intent requirement. The Appeals Chamber affirmed the Trial Chamber’s definition, articulating a two-part test. First, the Court established that the *actus reus* (the act) of aiding and abetting consists of “practical assistance, encouragement, or moral support which has a substantial effect on the perpetration of the crime.”[26] Second, the Court clarified that the *mens rea* (the mental state) element requires that the accused “(i) was aware of the essential elements of the crime committed by the principal perpetrator… and (ii) was aware that his acts would assist in the commission of the crime by the principal perpetrator.”[27] Crucially, this standard does not require that the accused share the principal perpetrator’s specific intent.

The SCSL found that, although Taylor neither exercised formal command over the RUF or AFRC, nor was he physically present at the crime scenes, he provided sustained practical assistance—including arms, ammunition, communications equipment, operational guidance, personnel, a safe haven for RUF leaders, as well as funding and political support—that had a substantial effect on the commission of crimes by the RUF.[28] The Court, therefore, was satisfied that Taylor’s assistance facilitated the commission of these crimes, thereby satisfying the requisite *actus reus* limb of liability.[29]

Furthermore, the evidence was overwhelming that Taylor was fully aware of the RUF’s brutal methods and that his actions evinced the requisite mental element of

---

[23] Human Rights Watch (2012).

[24] Jalloh (2016).

[25] Special Court for Sierra Leone (2012), para. 6096.

[26] Id., para. 6910.

[27] Special Court for Sierra Leone (2013), paras. 481–482.

[28] Special Court for Sierra Leone (2011), paras. 149, 154, 158, 163–165.

[29] Id., para. 39.

aiding and abetting.[30] He knew they were committing murder, rape, mutilations, and enslavement, and he knew his support was facilitating these very acts. He thus satisfied the *mens rea* requirement too. Taylor's guilt was not for ordering or instigating the crimes, as the Court acknowledged, but for knowingly and substantially contributing to the criminal enterprise that carried them out, making him as culpable as if he were on the front lines.[31]

On appeal, the Appeals Chamber cemented the governing legal standard for aiding and abetting.[32] Rejecting the ICTY Appeals Chamber's approach in *Perišić*, it held that "specific direction" is not an element of aiding and abetting under customary international law.[33] The Appeals Chamber did not accept Taylor's submission that it was required to find that he had provided assistance to the physical actor who actually committed each underlying crime. Instead, the Appeals Chamber made clear that liability for aiding and abetting arises where the accused provides assistance that has a "substantial effect on the commission of the crime" and does so with knowledge that such assistance will facilitate it.[34] This was a largely unprecedented clarification of accessorial liability in the context of a head of state's actions. By dismissing a heightened "specific direction" requirement, the Appeals Chamber preserved a doctrine capable of capturing forms of participation characteristic of contemporary conflicts, in which atrocities are often enabled by actors operating at a distance.[35] As noted by Kirsten Keith, former Legal Officer for the Prosecutor, the Court's ruling "makes patent that one does not have to be directly involved in a conflict to be held accountable for violations of the laws of war."[36]

In the end, the *Taylor* judgment confirmed that Article 6(1) of the SCSL Statute extends to those who materially support crimes from outside the immediate theatre of violence, provided their contribution is substantial and accompanied by the requisite knowledge.[37] The judgment helped clarify the boundaries between modes of liability, particularly when a perpetrator is not physically present but provides support for the commission of the crimes. The Court's decision also shed light on the fact that absence does not shield liability for aiding and abetting. Taylor operated from Liberia, not from Sierra Leone, where the crimes occurred.

4.1.1.3 Child Soldier Recruitment and Use

One of the most horrifying hallmarks of the Sierra Leonean conflict was the systematic recruitment and use of child soldiers. The RUF and other factions forcibly

[30] Special Court for Sierra Leone (2012), paras. 6955–6958, 6977.

[31] Westervelt (2012).

[32] Special Court for Sierra Leone (2013) 436, 475–482.

[33] Id., para. 479.

[34] Id., para. 480.

[35] Id.

[36] Keith (2012), p. 109.

[37] Special Court for Sierra Leone (2013), paras. 482–483.

conscripted thousands of children, some as young as nine, into their ranks, often after forcing them to kill their own family members to sever community ties. These children, organized into "Small Boy Units," were frequently drugged with cocaine or amphetamines, subjected to brutal initiation rituals, and deployed as ruthlessly effective and expendable fighters.[38]

The Trial Chamber convicted Taylor on Count 9 for the war crime of "enlisting, conscripting or using children under the age of 15 years to participate actively in hostilities"[39] under Article 4(c) of the SCSL Statute. The evidence demonstrated that Taylor was not only aware of this practice but that his support directly enabled it. The Trial Chamber found that RUF and AFRC forces systematically recruited and deployed child soldiers and that the weapons supplied by Taylor were placed in the hands of children, while the operational support he provided helped sustain the very units in which they served. The Court held that such conduct formed part of the broader pattern of abuses for which Taylor bore responsibility under Article 6(1) of the SCSL Statute.[40]

While the prohibition on using child soldiers was already an established norm of international law, Taylor's conviction was a landmark moment for its enforcement. The SCSL's findings are notable in light of the mode of participation at issue: Taylor's liability arose through assistance and support rather than direct involvement in recruitment on the ground. In this respect, the judgment demonstrated that criminal responsibility for the recruitment and use of child soldiers is not confined to immediate perpetrators or field commanders, but may extend to senior political actors whose conduct substantially contributes to the maintenance of the structures in which such practices occur. As the U.N. Office of the High Commissioner for Human Rights noted, the verdict sent a powerful message that "the recruitment and use of children in armed conflict is a serious crime and those in command who are responsible will be brought to justice."[41]

4.1.1.4 Procedural and Institutional Innovation

The *Taylor* proceedings were conducted outside Sierra Leone, following the transfer of the trial from Freetown to The Hague for security reasons. This transfer was authorized by U.N. Security Council Resolution 1688 (2006), which requested the International Criminal Court (ICC) to provide courtroom and detention facilities while preserving the jurisdiction and legal identity of the Special Court for Sierra Leone, which had itself only been created in 2002. The ICC thus acted solely as a host institution, and the proceedings remained governed by the Statute and Rules of the

---

[38] Jalloh (2012).

[39] Special Court for Sierra Leone (2012), para. 1607.

[40] Id., para. 1596.

[41] Office of the United Nations Commissioner for Human Rights (2013).

SCSL. The arrangement hence demonstrates how an internationalized tribunal may operate extraterritorially without altering its mandate or institutional character.[42]

4.1.1.5 Blood Diamonds

The civil war in Sierra Leone was intrinsically linked to the country's vast diamond wealth. So-called blood diamonds formed the economic counterpart to Taylor's support for the RUF and AFRC and were used as a form of payment.[43] The *Taylor* case was the first time an international tribunal judicially established the direct nexus between the illegal exploitation of natural resources and the commission of mass atrocities.

The SCSL found that rebel control over Sierra Leone's diamond-producing areas generated a flow of rough diamonds to Taylor through cross-border channels linking Sierra Leone and Liberia.[44] The judicial treatment of the issue hence became a landmark aspect of the Court's final judgment. The Trial Chamber's judgment meticulously detailed how diamonds were not merely a byproduct of the conflict but its very fuel. The RUF, with Taylor's support, seized control of the diamondiferous areas of the Kono and Tongo districts of Sierra Leone.[45] These were not sophisticated mining operations but brutal enterprises where civilians were enslaved and forced to dig for diamonds, with those suspected of hiding stones often summarily executed. In its sentencing judgment, the Court found that there was a continuous supply by the RUF of diamonds mined in Sierra Leone to Charles Taylor "often in exchange for arms and ammunition."[46] This, the Trial Chamber concluded, was conducted both directly and through Taylor's intermediaries,[47] though Taylor's role was that of the principal facilitator and beneficiary. The judgment established that he created a reciprocal relationship with RUF, through which he provided a constant supply of arms, ammunition, and operational support in exchange for diamonds.[48]

These were not isolated transactions but a cornerstone of Taylor's strategy. As Global Witness reported at the time of his judgment, Taylor was the RUF's "chief banker, quartermaster and mentor."[49] The diamonds, smuggled out of Sierra Leone and into Liberia, were sold on the international market with the proceeds used to purchase more weapons, enriching Taylor and perpetuating the region's cycle of violence.[50] This was sometimes conducted through a Belgian diamond dealer known

---

[42] Special Court for Sierra Leone (2011), *para.* 154.

[43] *Id.*, para. 158.

[44] Smillie (2000); Special Court for Sierra Leone (2011), paras. 163–165.

[45] Lallemand (2002).

[46] Special Court for Sierra Leone (2012), para. 6143.

[47] Id., paras. 6145–6146.

[48] Special Court for Sierra Leone (2011), *paras.* 163–165.

[49] Global Witness (2012).

[50] Id.

as Alpha Bravo, the Court also found.[51] In an effort to halt the smuggling of blood diamonds at the time, the United Nations imposed sanctions on the Liberian diamond trade in 2001. To compensate for the loss of diamond revenue caused by these sanctions, Taylor shifted his funding sources by selling Liberia's forests to logging companies,[52] though this did not have the same level of associated criminality attached to it for the purposes of the prosecution. Overall though, the picture was a bleak one, as the direct link between natural resource exploitation and the commission of mass atrocities became a central theme of the case. This solidified the concept of "blood diamonds" in both legal and public consciousness and established a clear precedent for holding leaders accountable for their role in financing conflicts through the trade of resources forcibly extracted.

4.1.2 *Prosecutor v. Brima, Kamara & Kanu*[53]

Indictments: 7 March 2003 against Alex Tambo Brima and Ibrahim (Brima) Bazzy Kamara; 23 September 2003 against Santigie Borbur Kanu

Arrest of Brima and Kamara on 10 March 2003; transfer of Kanu immediately upon indictment to the SCSL from Pademba Road Prison, where he had been awaiting trial on treason charges

Trial began: 7 March 2005

Indictment amended on 6 May 2004 to include new Count 8, other inhumane act (forced marriage) as a crime against humanity

Trial Chamber judgment: 20 June 2006

Appeals Chamber judgment: 22 February 2008

A pathbreaking judgment by the Appeals Chamber of the Special Court for Sierra Leone on 22 February 2008 established, for the first time, that the practice of "forced marriage" should be considered as one of the "other inhumane acts" constituting a crime against humanity in the statutes of the modern tribunals. In this case, the relevant governing document was the SCSL Statute, where the general category of "other inhumane acts" is listed in subsection (i) of Article 2, Crimes Against Humanity.[54]

Understanding the full character of forced marriage was fundamental to achieving accountability for the horrendous treatment of women and girls during the civil war that raged in Sierra Leone from 1991 to 2002.[55] In *Prosecutor v. Brima, Kamara &*

[51] Special Court for Sierra Leone (2012), para. 6150.

[52] Global Witness (2012).

[53] Special Court for Sierra Leone (2026a).

[54] Special Court for Sierra Leone (2002b), art. 2(i).

[55] Extract from Gong-Gershowitz (2009), p. 54: "Indeed, thousands of women and girls were abducted by rebels and subjected to constant sexual violence during the decade-long civil war

Kanu, the SCSL Trial Chamber had convicted three officials (Brima, Kamara, and Kanu) of the Armed Forces Revolutionary Council (AFRC) for the crime against humanity of "sexual slavery" in their practice of forced marriage instituted by AFRC forces deployed in the field. However, the Trial Chamber narrowed the concept of forced marriage essentially to a practice of sexual enslavement when, as argued in Judge Teresa Anne Doherty's strong Partly Dissenting Opinion, the victims endured mental and moral suffering arising from a host of abuses and duties which point towards a designation of forced marriage as a far broader crime against humanity among "other inhumane acts" and not as a crime confined within the more narrowly defined crime against humanity of sexual violence.[56]

The Appeals Chamber wrote, "While forced marriage shares certain elements with sexual slavery such as non-consensual sex and deprivation of liberty, there are also distinguishing factors. First, forced marriage involves a perpetrator compelling a person by force or threat of force, through the words or conduct of the perpetrator or those associated with him, into a forced conjugal association with another person resulting in great suffering, or serious physical or mental injury on the part of the victim. Second, unlike sexual slavery, forced marriage implies a relationship of exclusivity between the 'husband' and 'wife,' which could lead to disciplinary consequences for breach of this exclusive arrangement. These distinctions imply that forced marriage is not predominantly a sexual crime. The Trial Chamber, therefore, erred in holding that the evidence of forced marriage is subsumed in the elements of sexual slavery."[57]

The appeals judges continued, "In light of the distinctions between forced marriage and sexual slavery, the Appeals Chamber finds that in the context of the Sierra Leone conflict, forced marriage describes a situation in which the perpetrator through his words or conduct, or those of someone for whose actions he is responsible, compels a person by force, threat of force, or coercion to serve as a conjugal partner resulting in severe suffering, or physical, mental or psychological injury to the victim."[58] The evidence of the broader context of forced marriage showed "that victims of forced marriage endured physical injury being subjected to repeated acts of rape and sexual violence, forced labour, corporal punishment, and deprivation

in Sierra Leone. Abducted women and girls were assigned 'husbands' and forced to become the husbands' sex slaves. In addition to suffering horrific sexual violence, victims were also made to perform forced labor such as cooking, washing, carrying loads, and farming. These atrocities were committed against Sierra Leonean women and girls on a massive scale. In 2002, Physicians for Human Rights ('PHR') calculated that as many as 215,000 to 257,000 women and girls may have been subjected to sexual violence in the conflict period. According to field research conducted in 2000 under a project co-funded by the UN mission in Sierra Leone, seventy-three percent (73%) of women interviewed (twenty percent of whom were girls between six and seventeen years old) reported having experienced human rights abuses; forty-seven percent (47%) reported having been raped; and twenty percent (20%) reported having been gang raped. Forty-one percent (41%) of the interviewees reported having been abducted, and three percent said they were forced to marry their abductor." (citations omitted)

[56] Doherty opinion is reprinted in Van Schaack and Slye (2007), pp. 825, 836–837.

[57] Van Schaack and Slye (2007), p. 637; Special Court for Sierra Leone (2008), para. 195.

[58] Special Court for Sierra Leone (2008), para. 196.

of liberty. Many were psychologically traumatized by being forced to watch the killing or mutilation of close family members, before becoming 'wives' to those who committed these atrocities and from being labelled rebel 'wives' which resulted in them being ostracised from their communities. In cases where they became pregnant from the forced marriage, both they and their children suffered long-term social stigmatisation."[59]

Building upon the SCSL Appeals Chamber's judgment in *Prosecutor v. Brima et al*, the Extraordinary Chambers in the Courts of Cambodia and the International Criminal Court convicted leaders charged with the crime of forced marriage in judgments handed down in the early 2020's. Those reinforcing judgments are further described below and in Chap. 5 where each court's imprint on international criminal justice is discussed.

4.2 Extraordinary Chambers in the Courts of Cambodia

The Extraordinary Chambers in the Courts of Cambodia (the "ECCC"), located in Phnom Penh, was officially established in 2006 following almost a decade of negotiations reaching back to 1997.[60] The hybrid tribunal undertook investigations of five cases pertaining to alleged atrocity crimes of the Pol Pot regime between 17 April 1975 and 6 January 1979. The ECCC held trials for three of the cases, decided not to convene trials for the final two cases following contentious disputes between the ECCC's national and international officials, delivered its final judicial judgment in 2022, and transitioned to a residual status in 2023.[61] While national political influence had a constraining impact on the operations of the ECCC, important practices and rulings emerged over the years to deeply impact the future of international criminal justice.

Before examining key elements of the jurisprudence of the ECCC, two significant features of its practice merit emphasis. First, there was a concerted effort by the Cambodian Government and the United Nations to enable as many average Cambodian citizens as possible to personally witness the trials and to learn about the proceedings in community settings. The public auditorium of the ECCC's courtroom (a repurposed former stage with public seating for over 300 people) was filled to capacity during most of the trial dates stretching from 2008 through 2022. A total of about 250,000 Cambodian visitors filled those seats during ECCC trials and other public court proceedings.[62] On a daily basis they were transported by bus from all corners of Cambodia to spend a day witnessing and listening to an ongoing trial, with the Khmer language either delivered live in the courtroom or with the spoken English or French translated into Khmer for the Cambodian visitors to hear on their

---

[59] Id., para. 199.

[60] Scheffer (2008); Scheffer (2012), pp. 341–406.

[61] Extraordinary Chambers in the Courts of Cambodia (2026b).

[62] United Nations General Assembly (2025), para. 13.

headphones. No other modern atrocity crimes tribunal experienced such a large total number of visitors over its operational life.

In addition, about 500,000 Cambodian citizens attended local educational events and other outreach activities in their own communities to learn about what was occurring in the Phnom Penh courtroom.[63] Thus, the participation of the general Cambodian public as eyewitnesses and students of all ages to the work of the ECCC was and remains unprecedented in the history of modern jurisprudence. The experience stands as a powerful example of international criminal justice reaching the people, individually and personally, whose society was devastated by the atrocity crimes allegedly committed by the defendants on trial and who were sitting within feet of each of them.

A second feature of the ECCC was its inclusion of "civil parties" in the trial framework, whereby qualified victims of the alleged atrocities were officially registered with the Court through procedures involving the Co-Investigating Judges—one Cambodian and one international—and which enabled victims, through the interventions of their civil party counsel, to testify to and enter into the record the injuries, deaths, property destruction, and grief and to seek reparations.[64]

The ECCC took 3936 victim statements and it heard testimony from 334 witness in its three trials—recorded online and in the archives of the tribunal.[65] A total of 74 civil parties participated in Case 001 against Kaing Guek Eav (Duch), while a total of 3869 civil parties participated in Case 002/01 and 3865 civil parties joined Case 002/02. (Examination of the judgments in these three cases follow.)[66] A representative small group of the civil parties would sit each day on the stage of the courtroom behind the Co-Prosecutors' and civil party counsel desks, while many other civil parties and victim survivors of the Pol Pot atrocities would occupy the auditorium seats beyond the bullet-proof glass shielding the theater platform upon which the courtroom actually sat.

These ancillary benefits for the public that the ECCC facilitated during its operative years demonstrated the value of international justice being physically rendered within the victim societies (in this instance, Cambodia) and with a sharp focus on the interests of victims as civil parties. The International Criminal Court also provides for civil party participation but at a distance, namely in The Hague. While the procedures for identifying qualified civil parties at the ECCC proved burdensome, costly, and time-consuming, the fact that such victim rights could be recognized was a significant leap in both theory and practice.[67]

Finally, while criminal tribunals focus overwhelmingly on findings of guilt or innocence of the defendant, the lack of any tangible reparations (other than a published apology by the convicted defendant) in the judgment of Case 001 (Duch)) led the ECCC judges to create an innovative reparations scheme that was used in the

---

63 Id.

64 Extraordinary Chambers in the Courts of Cambodia (2026f).

65 Extraordinary Chambers in the Courts of Cambodia (2026b).

66 See Hoven (2014).

67 Jarvis (2014).

Khieu Samphan/Nuon Chea trials of Cases 002/01 and 002/02: Governments and civil society were invited to secure pledges for reparation *projects* of considerable variety (in the arts, medical care, education, circulation of court judgments broadly among the general public, etc.) and those projects approved by the judges would be reflected as official reparations upon a guilty judgment which the ECCC then would authorize be implemented. This is precisely what occurred in both Cases 002/1 and 002/2.[68] Innovative in character, this reparations scheme can serve as a supplement to or be a realistic alternative to whatever financial resources can be secured for a reparations award.

4.2.1 *Prosecutor v. Kaing Guek Eav Alias Duch*[69]

Indicted: 31 July 2007

Arrested: By Cambodian authorities in 1999; transferred to ECCC custody on 31 July 2007

Trial began: 17 February 2009

Trial Chamber Judgment: 26 July 2010

Supreme Court Chamber Judgment: 3 February 2012

Kaing Guek Eav, known as "Duch," was an important Khmer Rouge figure in the Pol Pot regime as the commander of Tuol Sleng Prison, or S-21, the notorious detention center in Phnom Penh. He also was in charge of both S-24 (Prey Sar) work camp and Choeung Ek killings fields on the outskirts of Phnom Penh. During his four-year leadership of S-21, no less that 12,272 prisoners were held at S-21 and only a few escaped execution. Duch was convicted by the ECCC of crimes against humanity and war crimes and sentenced to life imprisonment. He died in prison at the age of 77 in September 2020.

In its 2012 judgment, the ECCC's Supreme Court Chamber (the appeals chamber of the tribunal) ruled on a number of legal issues that clarified and strengthened key elements of international criminal law, including which crimes against humanity that were charged against Duch constituted customary international law during the temporal jurisdiction of the ECCC, namely April 1975 through January 1979 when Pol Pot ruled Cambodia.

[68] Herman (2015); Jasini (2016); Extraordinary Chambers in the Courts of Cambodia (2026c).

[69] Extraordinary Chambers in the Courts of Cambodia (2026a).

4.2.1.1 Meaning of "Senior Leader" and Someone "Most Responsible" for the Atrocity Crimes

The modern atrocity crimes tribunals were built for the purpose of investigating and prosecuting only senior leadership and typically not the lower-ranking officers and soldiers who physically commit the crimes in the field during battle or the incited civilians wielding machetes during a genocide, such as occurred in Rwanda in 1994. The issue that can easily arise is who qualifies as a "senior leader" and/or someone who was "most responsible" for commission of the atrocity crimes. (Or, in the case of the Special Court for Sierra Leone, who had the "greatest responsibility.") Defense counsel predictably raise challenges to any presumption that their client falls within either category and the judges are left to determine the defendant's level of responsibility and thus culpability before the tribunal.

The Supreme Court Chamber of the ECCC provided important guidelines for that determination in terms of the "senior leaders of Democratic Kampuchea and those who were most responsible for the crimes and serious violations of Cambodian penal law, international humanitarian law and custom, and international conventions recognized by Cambodia, that were committed during the period of 17 April 1975 to 6 January 1979."[70] The appeals judges decided that

> "the term 'most responsible' cannot be a jurisdictional requirement for many reasons, including: the notion of comparative responsibility is inconsistent with the ECCC Law's prohibition of a defence of superior orders; and the determination of whether an accused is 'most responsible' requires a large amount of discretion. The Supreme Court Chamber therefore finds that the term 'most responsible' should be interpreted as a non-justiciable, policy guide for the Co-Investigating Judges and the Co-Prosecutors in the exercise of their discretion as to the scope of investigations and prosecutions. Regarding the term 'senior leaders,' the Supreme Court Chamber finds that it too, is a non-justiciable, policy guide, rather than a jurisdictional requirement, due, among other reasons, to the flexibility in the term's definition....Whether an accused is a senior leader or one of those most responsible are exclusively policy decisions for which the co-Investigating Judges and co-Prosecutors, and not the Chambers, are accountable."[71]

4.2.1.2 Enslavement

The Supreme Court Chamber defined with more precision than the Trial Chamber the meaning of the crime against humanity of "enslavement." It found that, "The definition of enslavement as a crime against humanity as it existed under customary international law from 1975-1979 is: 1) the exercise over persons of the powers that attach to the right of ownership (*actus reus*): and 2) intention to accrue some gain through exercise over persons of the powers that attach to the right of ownership (*mens rea*)."[72] In applying this definition to the facts of the *Duch* case and what occurred at S-21, the Supreme Court Chamber found "that there is no evidence of an

[70] Extraordinary Chambers in the Courts of Cambodia (2004), art. 1.

[71] Extraordinary Chambers in the Courts of Cambodia (2012), para. 10.

[72] Id., para. 16.

intention by the Accused to accrue some gain from the totality of S-21 detainees or of otherwise treating them as a commodity. Consequently, the Trial Chamber did not err in limiting its finding of enslavement only to those detainees at S-21 who had been subjected to forced labour."[73] The overall imprisonment of the detainees at S-21 did not constitute enslavement. The definition of "enslavement" in the Rome Statute of the International Criminal Court, finalized in 1998 and thus long before the Supreme Court Chamber's judgment in 2012, hewed closely to the customary international law standard of "right of ownership over a person," but included explicitly within that concept "the exercise of such power in the course of trafficking in persons, in particular women and children."[74]

4.2.1.3 Torture and Rape

During the temporal jurisdiction of the ECCC, namely the period of the Pol Pot regime's rule of Cambodia (1975–1979), the Supreme Court Chamber held that rape could be considered as constituting the crime against humanity of torture. Such an understanding of customary international law during that period thus opened the pathway for rape to be prosecuted by the ECCC. The Supreme Court Chamber wrote, "The Trial Chamber held that, with respect to the actus reus of torture, '[c]ertain acts are considered *by their nature* to constitute severe pain and suffering. These acts include rape […].' The Supreme Court Chamber agrees, and accordingly finds that the Trial Chamber did not err in subsuming an act of rape into the definition of torture as a crime against humanity."[75] The Supreme Court Chamber noted "that, at the time of the Accused's criminal conduct, it was clear that torture constituted a grave violation of an individual's fundamental human rights. This widespread recognition by the community of States of the gravity of torture demonstrates the foreseeability of criminal prosecution for such conduct as a crime against humanity."[76] Almost twenty years after the fall of Pol Pot's regime, a distinct crime against humanity of rape was included in the Rome Statute of the International Criminal Court alongside other specific acts and "any other form of sexual violence of comparable gravity."[77] Thus, by 1998 and the final drafting of the Rome Statute, rape had attained the stand-alone description of a crime against humanity under customary international law, which was required before including any specific crime in the Rome Statute's Article 7 listing of crimes against humanity. But the ECCC signaled support for that development by identifying rape as falling within the ambit of torture that could be prosecuted as a crime against humanity committed during the Pol Pot regime.

---

[73] Id., para. 17.

[74] International Criminal Court (2024), art. 7(2)(c).

[75] Extraordinary Chambers in the Courts of Cambodia (2012), para. 20.

[76] Extraordinary Chambers in the Courts of Cambodia (2012), para. 21.

[77] International Criminal Court (2024), art. 7(1)(g).

4.2.1.4 Persecution

Confirming that persecution was a recognized crime against humanity in 1975, the ECCC Supreme Court Chamber held "that the *mens rea* requirement is the 'deliberate' perpetration of an act or omission with the specific intent to persecute on racial, religious or political grounds."[78] As to the *actus reus* of persecution, the Supreme Court Chamber stated "that it constitutes an act or omission that denies or infringes a fundamental right laid down in customary international law or treaty law. The crux of that analysis lies in determining whether or not the act or omission, when considered cumulatively and in context, *is equal in gravity or severity to other underlying crimes against humanity*, such that the result is a gross or blatant breach of fundamental rights….[and] the persecutory act or omission must 'discriminate in fact' such that there are actual discriminatory consequences."[79]

4.2.1.5 Sentence

The Trial Chamber sentenced Duch to a 35-year sentence of imprisonment following his conviction on crimes against humanity and war crimes, a sentence that the Co-Prosecutors argued on appeal was too lenient. The Supreme Court Chamber agreed with them and articulated why Duch must be imprisoned for life. The appeals judges found that "the Trial Chamber attached undue weight to mitigating circumstances and insufficient weight to gravity of crimes and aggravating circumstances."[80] The Supreme Court Chamber held, "It is well-established in international jurisprudence that the primary factor in sentencing is the gravity of the convicted person's crimes. The Supreme Court chamber further observes that ad hoc tribunals have issued sentences of life imprisonment mostly in cases in which the convicted person exhibited particular cruelty or zeal in the commission of the crimes. In determining the appropriate sentence, the Supreme Court chamber will therefore consider the gravity of the crimes as well as any aggravating factors, such as the leadership role of KAING Guek Eav and the particularly cruel or zealous commission of his crimes."[81]

The Trial Chamber had described the "particularly shocking and heinous character" of Duch's conduct,[82] a description embraced by the appeals judges who concluded that with respect to aggravating factors, the "fact that he was not on the top of the command chain in the DK regime does not justify a lighter sentence. Indeed, there is no rule that dictates reserving the highest penalty for perpetrators at the top of the chain of command. KAING Guek Eav's sentence must be proportionate

[78] Extraordinary Chambers in the Courts of Cambodia (2012), para. 22.
[79] Id., para. 23.
[80] Id., para. 35.
[81] Id., para. 37.
[82] Id., para. 38.

to the crimes he committed, regardless of whether others may have committed more serious offenses."[83]

The Supreme Court Chamber built upon this assessment of sentencing in the *Nuon Chea/Khieu Sampan* appeals judgment delivered on 23 November 2016 (see below), where it ruled that, "The Supreme Court Chamber notes that the gravity of the crimes should be reflected in the sentence. In view of the massive scale of the crimes; the complete lack of consideration for the ultimate fate of the Cambodian population, especially the most vulnerable groups; the fact that the crimes were not isolated events, but occurred over an extended period of time; and the significant rules of the Accused, the Supreme Court Chamber considers that the imposition of a life sentence for each of the Accused is appropriate and therefore confirms the sentence imposed by the Trial Chamber."[84]

4.2.1.6 Civil Party Applicants—Bonds That Tie

As noted above, the role of civil parties in the cases adjudicated by the ECCC was relatively novel and of significant character throughout the work of that tribunal, which was situated where the civil parties lived, namely in Cambodia, and that fact alone facilitated many individuals to step forward. Assessing the authenticity of civilians who are family or extended family of victims of atrocity crimes and who have suffered injury, particularly lasting trauma, because of their own exposure to the fate of a particular victim is not altogether an easy task. It consumed an enormous amount of time and energy at the ECCC, particularly in the Co-Investigators' offices where the assessments and key decisions were made.

The Supreme Court Chamber had an opportunity to speak to this process in its final ruling on the *Duch* case in 2012. The judges focused on the bonds that tie family members together: "The Supreme Court Chamber notes that bonds of affection and dependence are dynamics that usually exist among close family members. Therefore, the forced disappearance, imprisonment, torture and eventual murder of a family member will likely bring about suffering, anguish and other kinds of injury, such as financial damage, to the victim's close family members."[85] Further, the Trial Chamber had accepted a "broad notion of de facto immediate family members, but nonetheless later found that 'only in exceptional circumstances' will non-immediate family members be considered to have had 'special bonds of affection or dependence' with the direct victim…[This conclusion] does not infringe on the rights of the Civil Party Appellants because the formulation of a presumption lies in the area of the court's discretion and not the parties' right to benefit from it."[86]

[83] Id., para. 39.

[84] Extraordinary Chambers in the Courts of Cambodia (2016b), para. 107.

[85] Extraordinary Chambers in the Courts of Cambodia (2012), para. 54.

[86] Extraordinary Chambers in the Courts of Cambodia (2012), para. 55.

4.2.2 *Prosecutor v. Nuon Chea and Khieu Samphan*[87]

(Supreme Court Chamber Appeal Judgement (2016) in Case 002/01)

Indicted: 15 September 2010
Arrested: 19 November 2007
Trial began: 27 June 2011
Trial Chamber Judgment: 7 August 2014
Supreme Court Chamber Judgment: 23 November 2016

The two most senior surviving Khmer Rouge leaders of the Pol Pot regime who remained alive long enough to be tried and convicted by the ECCC were Nuon Chea, known as "Brother Number Two" to Pol Pot, and Khieu Samphan, Chairman of the State Presidium of Democratic Kampuchea during the regime. In 2014 the Trial Chamber found both men guilty of the crimes against humanity of extermination (encompassing murder), persecution on political grounds, and other inhumane acts (comprising forced transfer, enforced disappearances and attacks against human dignity) and sentenced each of the accused to life imprisonment. The crimes against humanity were committed in 1975 during the forced evacuation of about two million people from Phnom Penh in April 1975 (Population Movement Phase One) and the transfer of at least 300,000 to 400,000 people in various parts of the country and over a long period of time (Population Movement Phase 2). Following appeals by both of the accused, the Supreme Court Chamber delivered its judgment on 23 November 2016.[88]

4.2.2.1 Definitional Parameters of Certain Crimes against Humanity

The Supreme Court Chamber found that for crimes against humanity:

(i) "Criminal responsibility for murder…may arise even if the perpetrator acts with less than direct intent."[89]
(ii) "[U]nlike for murder, extermination requires a demonstration of direct intent to kill on a large scale"[90] and, lacking evidence to that effect, the deaths arising from the evacuation of Phnom Penh were not considered extermination.[91] But the killing of at least 250 Lon Nol soldiers in April 1975 at Tuol Po Chrey was

[87] Extraordinary Chambers in the Courts of Cambodia (2026d).
[88] See summary at Extraordinary Chambers in the Courts of Cambodia (2016b); full judgment at Extraordinary Chambers in the Courts of Cambodia (2016a).
[89] Extraordinary Chambers in the Courts of Cambodia (2016b), para. 33.
[90] Id., para. 38.
[91] Id., para. 41.

accomplished "with direct intent to kill on a large scale" and constituted "the *minimum* number of deaths" to qualify as extermination.[92]

(iii) The forcible eviction of at least two million people from Phnom Penh was done under conditions that constituted other inhumane acts, which included "terrifying and violent circumstances and without prior warning" and "in the course of the evacuation, people were killed and died because of the conditions that were inflicted upon the population," and thus such acts "caused serious mental and physical suffering and injury and affected a large number of individuals."[93]

(iv) Regarding Population Movement Phase Two, the Supreme Court Chamber found other inhumane acts occurred during that situation as well. These included "findings that those people who were displaced endured poor conditions resulting from lack of food, water and hygiene facilities. Some families were separated and some deaths occurred during the transfers. The Supreme Court considers that these circumstances, which affected a large number of people, are sufficient to amount to the crime of other inhuman acts."[94]

(v) The Supreme Court Chamber embraced the Trial Chamber's definition of persecution, namely that "the group that is the object of political persecution may also include groups whose members do not necessarily hold any common political views, but who are persecuted because of the perpetrator's political agenda or motivation."[95] "New People," who included all those who were living in Phnom Penh on 17 April 1975, "were targeted because of who they were perceived to be and what they were seen to represent."[96] That pointed to discriminatory conduct rising to persecution. However, regarding Population Movement Phase Two, the Supreme Court Chamber did not discover the discriminatory intent that would evoke the crime against humanity of persecution.

4.2.2.2 Joint Criminal Enterprise

The ECCC Supreme Court Chamber, like the Trial Chamber, fully embraced the joint criminal enterprise theory to establish individual criminal responsibility that had been developed in the jurisprudence of the International Tribunal for the former Yugoslavia (ICTY), and upheld it against Nuon Chea and Khieu Samphan in connection with Population Movement Phase One but rejected its application regarding Population Movement Phase Two. In examining the mode of liability, the Supreme Court Chamber wrote: "Even though the term 'JCE' was coined by the ICTY, the underlying notion had already emerged in the post-World War II case law. Notably, after World War II, accused were convicted of crimes they had not committed with

[92] Id., para. 44.
[93] Id., para. 52.
[94] Id., para. 53.
[95] Id., para. 55.
[96] Id., para. 58.

their own hands because these crimes had been encompassed by a criminal common purpose to which the accused had made a contribution."[97]

The appeals judges continued, "The common purpose must be criminal in character. This means that, either, it must in itself amount to the commission of one or more crimes, or the implementation of the common purpose must involve the commission of one or more crimes.... The question is thus whether, under customary international law as it existed in 1975, liability could be imputed for crimes that merely resulted from the implementation of a common purpose, but were not encompassed by it."[98] The Supreme Court Chamber agreed with the Trial Chamber that in 1975 "there was, indeed, no basis under customary international law for liability for crimes not encompassed by the common purpose."[99] That form of liability under joint criminal enterprise—for crimes not encompassed by the common purpose but nonetheless inflicted upon victims in pursuit of the common purpose—would only be found to exist in customary international law by the 1990s and affirmed in the jurisprudence of the ICTY.

The Supreme Court Chamber embraced the modality of joint criminal enterprise, albeit truncated from its ICTY formulation, by finding "that a common purpose 'amounts to' the commission of a crime if the crime is one of the primary objectives of the common purpose. In contrast, a common purpose 'involves' the commission of crimes if the crimes are not the immediate goal of the transaction, but are seen as a means to achieve an ulterior objective. Whether a crime was encompassed by the common purpose is primarily a question of fact. Relevant factors will be, for example, the overall objective of the common purpose and the likelihood that it may be attained only at the cost of the commission of crimes."[100]

Determining an individual's contribution to the common purpose of the joint criminal enterprise led the Supreme Court Chamber to support the Trial Chamber's view: "[A]n accused's contribution must be 'significant, but not necessarily indispensable.'[101] The Trial Chamber also correctly considered that a contribution to the JCE may take many forms. Even activities that are prima facie unrelated to the commission of crimes may be taken into account when determining whether the accused made a significant contribution. That said, a determination should always be based on an assessment of *all* activities of the accused person(s) that the Chamber has found to have been established."[102]

[97] Id., para. 65.

[98] Id., para. 66.

[99] Id., para. 67.

[100] Id., para. 68.

[101] Id., para. 86.

[102] Id.

4.2.3 *Prosecutor v. Khieu Samphan*[103]

(Supreme Court Chamber Appeal Judgement (2022) in Case 002/02)

Indicted: 15 September 2010
Arrested: 19 November 2007
Trial began: 17 October 2014
Trial Chamber Judgment: 16 November 2018
Supreme Court Chamber Judgment: 22 September 2022

Nuon Chea's death in August 2019 ended his participation in an appeal of the Trial Chamber judgment in Case 002/02, which found him guilty of genocide, crimes against humanity, and war crimes. But Khieu Samphan proceeded with his appeal of the Trial Chamber judgment, which also had found him guilty of genocide of such atrocity crimes. On 22 September 2022, the Supreme Court Chamber rendered its 862-page judgment against Khieu Samphan for atrocity crimes committed in numerous security centers and forced labor worksites, cooperatives at Tram Kak, egregious mistreatment of people throughout Cambodia, and internal purges.[104] The Supreme Court Chamber affirmed practically all of the Trial Chamber's judgment. Here we explain some of the findings of the Supreme Court Chamber that either elaborate upon the Trial Chamber judgment or provide some variation worth noting as a matter of understanding international criminal law. Then we provide some of the key views of the Trial Chamber in 2019, affirmed by the Supreme Court Chamber in 2022, about the crime of genocide.

4.2.3.1 Extermination of the Vietnamese as a Crime against Humanity

Killings of ethnic Vietnamese were found to have occurred at a number of locations in Cambodia. The Supreme Court Chamber confirmed that these multiple killings constituted extermination because the Trial Chamber had aggregated such killings in multiple areas and found "that they were part of the same murder operation."[105]

4.2.3.2 Political Persecution at Cooperatives and Security Centres

The Supreme Court Chamber concluded "that the fact that people were arrested *en masse* does not preclude a finding of persecution on political grounds, as long as

[103] Extraordinary Chambers in the Courts of Cambodia (2022a).
[104] Extraordinary Chambers in the Courts of Cambodia (2022a).
[105] Extraordinary Chambers in the Courts of Cambodia (2022b), para. 34.

members of the targeted group were arrested because they belonged to the targeted group."[106]

4.2.3.3 Other Inhumane Acts as Crimes against Humanity

The application of the principle of legality with regard to other inhumane acts requires that the category of other inhumane acts must be foreseeable and accessible to the accused, which it was in Khieu Samphan's case. The Supreme Court Chamber also explained "that it is not required that the particular conduct must be expressly criminalised under international law, as this would render the concept of other inhumane acts as a residual category unnecessary."[107]

Forced Marriage and Rape in the Context of Forced Marriage

The Supreme Court Chamber reiterated the Trial Chamber's ruling in its explanation of forced marriage as an inhumane act: "The Trial Chamber found that the regulation of marriage was one of the CPK's policies designed and implemented to achieve a socialist revolution in Cambodia. This policy involved the commission of the crime against humanity of other inhumane acts that occurred through conduct characterized by the Chamber as forced marriage and rape in the context of forced marriage. The Trial Chamber thus found Khieu Samphan guilty of committing these other inhumane acts as crimes against humanity through a joint criminal enterprise."[108] But the Supreme Court Chamber cited an error in the Trial Chamber's judgment regarding the male victims of forced marriages and clarified that the charges of rape should be understood as "being acts of forced sexual intercourse between male and female victims who had been forcibly married. This Chamber further finds that such forced acts violated the basic rights of physical integrity and human dignity applicable in 1975-1979 and are of comparable gravity. We thus conclude that this conduct, properly described as forced sexual intercourse in the context of forced marriage, fell within the scope of crime against humanity of other inhumane acts. The Supreme Court Chamber thus clarifies that the victims of forced sexual intercourse comprise both female and male victims."[109]

The Supreme Court Chamber reviewed the evidence and concluded "that it was in fact sufficient to support the conclusion that male victims experienced an impact comparable to that which female victims experienced when forced to engage in intercourse in the context of forced marriage. It follows that such forced sexual intercourse also constituted an inhumane act as to male victims…."[110]

---

[106] Id., para. 42 (iv).
[107] Id., para. 52.
[108] Id., para. 54.
[109] Id., para. 58.
[110] Id., para. 63.

4.2.3.4 Criminality of the Common Purpose in Joint Criminal Enterprise

Khieu Samphan repeatedly challenged the Trial Chamber's conclusion that the Communist Party of Kampuchea's plan for a socialist revolution was criminal in nature. "The Supreme Court Chamber recalls that, in order to give rise to criminal liability, the common purpose that is the object of the planned action among several persons must be of a criminal character, in the sense that it either amounted to or involved the commission of a crime. KHIEU Samphan claims that the common purpose of rapidly implementing socialist revolution in Cambodia was not criminal in nature, but rather was a purely political move. That characterisation ignores the fact that the underlying plan was to use any means necessary to achieve the socialist revolution in the country, including the crimes that were committed on a massive scale against the Cambodian people throughout the implementation process. This Chamber considers that by no stretch of the imagination could it be seriously stated that the [Communist Party of Kampuchea] revolution was implemented in a benevolent or altruistic manner. While there may have existed socialist revolutions that have taken place without bloodshed or criminal activity, this was not one of them. KHIEU Samphan's claim of error regarding the Trial Chamber's approach in determining the criminality of the common purpose [is] accordingly dismissed."[111]

4.2.3.5 Applicability of Joint Criminal Enterprise Liability to Crimes Committed with Indirect Intent (Dolus Eventualis)

> "[T]he Supreme Court chamber recalls its finding in Case 002/01 that liability under the JCE for crimes that fell outside the common purpose (i.e., JCE III) was not part of customary international law in 1975, and that liability under JCE before the ECCC could therefore only arise for crimes falling within the common purpose. The Trial Chamber incorrectly concluded that if the commission of a crime is merely foreseeable, that crime automatically falls outside the common purpose. This ignores situations where the probable commission of a crime was jointly and willingly agreed upon or accepted by all JCE participants. In such situations as the JCE participants share an agreement regarding the commission of a crime with *dolus eventualis* in furtherance of the common purpose, the crime is encompassed by the common purpose."[112]

4.2.3.6 Genocide

As noted above, the Supreme Court Chamber affirmed the Trial Chamber's findings on the crime of genocide and how to interpret its legal requirements. Nuon Chea was convicted of genocide with respect to the Cham (Muslim) and Vietnamese minority groups in Cambodia, while Khieu Samphan was convicted of genocide only with

[111] Id., para. 86.

[112] Id., para. 101.

respect to the Vietnamese protected group. The Trial Chamber confirmed, among many findings, the following key interpretations of the crime of genocide:

--"In the determination of what constitutes a protected group, the Chamber notes that the group must have a particular distinct identity and be defined 'as such' by its common characteristics rather than a lack hereof. A protected group cannot be defined by negative criteria."[113]

--"The Chamber finds that in order to establish the *actus reus* for genocide it is not required for there to be a 'numerical assessment of the number of people killed' nor does it have a 'numeric threshold.' The *actus reus* must in fact target a member or members of a group on the basis of their group membership."[114]

--"Genocide requires not only proof of the intent to commit the underlying act, but also proof of the specific intent to destroy the group, in whole or in part. This has been referred to as genocidal intent, *dolus specialis*, special intent or specific intent. The Chamber shall refer to this as specific intent."[115]

--"The Chamber concurs with the finding of the [International Court of Justice], based in part on the travaux preparatoires of the Genocide Convention, that the scope of that Convention was limited to the physical or biological destruction of the group to the exclusion of cultural genocide. Even when underlying acts of genocide do not 'directly concern the physical or biological destruction of members of the group [such as causing serious mental harm or forcible transfer of children],' those acts must be carried out 'with the intent of achieving the physical or biological destruction of the group, in whole or in part."[116]

--"Where a conviction for genocide relies on the intent to destroy a protected group 'in part,' the part must be a substantial part of the protected group, and the part targeted must be significant enough to have an impact on the group as a whole."[117]

--"In order to infer specific intent, the Chamber needs to consider 'whether all of the evidence, taken together, demonstrated a genocidal mental state.' Where an inference of specific intent is drawn, it must be the only reasonable inference available on the evidence. Factors relevant to this analysis may include the general context, the perpetration of other culpable acts systematically directed at the same group, the scale of atrocities committed, the systematic targeting of victims on account of their membership in a particular group, or the repetition of destructive and discriminatory acts. A Chamber can have regard to speeches made in public or in meetings to support a finding of specific intent. The existence of a plan or policy, while not a requirement of the crime of genocide, may support the inference that the perpetrator has the requisite specific intent."[118]

--"The NUON Chea Defence submits that physical perpetrators must also possess the specific intent for the crime of genocide. The Co-Prosecutors submit that physical perpetrators need not possess the specific intent in situations where they are used by members [such as Nuon Chea] of a joint criminal enterprise to commit genocide....The [Trial]Chamber notes that only one of the sources referenced by the NUON Chea Defence, the *Brdanin* Trial Judgement, supports its view that the person who physically carried out the crime must share the specific intent for genocide with the participants in a joint criminal enterprise. The [Trial] Chamber further notes that the ICTY Appeals Chamber subsequently clarified that the focus is on the mental state of the accused and the other alleged members of the [Joint Criminal Enterprise]

---

[113] Extraordinary Chambers in the Courts of Cambodia (2018), para. 793.

[114] Id., para. 796.

[115] Id., para. 797.

[116] Id., paras. 800–801.

[117] Id., para. 802.

[118] Id., para. 803.

and held that it is not the intent of the physical perpetrators of the underlying alleged genocidal acts, that is determinative.' The [Trial] Chamber concurs with this approach and finds that this is consistent with the object and purpose of the Genocide Convention."[119]

4.3 Special Tribunal for Lebanon

4.3.1 Prosecutor v. Ayyash et al. (2020)[120]

(Interloculatory Decision on the Applicable Law: Terrorism, Conspiracy, Homicide, Perpetration, Cumulative Charging, Case No. STL-11-01/I/AC/R176*bis* (Feb. 16, 2011)).

Indictment: 28 June 2011

Of the five defendants who originally stood trial before the Special Tribunal for Lebanon, all were tried in absentia and one, Salim Ayyash, was found guilty by the Appeals Chamber of acts of terrorism and international homicide and sentenced to life imprisonment in absentia on 11 December 2020. Ayyash was killed by Israel in November 2024. One of the five defendants died on 13 May 2016 during the proceedings, and three defendants were acquitted of all charges on 18 August 2020 by the Trial Chamber but two of those acquittals were reversed by the Appeals Chamber with guilty verdicts on 10 March 2022 and those convicted individuals remain at large as of this writing. Four additional defendants were charged with crimes of contempt of the Tribunal and obstruction of justice. They stood trial in person in the Tribunal courtroom. Two were convicted and sentenced with fines and two were acquitted.

The Special Tribunal for Lebanon (STL) was a hybrid court created under an international agreement between the United Nations, acting at the direction of the U.N. Security Council and negotiated by the U.N. Secretary-General, and the Government of Lebanon in 2006 to investigate and prosecute perpetrators of the car-bomb assassination of then Lebanese Prime Miniter Rafiq Hariri and 22 other victims in Beirut, Lebanon, on 14 February 2005. While other modern atrocity crimes tribunals exercised jurisdiction over multi-year situations of mass atrocities involving hundreds of thousands or even millions of victims, the STL had an exceptionally limited and sharp focus on the murder of one prominent political leader (and others) in an act that would be adjudicated under the Lebanese Criminal Code but using an international group of judges, prosecutors, and investigators in a tribunal situated in The Hague, far from the violence raging in Lebanon. The STL had the authority to try defendants *in absentia*, which reflected the French civil law heritage of Lebanon's past. Ultimately, the only litigation (other than contempt) before the STL was conducted against five

[119] Id., para. 804.

[120] United Nations (2023).

defendants *in absentia* and none of these indicted fugitives was ever captured and arrested to stand trial.

The significance of the STL in the advance of international justice occurred not in any final verdict delivered against defendants tried *in absentia.* Rather, in the most prominent case, namely *Prosecutor v. Ayyash et al*, the STL Appeals Chamber, led by President Antonio Cassese, who had also been the first president of the ICTY, delivered an interlocutory judgment in 2011,[121] many years before the initial major Trial Chamber judgment of the STL.[122] The issue before the appeals judges in 2011 was how the trial judges should interpret the relevant provisions on terrorism in the Lebanese Criminal Code and, in that respect, whether "the Tribunal also [should] take into account the relevant applicable international law?"[123]

In undertaking this request, the STL Appeals Chamber delivered an artful interlocutory decision that significantly and constructively shifted the boundaries of international justice with an explication of the meaning of "international terrorism" in the prosecution of indicted terrorists. While sustaining the legal basis of the STL Statute to charge and prosecute individuals only under the Lebanese Criminal Code, which includes "terrorism" among its crimes, the Appeals Chamber set forth a fulsome rationale for reading the Lebanese Criminal Code in the context of a modern interpretation of international terrorism. Essentially, the appeals judges wrote that Lebanese law cannot be interpreted without taking into account a) international law developments that Lebanon itself has been an active participant in, particularly with respect to commitments under relevant international treaties, and b) the march of customary international law in world affairs.

Reflecting the long-term significance of the Appeals Chamber decision, the following extracts from the decision explain the key elements of how a national legal system, like that found in Lebanon, should interpret and apply its domestic criminal law on terrorism with a modern understanding of international terrorism. This was essential because the STL, itself a novel mechanism of justice, was an international court that should not ignore developments in international law, particularly in treaties and customary international law, and how those developments impact national law. The Appeals Chamber boldly provided a modern legal interpretation of the crime of international terrorism that national courts across the world and international courts of present and future will understand the importance of in their deliberations.

The Appeals Chamber of the STL held as follows:

> 44. The clear language of Article 2 [of the STL Statute], which is unaffected by other contextual factors, therefore leads us to conclude that the Tribunal must apply the provisions of the Lebanese Criminal Code, and not those of international treaties ratified by Lebanon or customary international law to define the crime of terrorism.[124]
>
> 45. We note, however, that international conventional and customary law can provide guidance to the Tribunal's interpretation of the Lebanese Criminal Code. It is not a question of

[121] Special Tribunal for Lebanon (2011).

[122] See Special Tribunal for Lebanon (2020).

[123] Special Tribunal for Lebanon (2011), para. 42.

[124] Special Tribunal for Lebanon (2011), para. 44.

untethering the Tribunal's law from the Lebanese provisions referred to in Article 2. It is rather that as domestic law those Lebanese provisions may be *construed* in the light and on the basis of the relevant international rules. Thus when applying the law of terrorism, the Tribunal may "take into account the relevant applicable international law," but only as an aid to interpreting the relevant provisions of the Lebanese Criminal Code.[125]

....

83. ...[A]lthough it is held by many scholars and other legal experts that no widely accepted definition of terrorism has evolved in the world society because of the marked difference of views on some issues, closer scrutiny demonstrates that in fact such a definition has gradually emerged.[126]

......

85. ...[A] number of treaties, UN resolutions, and the legislative and judicial practice of States evince the formation of a general *opinio juris* in the international community, accompanied by a practice consistent with such *opinio*, to the effect that a customary rule of international law regarding the international crime of terrorism, at least *in time of peace*, has indeed emerged. This customary rule requires the following three key elements: (i) the perpetration of a criminal act (such as murder, kidnapping, hostage-taking, arson, and so on), or threatening such an act; (ii) the intent to spread fear among the population (which would generally entail the creation of public danger) or directly or indirectly coerce a national or international authority to take some action or to refrain from taking it; (iii) when the act involves a transnational element.[127]

....

91. ....To turn into an international crime, a domestic offence needs to be regarded by the world community as an attack on universal values (such as peace or human rights) or on values held to be of paramount importance in that community; in addition, it is necessary that States and intergovernmental organizations, through their acts and pronouncements, sanction this attitude by clearly expressing the view that the world community considers the offence at issue as amounting to an international crime.[128]

....

104. In the case of terrorism, demonstrating the requisite practice and *opinio juris sive necessitates*, namely the legal view that it is necessary and indeed obligatory to bring to trial and punish the perpetrators of terrorist acts, is relatively easy....[C]riminalization of terrorism has begun at the domestic level, with many countries of the world legislating against terrorist acts and bringing to court those allegedly responsible for such acts. This trend was internationally strengthened by the passing of robust resolutions by the UN General Assembly and Security Council condemning terrorism, and the conclusion of a host of international treaties banning various manifestations of terrorism and enjoining the contracting parties to cooperate for the repression of those manifestations. As a result, those States which had not already criminalized terrorism at the domestic level have increasingly incorporated the emerging criminal norm into domestic penal legislation and case-law, often acting out of a sense of international obligation.[129]

---

[125] Id., para. 45.

[126] Id., para. 83.

[127] Id., para. 85.

[128] Id., para. 91.

[129] Id., para. 104.

> ....
>
> 107. [T]he Appeals Chamber takes the view that, while the customary rule of an international crime of terrorism that has evolved so far only extends to terrorist acts *in times of peace*, a broader norm that would outlaw terrorist acts *during times of armed conflict* may also be emerging. As the ICTY and the SCSL have found, acts of terrorism can constitute war crimes, but States have disagreed over whether a distinct crime of terrorism should apply during armed conflict....[130]
>
> ....
>
> 108. ....[A]n overwhelming number of States currently takes the view that acts of terrorism may be repressed even in time of armed conflicts to the extent that such acts target civilians who do not take an active part in armed hostilities; these acts, in addition, could also be classified as war crimes (whereas the same acts, if they are directed against combatants or civilians participating in hostilities, may *not* be defined as either terrorist acts or war crimes unless the requisite conditions for war crimes were met)....[131]
>
> 109. Thus, the conclusion is warranted that a customary rule is incipient (*in statu nascendi*) which also covers terrorism in time of armed conflict (or rather, the contention can be made that the current customary rule on terrorism is being gradually amended)....[132]
>
> 111. In sum, the subjective element of the crime under discussion is twofold, (i) the intent or *dolus* of the underlying crime and (ii) the special intent (*dolus specialis*) to spread fear or coerce an authority. The objective element is the commission of an act that is criminalized by other norms (murder, causing grievous bodily harm, hostage taking, etc.). The crime of terrorism at international law of course requires as well that the terrorist act be transnational....[133]
>
> 124. ...[T]e allegations falling under the jurisdiction of the Tribunal have been uniquely regarded by the UN Security Council as a "threat to international peace and security" and have also justified the establishment of an international Tribunal entrusted with the task of prosecuting and trying the alleged authors of those facts. This patently proves that those terrorist attacks were considered by the Security Council as particularly grave acts of terrorism with international implications. Thus, faced with this criminal conduct and the Security Council's response to it, the Tribunal, while fully respecting Lebanese jurisprudence relating to cases of terrorism brough before Lebanese courts, cannot but take into account the unique gravity and transnational dimension of the facts at issue, which by no coincidence have been brought before an international court. The Tribunal therefore holds that it is justified in interpreting and applying Lebanese law on terrorism in light of international legal standards on terrorism, given that these standards specifically address transnational terrorism and are also binding on Lebanon.[134]

The Special Tribunal for Lebanon will not go down in history with a judicial record as voluminous and precedent-setting as the other modern atrocity crimes tribunals. But the STL broke new ground in how to bring international terrorists to justice and how to understand and define the crime of international terrorism. It also established

[130] Id., para. 107.

[131] Id., para. 108.

[132] Id., para. 109.

[133] Id., para. 111.

[134] Id., para. 124.

an important historical record of the events falling within its jurisdiction and their relevance to the rule of law. The progressive strengthening of international justice in the early twenty-first Century thus gained a strong ally.

4.4 Extraordinary African Chambers (EAC)

"I believe that the greatest lesson of Habré's trial is that justice is achievable, and by normal people. Every survivor can be Souleymane Guengueng, every activist can be a 'dictator hunter'."[135]—Reed Brody, Counsel and Spokesperson for Human Rights Watch.

4.4.1 Ministère of Public v. Hissein Habré (Hissène Habré)[136]

Indictment for war crimes and crimes against humanity: 2 July 2013

Arrested in Dakar: 30 June 2013

Trial began: 20 July 2015

Trial Chamber judgment: 30 May 2016

Appeals Chamber judgment: 27 April 2017

Hissène Habré served as President of Chad from 1982 until his overthrow in December 1990. His regime relied heavily on a centralized security apparatus, most notably the *Direction de la Documentation et de la Sécurité* (DDS)**,** a political police force responsible for surveillance, detention, and interrogation of perceived political opponents. Evidence later emerged that the DDS operated a network of detention facilities in which detainees were subjected to systematic torture, inhumane detention conditions, and extrajudicial killings. Thousands of individuals were arrested during Habré's rule, and many died in custody because of torture or deprivation.[137]

After being deposed by rebel forces led by Idriss Déby in December 1990, Habré fled to Senegal, where he lived in exile for more than two decades. He followed a well-established historical pattern of dictators seeking refuge abroad to evade accountability. Idi Amin fled Uganda in 1979 and ultimately settled in Saudi Arabia. Ferdinand Marcos was forced into exile in Hawaii after the collapse of his rule in the Philippines in 1986. Jean-Claude Duvalier fled Haiti for France in 1986 and remained there in exile for decades.[138] Mengistu Haile Mariam fled Ethiopia in 1991

---

[135] Brody (2017).

[136] Human Rights Watch (2016).

[137] Brody (2001).

[138] Human Rights Watch (2011).

and went into exile in Zimbabwe, where Ethiopian efforts to secure his extradition failed.[139] Charles Taylor, as described earlier in this chapter, left Liberia for Nigeria in 2003 while under mounting pressure and then remained there as international actors demanded his surrender to the Special Court for Sierra Leone.[140]

Beginning in 2000, victims of Habré's regime and human rights organizations initiated legal proceedings in Senegal, arguing that the country possessed jurisdiction over acts of torture under the United Nations Convention against Torture and Other Cruel, Inhuman or Degrading Treatment or Punishment (CAT).[141] Senegalese courts initially declined jurisdiction, leading victims and supporting organizations to pursue other avenues for accountability.[142]

The prosecution of Hissène Habré would likely not have occurred without the sustained mobilization of victims and civil society organizations over more than two decades. It reflects the indispensable role civil society has long played in securing justice for atrocity crimes. From the late 1990s onward, survivors of the Habré regime, supported by both Chadian and international human rights organizations, pursued a multifaceted campaign combining litigation, advocacy, and documentation of abuses. Central to this effort was the *Association des Victimes des Crimes et Répressions Politiques au Tchad* (AVCRP), founded by survivors of Habré's detention system.[143] One of its leading figures, Souleymane Guengueng, played a particularly important role. After surviving imprisonment and torture under the regime, Guengueng organized former detainees, collected testimonies, and helped initiate the first criminal complaints against Habré in Senegal in 2000. His activism helped transform individual experiences of repression into a collective legal claim for accountability.[144]

The victims' mobilization was closely supported by Chadian civil society organizations, particularly the Chadian Association for the Promotion and Defence of Human Rights (ATPDH), whose president Jacqueline Moudeina became one of the principal lawyers representing victims throughout the proceedings. Moudeina's work was instrumental in bringing together survivors, gathering documentary evidence, and maintaining the legal campaign during periods when prosecutions appeared unlikely. Her involvement also carried personal risk: she survived an assassination attempt in 2001 when security forces fired a grenade at a demonstration demanding Habré's prosecution.[145]

The campaign rapidly acquired an international dimension through the involvement of regional and global human rights organizations. The Dakar-based African Assembly for the Defence of Human Rights (RADDHO) provided logistical and legal support during the early proceedings in Senegal, helping victims navigate the

[139] Human Rights Watch (2003).

[140] Human Rights Watch (2005).

[141] United Nations (1987); Brody (2015).

[142] Brody (2015).

[143] Id.

[144] See United Nations Committee Against Torture (2006).

[145] See Brody (2001); Brody (2015).

Senegalese legal system and raising awareness of the case within West Africa. At the international level, Human Rights Watch (HRW) and the International Federation for Human Rights (FIDH) played particularly significant roles in transforming the case into a global human rights campaign. Reed Brody of HRW coordinated the international advocacy strategy, assisted victims' lawyers, conducted investigations into Habré's crimes, and pressed governments and international institutions to pursue prosecution. Through persistent advocacy before national courts, the African Union, and ultimately the International Court of Justice (ICJ), these organizations helped maintain political pressure for accountability even when legal avenues appeared blocked.

Civil society actors also contributed crucially to documenting the crimes of the Habré regime. Investigations conducted by Human Rights Watch in the early 2000s uncovered thousands of files belonging to the DDS pertaining to arrests, interrogations, and deaths in detention. These documents provided key evidence demonstrating the systematic nature of the repression and linking the detention system directly to the presidency. Later publications, including Human Rights Watch's extensive report *The Plain of the Dead* (2013), compiled hundreds of survivor testimonies and archival materials documenting the operation of the detention network. Such documentation helped establish the factual record that later underpinned the prosecution before the EAC.[146] At Habré's eventual trial, thousands of victims participated in the proceedings.[147]

The prosecution of Hissène Habré ultimately required the creation of a novel judicial mechanism. In 2012, Senegal and the African Union concluded an agreement establishing the Extraordinary African Chambers (EAC) within the Senegalese judicial system. The Chambers were mandated to prosecute the person or persons most responsible for crimes committed in Chad between 1982 and 1990 that constituted crimes against humanity, war crimes, or torture under international law.[148] This was the first time a strictly African Court prosecuted a former African head of state for international crimes. It also countered the widely held perception that such crimes can only be prosecuted through international courts.[149] The establishment of the EAC illustrates how international legal obligations clarified through inter-state litigation can lead to the creation of hybrid judicial mechanisms capable of prosecuting former heads of state for serious violations of international law.

The institutional design of the EAC incorporated elements of both domestic and international criminal justice standards. Although integrated into Senegal's national judiciary, the Chambers applied international criminal law and included judges drawn from several African states. This "hybrid" or "internationalized" model strengthened the role of nation-states to pursue justice against perpetrators of atrocity crimes found on their territory and within their jurisdiction. It also reinforced Senegal's

[146] Human Rights Watch (2013).

[147] Human Rights Watch (2015).

[148] Adjovi (2013), p. 1024.

[149] Mohr (2022).

responsibility under international law to either prosecute or extradite Habré (in other words, the principle of *aut dedere aut judicare*).

This responsibility was articulated in the proceedings before the ICJ in *Questions Relating to the Obligation to Prosecute or Extradite* (Belgium v. Senegal).[150] In 2000, victims of Habrés' crimes filed proceedings in Belgium under its then-expansive universal jurisdiction laws. Subsequently, Belgian authorities opened an investigation and, in 2005, issued an international arrest warrant against Habré and formally requested his extradition to stand trial in Belgium. When Senegal refused this request, Belgium instituted proceedings before the ICJ in 2009, alleging that Senegal had failed to comply with its obligations under the CAT by neither prosecuting Hissène Habré nor extraditing him to Belgium for trial. Belgium argued that Senegal, as a State Party to the CAT, was required to ensure that an alleged perpetrator of torture present within its territory would either be prosecuted by its competent authorities or extradited to another State willing to undertake the prosecution.[151]

In its judgment of 20 July 2012, the ICJ clarified the scope of these treaty obligations. The Court held that under Article 7(1) of the CAT, Senegal was under a binding obligation to submit the case to its competent authorities for prosecution if it chose not to extradite Habré.[152] This obligation arises once the alleged offender is present in the territory of a State Party and does not depend on the existence of a prior extradition request. The ICJ further concluded that Senegal had breached its obligations under the Convention by failing to take the necessary steps to initiate proceedings with sufficient promptness after allegations of torture had been brought to the attention of its authorities.[153] In the operative clause of the judgment, the Court therefore ordered Senegal to submit the case to its competent authorities for prosecution "without further delay" if it did not extradite Habré.[154]

The ICJ emphasized that the CAT establishes a system designed to ensure that alleged perpetrators of torture do not escape criminal accountability by remaining within the territory of a state unwilling to prosecute them. In essence, a state cannot present a safe haven for perpetrators of torture. Moreover, the ICJ held that the obligations created by the Convention are owed *erga omnes partes*, meaning that all States Parties have a legal interest in ensuring compliance with the CAT. (see Sect. 2.2) Consequently, Belgium was entitled to invoke Senegal's responsibility for non-compliance with the CAT even though the alleged crimes had not occurred on Belgian territory.[155]

---

150 International Court of Justice (2012).

151 Id., paras. 1–2, 48–50, 54–57.

152 Id., paras. 90–95.

153 Id., paras. 110–111.

154 Id., paras. 121–122.

155 Id., paras. 68–69.

The ICJ's decision played an important role in catalyzing the eventual prosecution of Habré. Shortly after the judgment, Senegal and the African Union finalized the agreement establishing the EAC, thereby creating the institutional framework through which Senegal ultimately fulfilled its international legal obligation to prosecute Habré.[156]

The *Habré* case became one of the most important precedents in international criminal law across several significant areas. A central feature of the EAC's judgment was the attribution of liability to Hissène Habré on three complementary bases of individual criminal responsibility. The Trial Chamber found Habré guilty as a direct perpetrator under Article 10(2) of the Statute of the Extraordinary African Chambers,[157] as a member of a Joint Criminal Enterprise (JCE),[158] and as a superior exercising command responsibility under Article 10(4) of the same Statute.[159] Through this layered framework, the EAC confirmed several forms of liability for crimes Habré directly ordered or participated in and for crimes committed by subordinates within the security apparatus operating under his authority.

4.4.1.1 Direct Responsibility

Although obviously not as often cited as ICTY jurisprudence, the *Habré* case is still very significant for its treatment of direct responsibility. The judgment identifies instances in which Habré was directly involved with crimes, including personally raping and torturing a detainee,[160] and directly ordering the execution of two individuals.[161] The Court concluded that these latter crimes, committed by members of the Chadian National Armed Forces (FANT), were not merely tolerated by the accused but carried out pursuant to his directives with the requisite intent.[162] The findings reinforced the principle that heads of state can be held responsible for direct acts of international crimes.

4.4.1.2 Joint Criminal Enterprise (JCE)

The Statute of the EAC does not contain an explicit provision on a joint criminal enterprise (JCE), but the Trial Chamber deduced the concept from the practice of international criminal tribunals and found it to be applicable to the case.[163] Thus,

[156] See Williams (2013); Perez-Leon-Acevedo (2020).

[157] Extraordinary African Chambers (2016), paras. 1819–1864.

[158] Id., paras. 1865–2170.

[159] Id., paras. 2171–2262.

[160] Id., paras. 1819–1840.

[161] Id., paras. 1844–1864.

[162] Id.

[163] Id., para. 1865.

the EAC could attribute individual responsibility to complex bureaucratic systems of oppression.

The judgment confirmed the existence of two criminal enterprises: The first one being the system of repression by the Chadian security apparatus, consisting of members of the DDS, the *Brigade Spéciale d'Intervention Rapide* (BSIR; Special Rapid Intervention Brigade), the Presidential Guard, the FANT, the *Renseignements Généraux (*RG; General Intelligence Service), *Service d'Investigation Présidentiel* (SIP; Presidential Investigation Service), and Habré's political party, the *Union Nationale pour l'Indépendance et la Révolution* (UNIR). The enterprise's common goal was the repression of any rebellion and the hindrance of the formation of any opposition.[164] In order to achieve this goal, the members of the enterprise intended to resort to crimes including homicide, summary executions, disappearance of individuals, torture and inhumane treatment.[165] The second criminal enterprise, within the first, was the organized system of mistreatment of prisoners within the DDS prisons.[166]

As to Habré's participation in the JCE, the judges found that he had created the majority of the aforementioned institutions implicated in the multiple waves of repressive efforts launched in Chad and controlled all of them.[167] He either gave direct orders to subordinates to arrest, detain, torture and execute individuals he perceived as adversarial or acted through the relevant hierarchy. He regularly visited DDS prisons for inspections and either gave direct instructions to interrogators or led interrogations himself.[168] His participation in achieving the JEC common goals was deemed central,[169] acting with full knowledge of the nature of the crimes committed[170] and explicit criminal intentions.[171]

4.4.1.3 Superior (Command) Responsibility

The Trial Chamber also held Habré responsible under the doctrine of command responsibility pursuant to Article 10(4) of the EAC's Statute, which established liability where a superior knew or had reason to know that subordinates were committing or about to commit crimes and failed to take necessary and reasonable measures to prevent those crimes or punish the perpetrators.[172]

---

[164] Id., para. 1928.

[165] Id., para. 1929.

[166] Id., para. 1933.

[167] Id., para. 2144.

[168] Id., para. 2145.

[169] Id., para. 2146.

[170] Id., para. 2152.

[171] Id., para. 2135.

[172] Id., paras. 2191–2262.

The EAC determined that Habré exercised effective authority and control over the DDS and all other relevant institutions of the Chadian security apparatus.[173] Evidence presented at trial demonstrated that Habré was a skilled and meticulous administrator who would read through all reports submitted to him in detail and make thorough annotations. He would "not sleep and only read reports."[174] He also was regularly provided with international reports from Amnesty International and other NGOs documenting those very crimes. As stated earlier, he also visited prisons himself and participated in or personally led interrogations.[175] The EAC concluded that, considering the large number, intensity, and variety of crimes that necessitated the implication of the Habré-controlled security apparatus and whose commission did not diminish during the eight years of Habré's rule, Habré had ample knowledge of the nature of those crimes.[176]

Habré never intervened to prevent any crimes of his subordinates.[177] The EAC also found a complete absence of punishment for those subordinates who directly committed the crimes. To the contrary, he would occasionally commend those individuals, thus creating a system of complete impunity and, arguably, encouragement.[178]

The EAC's reasoning regarding command responsibility aligns with the prior jurisprudence that emanated from both the ICTY and the International Criminal Court and reinforces the principle that omission is a ground for criminal responsibility. The EAC also rejected any argument that Habré's status as former head of state could shield him from liability. The decision adds to the important erosion of functional immunity (*ratione materiae*). Habré was ultimately sentenced to life imprisonment. The case demonstrated how doctrines developed in international criminal jurisprudence—particularly those relating to command responsibility and crimes against humanity—can be applied within a hybrid tribunal embedded in a domestic judicial system that exercises jurisdiction over international crimes. Habré, serving a life sentence in Dakar, Senegal, died on August 24, 2021.

References

Adjovi R (2013) Introductory note to the agreement on the establishment of the extraordinary African chambers within the Senegalese judicial system between the government of the Republic of Senegal and the African union and the statute of the chambers. Intl Legal Materials 52(4):1020–1036. https://doi.org/10.5305/intelegamate.52.4.1020

[173] Id., para. 2192.

[174] Id., para. 2131.

[175] Id., para. 2132.

[176] Id., para. 2133.

[177] Id., para. 2257.

[178] Id., paras. 2142–2143.

Britannica E (2026) Charles Taylor. Encyclopædia Britannica. Encyclopædia Britannica, Inc. Available via Encyclopædia Britannica, In. https://www.britannica.com/biography/Charles-Ghankay-Taylor. Accessed 30 Apr 2026

Brody R (2001) The prosecution of Hissène Habré: An "African Pinochet." New Eng L Rev 35: 321–345

Brody R (2015) Bringing a dictator to justice: the case of Hissène Habré. J Intl Crim Just 13:209–217. https://doi.org/10.1093/jicj/mqv005

Brody R (2017) Reed Brody: "The greatest lesson from Habré's trial is that justice is achievable." TRIAL International. https://trialinternational.org/latest-post/reed-brody-the-greatest-lesson-from-habres-trial-is-that-justice-is-achievable/. Accessed 6 Jun 2026

Bryant L (2012) Former Liberian leader convicted of war crimes. Voice of America. https://www.voanews.com/a/charles-taylor-found-guilty-of-war-crimes-crimes-against-humanity-149031235/370195.html. Accessed 30 Apr 2026

Crane DM (2019) Every living thing: facing down terrorists, warlords, and thugs in West Africa—a story of justice. Carolina Academic Press, Durham

Durotoye A (2015) Obasanjo's personal diplomacy, the Liberian civil war and Charles Taylor's asylum in Nigeria. Intl Affairs and Global Strategy 36:19–27. https://www.iiste.org/Journals/index.php/IAGS/article/view/25490/26194

Extraordinary African Chambers (2016) Ministère public c. Hissein Habré, dossier no. EAC-01/2015, jugement. Extraordinary African Chambers. Accessible via Legal Tools Database. https://www.legal-tools.org/doc/98c00a/. Accessed 30 Apr 2026

Extraordinary Chambers in the Courts of Cambodia (2007) Law on the establishment of extraordinary chambers in the courts of Cambodia for the prosecution of crimes committed during the period of democratic Kampuchea. Extraordinary Chambers in the Courts of Cambodia. https://www.eccc.gov.kh/sites/default/files/legal-documents/KR_Law_as_amended_27_Oct_2004_Eng.pdf. Accessed 8 May 2026

Extraordinary Chambers in the Courts of Cambodia (2012) Summary of appeal judgement, case file 001/18-07-2007-ECCC/SC (Kaing Guek Eav). Extraordinary Chambers in the Courts of Cambodia. https://www.refworld.org/jurisprudence/caselaw/eccc/2012/85016. Accessed 8 May 2026

Extraordinary Chambers in the Courts of Cambodia (2016a) Appeal judgement, case file/dossier no. 002/19-09-2007-ECCC/SC. Extraordinary Chambers in the Courts of Cambodia. https://www.legal-tools.org/doc/e66bb3/pdf/. Accessed 8 May 2026

Extraordinary Chambers in the Courts of Cambodia (2016b) Summary of the supreme court chamber appeal judgement pronounced on 23 November 2016, case 002/01, Nuon Chea and Khieu Samphân. Extraordinary Chambers in the Courts of Cambodia. https://www.eccc.gov.kh/sites/default/files/publications/Appeal%20Judgement%20SUMMARY%20-%20English.pdf. Accessed 8 May 2026

Extraordinary Chambers in the Courts of Cambodia (2018) Case 002/02 judgement, case file/dossier no. 002–19-09-2007/ECCC/TC, Nuon Chea and Khieu Samphân. Extraordinary Chambers in the Courts of Cambodia. https://www.legal-tools.org/doc/8v76lk/. Accessed 8 May 2026

Extraordinary Chambers in the Courts of Cambodia (2022a) Appeal judgment, case file/dossier no. 002/19-09-2007-ECCC/SC, Khieu Samphân. Extraordinary Chambers in the Courts of Cambodia. https://www.legal-tools.org/doc/409scyke/pdf. Accessed 8 May 2026

Extraordinary Chambers in the Courts of Cambodia (2022b) Summary of the appeal judgment in case 002/02, case file/dossier no. 002/19-09-2007-ECCC/SC, Khieu Samphân. Extraordinary Chambers in the Courts of Cambodia. https://archive.eccc.gov.kh/documents/1000257. Accessed 8 May 2026

Extraordinary Chambers in the Courts of Cambodia (2026b) Extraordinary Chambers in the Courts of Cambodia. https://www.eccc.gov.kh/en. Accessed 8 May 2026

Extraordinary Chambers in the Courts of Cambodia (2026b) Duch. Extraordinary Chambers in the Courts of Cambodia

Extraordinary Chambers in the Courts of Cambodia (2026c) Reparations. Extraordinary Chambers in the Courts of Cambodia. https://www.eccc.gov.kh/en/organisation/victim-and-witness-support/reparations. Accessed 8 May 2026

Extraordinary Chambers in the Courts of Cambodia (2026d) Trial 002/01. Extraordinary Chambers in the Courts of Cambodia. https://www.eccc.gov.kh/en/cases/case-002/trial-01. Accessed 8 May 2026

Extraordinary Chambers in the Courts of Cambodia (2026e) Trial 002/02. Extraordinary Chambers in the Courts of Cambodia. https://www.eccc.gov.kh/en/cases/case-002/trial-02. Accessed 8 May 2026

Extraordinary Chambers in the Courts of Cambodia (2026f) Victims support section. Extraordinary Chambers in the Courts of Cambodia. https://www.eccc.gov.kh/en/organisation/victim-and-witness-support/victims-support. Accessed 8 May 2026

Global Witness (2012) The Charles Taylor verdict: a Global Witness briefing on a dictator, blood diamonds and timber, and two countries in recovery. https://globalwitness.org/en/campaigns/conflict-diamonds/the-charles-taylor-verdict-a-global-witness-briefing-on-a-dictator-blood-diamonds-and-timber-and-two-countries-in-recovery/. Accessed 30 Apr 2026

Gong-Gershowitz J (2009) Forced marriage: a "new" crime against humanity? Northwestern J of Intl Human Rights 8(1):53–76. https://scholarlycommons.law.northwestern.edu/njihr/vol8/iss1/3/

Herman J (2015) Realities of victim participation: the civil party system in practice at the extraordinary chambers in the courts of Cambodia (ECCC). Restorative justice. Exchange. https://restorativejustice.org/rj-archive/realities-of-victim-participation-the-civil-party-system-in-practice-at-the-extraordinary-chambers-in-the-courts-of-cambodia-eccc/. Accessed 8 May 2026

Hoven E (2014) Civil party participation in trials of mass crimes: a qualitative study at the extraordinary chambers in the courts of Cambodia. J of Intl Crim Just 12(1):81–107. https://doi.org/10.1093/jicj/mqt047. Accessed 6 Jun 2026

Human Rights Watch (2003) Amin should have faced justice. https://www.hrw.org/legacy/press/2003/07/uganda072203.htm. Accessed 27 Mar 2026

Human Rights Watch (2005) Nigeria: Surrender Taylor to war crimes court. https://www.hrw.org/news/2005/08/11/nigeria-surrender-taylor-war-crimes-court. Accessed 30 Apr 2026

Human Rights Watch (2007) Q & A: Charles Taylor's trial before the Special Court for Sierra Leone. https://www.hrw.org/news/2007/05/31/q-charles-taylors-trial-special-court-sierra-leone. Accessed 27 Mar 2026

Human Rights Watch (2011) Haiti: Prosecute Duvalier. Human Rights Watch. https://www.hrw.org/news/2011/01/17/haiti-prosecute-duvalier. Accessed 27 Mar 2026

Human Rights Watch (2012) "Even a 'big man' must face justice": lessons from the trial of Charles Taylor. Human Rights Watch. https://www.hrw.org/report/2012/07/25/even-big-man-must-face-justice/lessons-trial-charles-taylor. Accessed 30 Apr 2026

Human Rights Watch (2013) The plain of the dead: the Chad of Hissène Habré (1982–1990). Human Rights Watch. https://www.hrw.org/reports/chad1213summary_english.pdf. Accessed 30 Apr 2026

Human Rights Watch (2015) Hissène Habré trial: witness hearings ending. Human Rights Watch.. https://www.hrw.org/news/2015/12/13/hissene-habre-trial-witness-hearings-ending. Accessed 27 Mar 2026

Human Rights Watch (2016) Q&a: the case of Hissène Habré before the extraordinary African chambers in Senegal. Human Rights Watch. https://www.hrw.org/news/2016/05/03/qa-case-hissene-habre-extraordinary-african-chambers-senegal. Accessed 8 May 2026

International Court of Justice (2012) Questions relating to the obligation to prosecute or extradite (Belgium v. Senegal), judgment International Court of Justice Accessible via ICJ Reports https://www.icj-cij.org/sites/default/files/case-related/144/144-20120720-JUD-01-00-EN.pdf. Accessed 30 Apr 2026

International Criminal Court (2024) Rome statute of the international criminal court. International Criminal Court. https://www.icc-cpi.int/sites/default/files/2024-05/Rome-Statute-eng.pdf. Accessed 8 May 2026

Jalloh CC (2011) Special court for Sierra Leone: achieving justice? Michigan J of Intl Law 32(3):395–460. https://repository.law.umich.edu/mjil/vol32/iss3/1

Jalloh CC (2012) Charles Taylor and the delayed special court for Sierra Leone judgment. International Justice Monitor. https://www.ijmonitor.org/2012/02/charles-taylor-and-the-delayed-special-court-for-sierra-leone-judgment/. Accessed 30 Apr 2026

Jalloh CC (2015) The law and politics of the Charles Taylor case. Denver J of Intl Law and Policy 43(3):229–276. https://digitalcommons.du.edu/cgi/viewcontent.cgi?article=1067&context=djilp

Jalloh CC (2016) Charles Taylor. In: Schabas WA (ed) The Cambridge companion to international criminal law. Cambridge University Press, Cambridge, pp 312–332

Jarvis H (2014) "Justice for the deceased": victims' participation in the extraordinary chambers in the courts of Cambodia. Genocide Stud Prev: Int J 8(2):19–27. https://doi.org/10.5038/1911-9933.8.2.4

Jasini R (2016) Victim participation and transitional justice in Cambodia: the case of the extraordinary chambers in the courts of Cambodia (ECCC). Impunity Watch. https://www.impunitywatch.org/wp-content/uploads/2022/08/ResearchReport_Victim_Participation_Cambodia_ECCC_2016_eng-1.pdf. Accessed 8 May 2026

Keith K (2012) Blood diamonds and war crimes: the case against Charles Taylor. Southern Cross University Law Rev 15:99–110. https://www7.austlii.edu.au/cgi-bin/viewdoc/au/journals/SCULawRw/2012/7.html

Kosovo Specialist Chambers and Specialist Prosecutor's Office (2026) Kosovo Specialist Chambers and Specialist Prosecutor's Office. https://www.scp-ks.org/en. Accessed 8 May 2026

Lallemand A (2002) Drugs, diamonds and deadly cargoes. Int Consort Investig JIsts. https://www.icij.org/investigations/makingkilling/drugs-diamonds-and-deadly-cargoes/. Accessed 30 Apr 2026

Mohr C (2022) The president on trial: prosecuting Hissène Habré edited by Sharon Weill, Kim Thuy Seelinger and Kerstin Bree Carlson. Intl Rev of the Red Cross 103(918):1067–1071. https://doi.org/10.1017/S1816383121000916

News BBC (2009) Charles Taylor 'duped' by Nigeria. http://newsbbccouk/2/hi/8352575stm. Accessed 30 Apr 2026

Office of the United Nations High Commissioner for Human Rights (2013) CRC welcomes Charles Taylor conviction as deterrent to use of children in armed conflict. https://www.ohchr.org/en/statements-and-speeches/2013/11/crc-welcomes-charles-taylor-conviction-deterrent-use-children-armed. Accessed 30 Apr 2026

Perez-Leon-Avecedo JP (2020) The Extraordinary African Chambers in the Senegalese courts and the development of international criminal law in Africa. In: Sarkin J, Siang'andu ETM (eds) Africa's role and contribution to international criminal justice. Intersentia, Cambridge, p 53–84. https://www.cambridge.org/core/books/abs/africas-role-and-contribution-to-international-criminal-justice/extraordinary-african-chambers-in-the-senegalese-courts-and-the-development-of-international-criminal-law-in-africa/40F32ECD7B675919869B05FCC41580F9

Reisman T (2015) Charles Taylor will remain in prison in the UK. International Justice Monitor. https://www.ijmonitor.org/2015/03/charles-taylor-will-remain-in-prison-in-the-uk/. Accessed 30 Mar 2026

Scheffer D (2008) The extraordinary chambers in the courts of Cambodia. In: Bassiouni MC (ed) International criminal law, vol 3, 3rd edn. Martinus Nijhoff Publishers, Leiden, pp 219–255

Scheffer D (2012) All the missing souls: a personal history of the war crimes tribunals. Princeton University Press, Princeton

Smillie I (2000) Diamonds: a guerilla's best friend. Humanitarian Exchange 16(2):5–6. https://odihpn.org/content/uploads/2003/06/humanitarianexchange016.pdf

Special Court for Sierra Leone (2002a) Agreement between the United Nations and the government of Sierra Leone on the establishment of a special court for Sierra Leone. Special Court for Sierra Leone. https://www.rscsl.org/Documents/scsl-agreement.pdf. Accessed 8 May 2026

Special Court for Sierra Leone (2002b) Statute of the special court for Sierra Leone. Special Court for Sierra Leone. https://www.rscsl.org/Documents/scsl-statute.pdf. Accessed 30 Apr 2026

Special Court for Sierra Leone (2004a) Charles Taylor is subject to criminal proceedings before the special court. Special Court for Sierra Leone. https://www.rscsl.org/Documents/Press/2004/pressrelease-053104.pdf. Accessed 30 Apr 2026

Special Court for Sierra Leone (2004b) Prosecutor v. Charles Ghankay Taylor, case no. SCSL-03-01-I, decision on immunity from jurisdiction. Special Court for Sierra Leone. https://docs.rscsl.org/document/SCSL-03-01-0059. Accessed 30 Apr 2026

Special Court for Sierra Leone (2007) Fourth annual report of the president of the special court for Sierra Leone. Special Court for Sierra Leone. https://rscsl.org/Documents/AnRpt4.pdf. Accessed 30 Apr 2026

Special Court for Sierra Leone (2008) Prosecutor v. Brima, Kamara, and Kanu, case no. SCSL-04-16-A, judgment. Special Court for Sierra Leone. https://docs.rscsl.org/document/SCSL-04-16-0675/14250. Accessed 8 May 2026

Special Court for Sierra Leone (2011) Prosecutor v. Charles Ghankay Taylor, case no. SCSL-03-01-T, judgement summary. Special Court for Sierra Leone. https://www.refworld.org/jurisprudence/caselaw/scsl/2012/85716. Accessed 30 Apr 2026

Special Court for Sierra Leone (2012) Prosecutor v. Charles Ghankay Taylor, case no. SCSL-03-01-T, judgement. Special Court for Sierra Leone. https://docs.rscsl.org/document/SCSL-03-01-1281. Accessed 30 Apr 2026

Special Court for Sierra Leone (2013) Prosecutor v. Charles Ghankay Taylor, case no. SCSL-03-01-A, judgment. Special Court for Sierra Leone. https://docs.rscsl.org/document/SCSL-03-01-1389. Accessed 30 Apr 2026

Special Court for Sierra Leone (2026a) AFRC: the prosecutor vs. Alex Tamba Brima, Ibrahim Bazzy Kamara and Santigie Borbor Kanu. https://rscsl.org/the-scsl/cases/afrc-the-prosecutor-vs-alex-tamba-brima-ibrahim-bazzy-kamara-and-santigie-borbor-kanu/. Accessed 8 May 2026

Special Court for Sierra Leone (2026b) Charles Taylor. https://rscsl.org/the-scsl/cases/charles-taylor/. Accessed 8 May 2026

Special Tribunal for Lebanon (2011) Interlocutory decision on the applicable law: Terrorism, conspiracy, homicide, perpetration, cumulative charging with corrected front page, case no. STL-11-01/I. Special Tribunal for Lebanon. https://www.legal-tools.org/doc/4c16e9/pdf. Accessed 8 May 2026

Special Tribunal for Lebanon (2020) Judgment, case no. STL-11-01/T/TC. Special Tribunal for Lebanon. https://www.legal-tools.org/doc/gcoqu8/pdf/. Accessed 8 May 2026

Special Tribunal for the Crime of Aggression against Ukraine (2026) Special Tribunal for the Crime of Aggression against Ukraine. https://www.coe.int/en/web/special-tribunal-ukraine. Accessed 8 May 2026

United Nations (1987) Convention against torture and other cruel, inhuman or degrading treatment or punishment, adopted by the general assembly of the United Nations on 10 December 1984. United Nations Treaty Series. United Nations. Accessible via United Nations Treaty Collection, In. https://treaties.un.org/pages/showDetails.aspx?objid=080000028003d679. Accessed 30 Apr 2026

United Nations (2023) Justice served: Lebanon's special tribunal closes. UN News. https://news.un.org/en/story/2023/12/1145217. Accessed 8 May 2026

United Nations Committee Against Torture (2006) Guengueng et al. v. Senegal, decision, communication no. 181/2001. United Nations Committee Against Torture. https://juris.ohchr.org/casedetails/116/en-US. Accessed 30 Apr 2026

United Nations General Assembly (2025) Extraordinary chambers in the courts of Cambodia—residual functions: report of the secretary-general. United Nations General Assembly Accessible via UNDOCS. https://docs.un.org/en/A/79/827. Accessed 6 Jun 2026

Van Schaack B, Slye RC (2007) International criminal law and its enforcement: cases and materials. Foundation Press, New York

Wenaweser C, Alavi S (2026) A special tribunal for the crime of aggression against Ukraine: origins, debates, and implications. Yale Journal of International Law. https://yjil.yale.edu/posts/2026-02-07-a-special-tribunal-for-the-crime-of-aggression-against-ukraine-origins-debates-and. Accessed 8 May 2026

Westervelt E (2012) Former Liberian leader convicted of war crimes. NPR. https://www.npr.org/2012/04/26/151470775/former-liberian-leader-convicted-of-war-crimes. Accessed 27 Mar 2026

Williams S (2013) The extraordinary African chambers in the Senegalese courts: an African solution to an African problem? J of Intl Crim Just 11(5):1139–1160. https://doi.org/10.1093/jicj/mqt060

Chapter 5
International Criminal Court: Permanent Access to Criminal Justice

The International Criminal Court (ICC)[1] is the most significant criminal tribunal created during the modern period spanning from 1993 to 2025. In contrast to all of the other tribunals, the ICC is a permanent court of expanding territorial jurisdiction with the ratification or accession of each new country to the Rome Statute of the ICC,[2] the widest range of atrocity crimes in its subject matter jurisdiction (genocide, crimes against humanity, war crimes, and aggression), and a temporal jurisdiction that under certain procedures can reach back to 2002 (the year the Rome Statute entered into force and the ICC started its operations) and that locks in a perpetual set of obligations and rights for States Parties and their peoples into the future.

The jurisprudence of the ICC has emerged slowly because the case load of the Court has been limited during its first 23 years of operation. By May 2026, 61 arrest warrants and 34 cases existed at the ICC. There had been a total of 74 defendants charged, with 33 of them still at large. A total of 13 convictions and four acquittals had been rendered. There remained only one situation under preliminary examination while a total of 13 situations were under official investigation. The 2026 budget for the ICC was € 196,852,900.[3] Despite the seemingly paltry number of convictions at the ICC after 24 years of operation that began on 1 July 2002, several significant perpetrators of atrocity crimes were brought to justice and important principles of international criminal law were strengthened by the ICC's jurisprudence during these years. The following three cases—one fully adjudicated, another on appeal, and a third awaiting enforcement of arrest warrants—reflect both the magnitude of the situations under investigation by the ICC and some key legal developments arising from the judgments of the ICC.

---

[1] See International Criminal Court (2026c).

[2] International Criminal Court (2021b).

[3] See International Criminal Court (2026a); International Criminal Court (2026c).

D. J. Scheffer and M. S. Ellis, *The Story of Modern International Justice, 1993-2025*,
https://doi.org/10.1007/978-3-032-33243-1_5

5.1 Prosecutor v. Dominic Ongwen

Situation: Uganda

Warrant of Arrest: under seal on July 8, 2005; unsealed on 13 October 2005

Transferred to ICC Detention Centre in The Hague: 21 January 2015

Trial began: 6 December 2016

Verdict: 4 February 2020

Sentence: 6 May 2021

Appeals Judgment: 15 December 2022

Reparations Order: 28 February 2024

Appeals Judgment on Reparations: 7 April 2025

During the rebellion by the Lord's Resistance Army (LRA), a non-state militia, against the government of Uganda and that country's armed forces, and specifically from 1 July 2002 to 31 December 2005 in northern Uganda, one notorious LRA commander committed a multitude of crimes against humanity and war crimes that finds few equals in the modern history of the atrocity crimes tribunals. Dominic Ongwen, who originally had been abducted as a child soldier by the LRA and rose in its ranks to become one of LRA leader Joseph Kony's top commanders, was convicted on 61 counts of such atrocity crimes.[4] As he led LRA militia on rampages across Ugandan territory, there was no seeming restraint shown by either Ongwen personally or by his LRA militia in their criminal treatment of Ugandan civilians. The Trial Chamber convicted Ongwen primarily of sexual and gender-based crimes, including forced marriage, torture, rape, sexual slavery, and forced pregnancy (Article 8(2)(b)(xxii) of the Rome Statute), and of enslavement (Article 7(1)(c) of the Rome Statute) and outrages upon personal dignity (Article 8(2)(b)(xxi) of the Rome Statute). Ongwen also was convicted for engaging in the conscription of children under age 15 into the LRA's "Sinai brigade" and then using them actively in hostilities—an explicit war crime under the Rome Statute (Article 8(2)(b)(xxvi)).

The Appeals Chamber of the Special Court for Sierra Leone in 2008 had earlier blazed a judicial trail for the crime against humanity of forced marriage to be defined as an "other inhumane act" under the Statute of the Special Court for Sierra Leone.[5] The ICC fully embraced such a characterization, thus locking it into the framework of international criminal law. As stated in the official Summary of the Judgment of the Appeals Chamber in *Ongwen*,

> 42.....[T]he Appeals Chamber finds that convicting an accused of forced marriage as a form of other inhumane acts under article 7(1)(k) of the [Rome] Statute is not *ultra vires* and does not violate the principle of *nullum crimen sine lege*. In this regard, the Appeals Chamber notes that article 7(1)(k) of the statute provides for the category of crimes called 'other inhumane act', which is designed to criminalise an act that does not specifically qualify as

[4] International Criminal Court (2021d).

[5] Special Court for Sierra Leone (2026); pp. XX of this book.

any of the crimes under article 7(1) of the Statute. The Appeals Chamber finds that the scope of 'other inhumane acts' as prescribed under article 7(1)(k) of the [Rome] Statute and the Elements of Crimes is sufficiently clear and precise to satisfy the principle of *nullum crimen sine lege*. In addition, since it is an open provision – meaning that different types of conduct may amount to other inhumane acts as long as they satisfy the elements of article 7(1)(k) of the Statute – the Appeals Chamber considers that in order to determine whether a specific conduct may qualify as a form of other inhumane acts, a chamber may have recourse to relevant international instruments, such as conventions and treaties.

43. The Appeals Chamber also concurs with the Trial Chamber's finding that the central element of forced marriage is the imposition of a conjugal union and the resulting spousal status on the victim. In this regard, the Appeals Chamber notes that the notion of 'conjugal union' is associated with the imposition of duties and expectations generally associated with 'marriage', which may be established on the facts of the case.[6]

The ICC Appeals Chamber ruled for the first time under international criminal law on a forced pregnancy charge and adjudicated it as both a crime against humanity (Article 7(1)(g) of the Rome Statute) and as a war crime (Article 8(2)(vi) of the Rome Statute). Never before had an international court convicted an individual for violating a woman's reproductive capacity. The Appeals Chamber found "that the crime of forced pregnancy seeks to protect, among others, the woman's reproductive health and autonomy and the right to family planning….Regarding the Defence's argument that the Trial Chamber failed to consider the national law of Uganda on abortion in accordance with article 7(2)(f) of the Statute,[7] the Appeals Chamber finds that this provision was inserted to alleviate the concerns raised by some States that the forced pregnancy provision might be interpreted as interfering with the States' approach to abortion…. [T]he Appeals Chamber concludes that the Trial Chamber was not required to consider Ugandan law on abortion in its assessment of this crime."[8]

The Appeals Chamber strengthened the set of sexual and gender-based crimes for purposes of prosecution by distinguishing among the crimes of forced marriage, forced pregnancy, rape, and sexual slavery. Each of these crimes need to be understood as having distinct elements of crime to prove and as protecting unique interests.[9]

In the sentencing of defendant Ongwen, the Trial Chamber modified what could have been a sentence of life imprisonment to a 25 year term of imprisonment due to his childhood life "in the extremely violent environment of the LRA."[10] As one legal scholar, Cóman Kenny, wrote, "The case breaks new ground in international criminal justice by finding that Ongwen's experience as a child soldier justified a

[6] International Criminal Court (2022b), paras. 42–43.

[7] The definition of forced pregnancy in the Rome Statute is: 'Forced pregnancy' means the unlawful confinement of a woman forcibly made pregnant, with the intent of affecting the ethnic composition of any population or carrying out other grave violations of international law. This definition shall not in any way be interpreted as affecting national laws relating to pregnancy;" Article 7(2)(f) of the Rome Statute.

[8] International Criminal Court (2022b), para. 45.

[9] International Criminal Court (2022a), paras. 41, 1042–1068, 1677–1683.

[10] International Criminal Court (2021c), paras. 386, 388.

reduction in his sentence even though it was found not to have resulted in a mental disease or disorder or to have had any lasting consequences from that perspective."[11]

Another "first" for the ICC in the *Ongwen* verdict was that the judges did not accept the victimization of Ongwen as a defense to the charges against him. Any claimed mental disease or defect would not succeed to exclude criminal liability, particularly in the context of atrocity crimes. The Appeals Chamber favorably observed that

> the Trial Chamber explicitly noted the Defence's submissions emphasizing that Mr. Ongwen was himself a victim of crimes, on account of his abduction at a young age by the LRA. The Trial Chamber recalled that it had duly considered the facts underlying these submissions, and also noted the potential relevance of these facts to both grounds excluding criminal responsibility. While acknowledging that Mr Ongwen had been abducted at a young age by the LRA, the Trial Chamber noted that the accused committed the relevant crimes when he was an adult and, importantly, that, in any case, the fact of having been (or being) a victim of a crime does not constitute, in and of itself, a justification of any sort for the commission of similar or other crimes.[12]

Cóman Kenny aptly summed up the *Ongwen* case: "In sum, the *Ongwen* case demonstrates how far the ICC has progressed in relation to sexual and gender-based violence and should stand as a strong precedent on forced marriage and forced pregnancy. Nonetheless, there remains a great deal of work to be done in this regard. Additionally, Ongwen's invocation of grounds for excluding responsibility, particularly given his own victimhood, have served to chalk a faint outline on mental disease or defect and duress, as defenses in international criminal law."[13]

On February 28, 2024, the ICC Trial Chamber delivered an Order on Reparations for the benefit of the victims of Ongwen's crimes against humanity and war crimes.[14] The ICC imposed a financial liability on Ongwen of Euro 52,429,000 and ordered collective community-based reparations of rehabilitation and symbolic/satisfaction measures. The latter consists of collective rehabilitation programs as well as a symbolic award of Euro 750 for each eligible victim. The Trial Chamber also ordered other community symbolic measures. The Appeals Chamber confirmed the Trial Chamber award on 7 April 2025.[15] How the Trust Fund for Victims,[16] which is the primary vehicle for raising funds for reparations awards that have been ordered by the ICC, can possibly achieve such an unprecedented financial amount remains uncertain.[17] But the reparations order marked a new plateau of reckoning for international criminal justice: remedies that include substantial financial amounts aimed at rectifying the injury and damages inflicted upon the victims of atrocity crimes. This reflects two fronts in achieving justice: determining guilt or innocence of the perpetrator of atrocity crimes and meeting the needs of those individuals victimized by the commission of such atrocity crimes.

---

[11] Kenny (2024), p. 158; see International Criminal Court (2021c), para. 83.

[12] International Criminal Court (2022b), para. 63.

[13] Kenny (2024), p. 160.

[14] International Criminal Court (2024a).

[15] International Criminal Court (2025b).

[16] Trust Fund for Victims (2024).

[17] Scheffer (2020); Scheffer, Kaeb, and Babin (2024).

5.1.1 *Prosecutor v. Ali Muhammad Ali Abd-Al-Rahman*

Situation: Darfur, Sudan

First warrant of arrest: 27 April 2007; second warrant of arrest made public 11 June 2020

Following voluntary surrender, transferred to ICC Detention Centre in The Hague: 9 June 2020

Trial began: 5 April 2022

Trial Chamber Conviction: 6 October 2025

Sentence: 9 December 2025

The atrocity crimes committed in Darfur, Sudan, in the early 2000's led the U.N. Security Council in Resolution 1593[18] to refer the situation to the ICC on 31 March 2005, for investigation and prosecution of any charged individuals. That referral under the authority of Chap. 7 of the U.N. Charter overcame the fact that Sudan had not acceded to the Rome Statute of the ICC and thus, prior to Resolution 1593, the country escaped the jurisdiction of the ICC. The atrocity crime most commonly associated with the situation in Darfur during that period is genocide, which has been charged by the ICC against Omar Haman Ahmad Al Bashir, the President of the Republic of Sudan during the violent years of 2003 to 2008.[19] As of this writing, Al Bashir remains at large and thus no trial has been held yet to prosecute him.

Ali Muhammad Ali Abd-Al-Rahman, known in the field as "Ali Kushayb," was one of the senior leaders of the *Janjaweed* militia which collaborated with Government of Sudan forces to attack civilian populations in Darfur and the rebel forces of the Sudan Liberation Movement/Army and the Justice and Equality Movement. The ICC focused on a relatively short period of time (August 2003 to March 2004) when Ali Kushayb was leading the *Janjaweed* in commission of war crimes and crimes against humanity against primarily the Fur tribe living in Darfur. He was not charged with genocide.[20] But the magnitude of his war crimes and crimes against humanity led to a guilty verdict by an ICC Trial Chamber that reflected the ICC's capacity to hold a mastermind of atrocity crimes accountable under the expanding reach of international criminal law.[21]

In sum, Ali Kushayb was convicted as (1) a *direct perpetrator* of murder and torture as crimes against humanity and war crimes, as well as outrages upon personal dignity as a war crime and persecution as a crime against humanity; (2) *a co-perpetrator* for the joint commission with *Janjaweed* and/or Government of Sudan Forces, in relation to at least 200 captives and/or detainees during two operations, of murder, attempted murder and torture as war crimes and crimes against humanity,

[18] United Nations Security Council (2005).

[19] See International Criminal Court (2021a).

[20] See Id.

[21] International Criminal Court (2025a).

outrages upon personal dignity as a war crime, and persecution as a crime against humanity; and (3) for *ordering* the *Janjaweed* to commit during an operation murder and rape as war crimes and crimes against humanity, attack a civilian population, commit outrages upon personal dignity, pillage and destroy the enemy's property as war crimes, and forcibly transfer a population and commit persecution and other inhumane acts as crimes against humanity.

Following an exhaustive examination of the evidence pointing to war crimes and crimes against humanity, the Trial Chamber rendered the comprehensive verdict of guilty described above against Ali Kushayb and sentenced him to 20 years of imprisonment. As of this writing, he is appealing that verdict and the Appeals Chamber will render its final judgment in due course. The Trial Chamber explained the law underpinning its findings of guilt in its 2025 judgment and provided important clarity in the prosecution of atrocity crimes.

With respect to the requirement that crimes against humanity be directed against any civilian population, the Trial Chamber "recalls that when crimes against humanity are alleged to have been committed during an armed conflict, as in this case, it is not necessary to prove that all individual victims were civilians within the meaning of international humanitarian law. There is no legal requirement that the 'main aim or object of the relevant acts was to attack civilians'. The question of whether the attack was directed at a civilian population is a factual issue to be assessed by the [Trial] Chamber."[22] The civilian population retains its civilian character despite the presence of some fighters among it: "The [Trial] Chamber finally recalls that even if there were some fighters among the detainees, this does not affect the civilian character of the population that was being attacked in terms of article 7(1) of the [Rome] Statute."[23]

Earlier in the judgment, "the [Trial] Chamber recalls that it is not [a] requirement that all civilians within the population be targeted or that all individual victims were civilians within the meaning of international humanitarian law, to conclude that the attack was directed against a civilian population. The [Trial] Chamber also recalls that the (alleged) presence within a civilian population of individuals who do not fall under the definition of 'civilians' does not deprive the population of its civilian character and that 'the difficulty in distinguishing combatants from civilians may be a relevant consideration when determining whether the civilian population as such was the object of the attack. At the same time, [...] such difficulties cannot justify the targeting of an entire ethnic group without distinction between civilians and combatants.' There is no legal requirement that the 'main aim or object of the relevant acts was to attack civilians' as '[a]n attack directed against a civilian population may also serve other objectives or motives'. See para. 694 above."[24]

Paragraph 694 of the Trial Chamber judgment articulated the broader principle:

[22] Id., para. 818 (citations omitted).

[23] Id., para. 822 (citations omitted).

[24] Id., fn. 2605.

"694. Article 7(1) of the [Rome] Statute requires that the attack must be 'directed against any civilian population', namely a collective, as opposed to individual civilians. By using the term 'any'civilian population, Article 7(1) of the Statute is not limited to populations defined by a common nationality, ethnicity, or other similar distinguishing features. There is no legal requirement that the 'main aim or object of the relevant acts was to attack civilians' as '[a]n attack directed against a civilian population may also serve other objectives or motives'.

The question of whether the attack was directed at a civilian population is a factual issue to be assessed by the Chamber."[25]

The power of public speech by leaders can create the context for commission of atrocity crimes and incite perpetrators to follow through with the incendiary rhetoric. The Trial Judgment explained how this can unfold:

> 826. The content of those speeches, including the use of 'amsah aksah', were explicit orders to:
>
> - take no prisoners and kill anyone, including civilians: 'wipe out and sweep away the Fur do not keep anyone alive', '[President Al-Bashir said that] no stone, no trees, no plant, no human beings [would] be left safe and that he [did not] want any prisoner or casualties or wounded in the Darfur war', '[the Accused said that the 'motto' was] [c] ut the straw, eat it raw. Don't leave anyone behind, and bring no one alive', 'never bring someone alive';
> - destroy everything and 'wipe out' entire areas: 'not even a single tree should be standing there';
> - act without any limits: 'Bring him alive, eat him alive, fresh', '[amsah aksah' means] there are no restrictions or limits that govern military and combat operations', 'the fighters should be, of course, free to do what they do. There are no limits, so they can do what they like', '[amsah aksah] these words mean genocide and killing prisoners'; and
> - looting and pillaging: 'the Fur and their money were war booty [sic] or a "prize" for the *Janjaweed*'.
>
> 827. 'Amsah aksah', also used as a 'motto' by the fighters, [Government of Sudan] Forces and *Janjaweed* alike, when they 'carried out the work' on the battleground, was described by witnesses as meaning that the fighters could do what they like, without any limit.
> 828. The Chamber is satisfied that the language used by [Government of Sudan] officials and *Janjaweed* leaders, including the Accused, dehumanised the non-Arab tribes targeted, who would be the future victims of the crimes. In the speeches, they were represented as objects, a 'booty' or a 'war prize', or something that could be eaten; they were placed on the same level as 'trees' and 'stones'; they were described as something that the fighters could do what they wanted with, with no limits. The non-Arab tribes targeted and the places they lived in were also repeatedly represented, as something that needed to be 'cleaned'.
> 829. In addition, the speeches and instructions were given in a specific context. These preparatory meetings and speeches coincided with the distribution of military equipment, weapons or money by the [Government of Sudan] and/or immediately preceded attacks and lootings. They were made in the historical context of pre-existing tribal tensions between non-Arab tribes and Arab tribes. They were addressed to fighters comprised of [Government of Sudan] forces and *Janjaweed* specifically selected on the basis of their belonging to Arab tribes. Therefore, those speeches, addressed to fighters member [sic] of Arab tribes, in this specific context of pre-existing tribal tensions, and which dehumanised members of non-Arab tribes, encouraged, as intended, the commission of crimes against them."[26]

[25] Id., para. 694 (citations omitted).

[26] Id., paras. 826–829 (citations omitted).

With respect to the war crime of destroying an enemy's property, the Trial Chamber offered an instructive summation:

> 857. There is no indication in the evidence that the property destroyed, which was of a civilian nature, served any military purpose or constituted a military objective, and a reasonable person could therefore not have believed that the property destroyed qualified as such. The Chamber further notes that there was no evidence of a rebel presence in these locations at the relevant time. Importantly, the Chamber observes that Kodoom and Bindisi were under the control of the attacking forces (i.e. the *Janjaweed*) when the properties were being destroyed. The Chamber therefore finds that the property destroyed was protected from that destruction under international humanitarian law. Similarly, there is no evidence that the destruction was required by military necessity. The Chamber is therefore satisfied that the third and fifth legal elements of destruction of an adversary's property as a war crime, respectively, that the destroyed property was protected from that destruction under the international law of armed conflict, and that the destruction was not required by military necessity, are met."[27]

In determining rape as both a crime against humanity and a war crime in the circumstances of Darfur and Ali Kushayh's leadership of the *Janjaweed*, the Trial Chamber viewed the issues in these words:

> 868. The Chamber notes that these acts [rape] were committed concomitantly with an attack directed against the civilian population, including the burning of houses and properties, the shooting and killing of many inhabitants, the looting and the beating of people. In addition, several of these rapes were committed in circumstances which included: (i) the use of physical force and sharp objects; (ii) the use of explicit threats and other violent and derogatory language; (iii) the commission by several members of the *Janjaweed* successively or simultaneously; (iv) the perpetration out in the open for other women to watch; and (v) the commission against girls between 15 and 18 years of age. On the basis of these facts, the Chamber is satisfied that second element of rape as a crime against humanity, pursuant to Article 7(1)(g) [of the Rome Statute], and rape as a war crime, pursuant to Article 8(2)(e)(vi) [of the Rome Statute], i.e. that the invasion was committed by force, or by threat of force or coercion, is met.[28]

Torture as both a crime against humanity and a war crime can be entirely plausible and was shown as such by the Trial Chamber in this passage describing what constitutes torture as acts by both the *Janjaweed* under Ali Kushayh's command and by the Government of Sudan (GoS) Forces:

> "873. The Chamber recalls that, over the course of at least two days between late February and early March 2004, members of the *Janjaweed* and GoS Forces verbally and physically abused at least 100 predominantly Fur men and boys, at Mukjar police station. This included beating the detainees using sticks and whips, burning them, shaving their heads and severing their ears. In addition, the conditions of their detention were inhumane: the cells were overcrowded, dirty and hot; the detainees were given little to no food or water; they were forced to urinate and defecate in the cells; and they were not provided any medical treatment. The Chamber also found that, as a result of these dire conditions of detention and the abuse inflicted by the *Janjaweed* and GoS Forces, at least three man [sic] detained at Mukjar police station died.

---

[27] Id., para. 857 (citations omitted).

[28] Id., para. 868 (citations omitted).

874. The Chamber found that, between 5 and 7 March 2004, members of the *Janjaweed* and GoS Forces also physically abused at least 100 Fur men and boys arrested during the search and arrest operation in different areas of Deleig. The *Janjaweed* and GoS Forces kicked, beat, whipped and stabbed the detainees. The Chamber also found that the *Janjaweed* and GoS forces [sic] brought the detainees to an open area near Deleig police station where they were made to lie face down on the ground in the hot sun for prolonged periods of time. While the detainees were lying on the ground, members of the *Janjaweed* walked on their backs, stomped on them, and hit them with fist, whip and stick. The Chamber recalls that the detainees inside Deleig police station were beaten, whipped and pulled by the neck while tied with a metallic-type rope. In addition, the victims were detained in intolerable conditions: the small cell was so over overcrowded that it was hard to breathe, the detainees were denied food and water, and had to defecate where they crouched. Finally, the Chamber recalls that the acts of torture and mistreatment committed by the *Janjaweed* left many victims with long term psychological and physical harms.

875. On the basis of these facts, the Chamber is satisfied that the first legal element of torture as a crime against humanity, pursuant to Article 7(1)(f) of the [Rome] Statute, and torture as a war crime, pursuant to Article 8(2)(c)(i) of the [Rome] Statute, namely that the perpetrator inflicted severe physical or mental pain or suffering on the victim, is met with respect to victims of both the Mukjar and Deleig Operations."[29]

There can arise confusion or lack of knowledge about what "outrages upon personal dignity as a war crime" really means in the practice of international criminal law. The Trial Chamber elucidated some examples in its judgment:

"899. The Chamber finds that the nature of the detention, mistreatment and rape, the manner in which it was imposed and the use of derogatory expressions by the members of the *Janjaweed* humiliated, degraded or otherwise violated the dignity of the detained Fur men, women and children. In relation to the severity, the Chamber is satisfied that the conduct of the members of the *Janjaweed* in Bindisi was of such degree as to be generally recognised as an outrage upon personal dignity.

900. On the basis of these facts, the Chamber is persuaded that the first and second legal elements of outrages upon personal dignity as a war crime are met, namely that the *Janjaweed* humiliated, degraded or otherwise violated the dignity of one or more persons and that this conduct was such that the humiliation, degradation and other violations of dignity each victim suffered reached the degree of severity that constitutes an outrage upon personal dignity, with respect to the inhabitants of Bindisi and the surrounding areas..."[30]

One key attribute that can arise in the context of "outrages upon personal dignity as a war crime" is humiliation of the victims. The Trial Chamber offered illustrative examples of how humiliation can be part of the definition of such outrages upon personal dignity:

"903. In establishing that the severity of the humiliation was of such a degree so as to be generally recognised as an outrage upon personal dignity, the Chamber reiterates that the members of the *Janjaweed*, the Police and the [Central Reserve Forces] physically and verbally abused the detainees, including young boys. This humiliation included: (i) physical assault and mistreatment; (ii) use of derogatory expressions to degrade and threaten such as nujus, tora bora and abid; (iii) photographing and filming the detainees whilst being called tora bora and accused of being rebels, followed by threats of being destroyed by Minister

[29] Id., paras. 873–875 (citations omitted).

[30] Id., paras. 899–900 (citations omitted).

Harun and other government officials; (iv) forcing detainees to lie face down and not raise their heads, stacking detainees on top of one another; and mistreating them as they were thrown onto the back of vehicles; and (v) shaving the heads and severing the ears of some detainees, causing bleeding.

904. Further, regarding the conduct which humiliated and degraded the detainees in Mukjar, the Chamber reiterates that, on or about 1 March 2004, the *Janjaweed* and GoS Forces: (i) physically abused detainees by beating them, striking them with sticks, and whips; (ii) denied umdah Yahya Ahmad Zarruq permission to get dressed properly; and (iii) loaded the detainees, including the umdahs, onto the vehicles where they were beaten and told they would be killed.

905. Considering the above, the Chamber is satisfied that the circumstances of the detention, the mistreatment the detainees endured, and the derogatory expressions used towards them at Mukjar police station humiliated and degraded the personal dignity of the detained Fur men, boys and umdahs. The Chamber recalls that the severity of the abuse inflicted by the perpetrators was of such intensity that the detainees were shouting and crying, whilst some read verses from the Qur'an, some were left with wounds, in agony and the skin of some detainees started to peel off, leaving them disfigured. The level of violence employed, the public nature of the violence, the helplessness of the detainees, their vulnerability, and the filming of the detainees during Minister Harun's visit on or around 1 March 2004, render the degree of degrading conduct so severe as to be generally recognised as an outrage upon personal dignity."[31]

5.1.2 Prosecutor v. Vladimir Vladimirovich Putin

Warrant of arrest issued: 17 March 2023

The International Criminal Court's arrest warrant against Vladimir Putin, President of the Russian Federation, is a landmark development in international criminal law with profound historical significance. It marks the first time a leader of a permanent member of the U.N. Security Council has been indicted by the ICC and only the second time the ICC has issued an arrest warrant against a sitting head of state - the first being against Omar Al Bashir, then President of Sudan, in 2009.[32]

5.1.2.1 Jurisdiction

The arrest warrant is grounded in territorial rather than nationality jurisdiction, enabling the ICC to prosecute crimes committed on Ukrainian territory despite Russia not being a State Party to the Rome Statute. Russia's relationship with the ICC had already deteriorated significantly long before 2022, when the invasion of Ukraine began. Indeed in 2016, it withdrew its signature from the Rome Statute following the

[31] Id., para. 903–905 (citations omitted).

[32] Gehani (2023).

ICC Prosecutor's determination that Russia's actions in Crimea since 2014 amounted to an "ongoing state of occupation."[33]

Ukraine, however, had already brought itself within the ICC's jurisdiction by lodging two declarations per Article 12(3) of the Rome Statute, which allows non-party States to accept the Court's jurisdiction with respect to a specific crime. In 2014, Ukraine first accepted the ICC's jurisdiction in relation to alleged crimes committed from 21 November 2013 to 22 February 2014.[34] The second declaration, lodged in the aftermath of the occupation of Crimea and the outbreak of hostilities in eastern Ukraine, extended this acceptance on an open-ended basis to encompass ongoing alleged crimes committed throughout the territory of Ukraine from 20 February 2014 onwards.[35] On 1 January 2025, Ukraine formalized its relationship with the ICC by becoming the 125th member of the ICC.

The arrest warrant against Vladimir Putin also underscores the extraordinary efforts required to build a case file prior to indictment. The ICC spent several years gathering its evidence. In December 2020, the ICC Prosecutor announced the conclusion of her preliminary examination, finding reasonable grounds to believe that war crimes and crimes against humanity had been committed in Ukraine, and formally requested authorization from the judges of the Pre-Trial Chamber to open an investigation.[36] Nearly two years later, on the day after the start of the Russian invasion of Ukraine on 28 February 2022, the ICC Prosecutor confirmed that the ICC could exercise jurisdiction over acts of genocide, crimes against humanity, or war crimes committed within Ukraine since 20 February 2014.[37]

5.1.2.2 The Basis for the Warrant of Arrest

Russia's war against Ukraine also prompted an unprecedented joint referral to the ICC by 43 nations, removing the procedural requirement for Pre-Trial Chamber authorization and accelerating the investigation.[38] However, despite the extensive evidentiary investigation and the overwhelming calls from States for the ICC to pursue indictments against Russian military and political leaders, there remained the question of exactly what the indictments would entail. In the end, President Putin made the decision much easier.

In May 2022, Putin signed a decree simplifying the adoption of Ukrainian children by Russian families, accompanied by added state financial incentives.[39] Then, in February 2023, came a report that would prove pivotal. The Yale School of Public Health's Humanitarian Research Lab released a landmark report highlighting that the

---

[33] International Criminal Court (2016), paras. 158, 173; see Kersten (2023).

[34] Marchuk & Wanigasuriya (2022).

[35] International Criminal Court (2026e).

[36] Parliamentarians for Global Action (2026).

[37] Khan (2022).

[38] Marchuk and Wanigasuriya (2022).

[39] Euronews (2024).

Russian federal government had systematically transferred at least 6000 Ukrainian children to facilities in Russia-occupied Crimea and mainland Russia identifying 43 such sites.[40] A later report found as many as 210 sites.[41]

The scale and organization of the operation were staggering. Children were transported across vast distances - from Russian-occupied Crimea to Siberia—and subjected to re-education programs, including military conditioning.[42]

Yale's researchers found that Russia deliberately targeted the most vulnerable - these included orphans, children with disabilities, children from low-income families, and children with parents in the military.[43] The documented abuses were severe. Children were not only physically abused, but they were also denied communication with their families in Ukraine and given inadequate access to food and care after being taken to Russia.[44] But what stands out as another clear violation of international law is that Russia has refused to provide Ukrainian authorities with the list of children it has taken.[45] The Ukrainian government also handed more than 1000 pages of documents over to the ICC regarding the alleged forcible deportation of children to Russia.[46]

A later report by the Independent International Commission of Inquiry on Ukraine (the "Commission") regarding the deportation and transfer of 1205 children from Russian-occupied areas in Ukraine would add further weight to Russia's alleged crimes.[47]

The Commission concluded that:

> The Russian authorities committed crimes against humanity by deporting children to the Russian Federation or forcibly transferring them to other areas they occupied in Ukraine. They also committed crimes against humanity of enforced disappearance of children by deliberately withholding information about their fate and whereabouts to the parents or legal guardians. In addition, they committed a war crime of unjustifiable delay in the repatriation of civilians by not facilitating the return of children."[48]

The Commission submitted 39 written requests to Russian authorities requesting information about the children and other concerns, and they have never received a reply.

The die had been cast. There was ample evidence to issue arrest warrants for innumerable other crimes committed against Ukraine. In fact, other arrest warrants were issued against Viktor Sokolov, Sergei Kobylash, Sergei Shoigu and Valery

---

[40] Yale School of Public Health Humanitarian Research Lab (2023).

[41] Yale School of Public Health Humanitarian Research Lab (2025b).

[42] Yale School of Public Health Humanitarian Research Lab (2023).

[43] Yale School of Public Health Humanitarian Research Lab (2025a).

[44] Id.

[45] Id.

[46] Leff, Kelemen, and Maynes (2023).

[47] United Nations (2023b).

[48] Office of the United Nations High Commissioner for Human Rights (2026).

Gerasimov for other crimes.[49] However, crimes against innocent children were the emotive action needed to give moral support to the ICC from the larger international community to act against Putin. Under international law, children are a particularly protected group and their transfer from occupied territory is presumptively unlawful.

Within the Trump Administration of the U.S. Government, the forced removal of Ukrainian children by Russia was impossible to ignore. First Lady Melania Trump took it upon herself to act by writing a personal letter to Vladimir Putin,[50] establishing a direct line of communication with the Kremlin and facilitating four separate rounds of child reunifications. While the Trump Administration broadly sought constructive ties with Russia, the First Lady's persistent focus on the abducted children stood as a quiet but unmistakable acknowledgment that acts against children were wrong and that the White House was paying attention. However, notably, she avoided directly naming Russia as the abductor and did not reference the ICC arrest warrant against Putin related to the deportations.

On 17 March 2023, Pre-Trial Chamber II issued warrants of arrest against Vladimir Putin and Maria Lvova-Belova.[51] As for the arrest warrant against Putin, the Court relied on Article 27 of the Rome Statute which excludes head of state immunity[52] and clarified that Russia's non-party State status did not affect jurisdiction once it had jurisdiction under Article 12 of the Statute.[53]

The legal charges of war crimes contained in the arrest warrant were precise. Filed under Articles 8(2)(a)(vii) and 8(2)(b)(viii) of the Rome Statute, they related to the alleged unlawful deportation and transfer of civilians - specifically children - in territories under Russian control since February 2022.[54] The provision reflects one of the most settled prohibitions in the law of occupation: the removal of protected persons from occupied territory.[55] The focus of the warrant was not on incidental displacement, but on the organized transfer and relocation of children from occupied territories.

As then ICC Prosecutor Karim Khan emphasized: children must not be treated as "spoils of war."[56] The ICC made the warrants public "in the interests of justice," recognizing that public awareness could contribute to the prevention of further commission of crimes.[57]

---

49 The Putin and Lvova-Belova warrants were only the beginning. The ICC also issued arrest warrants for Viktor Sokolov, Sergei Kobylash, Sergei Shoigu, and Valery Gerasimov, all officers in the Russian military in the context of the situation in Ukraine for alleged international crimes committed from at least 10 October 2022 until at least 9 March 2023. Shoigu (former Defence Minister) and Gerasimov (Chief of the General Staff) were specifically accused of overseeing missile strikes on civilian infrastructure including power plants.

50 Gonnella-Platts (2025).

51 International Criminal Court (2023).

52 Gaeta (2009).

53 Jackson (2023).

54 Joldoshev (2024).

55 United Nations (1949), art. 49.

56 United Nations (2023b).

57 Id.

Like the *Hissène Habré* case examined in Chap. 3, Putin was charged with both direct and indirect criminal responsibility. And because the ICC does not recognize head of state immunity, and Russia's alleged crimes were committed on Ukrainian territory, there are no legal restrictions on issuing an arrest warrant against Putin in the Ukraine situation.

5.1.2.3 Issues of Enforceability

However, as discussed in Chapter 6 about the Special Tribunal for the Crime of Aggression against Ukraine, Article 63(1) of the Rome Statute requires the accused to be "present" before the trial can proceed.[58] The ICC does not provide for trials *in absentia* where the accused has never appeared before the Court.[59] Without arrest and surrender, and initial appearance, the proceedings cannot move forward.[60]

Thus, the most challenging barrier to the effectuation of the ICC's arrest warrant against Putin remains its enforcement. The ICC has no police force and nor does it have an army. The ICC relies entirely on the international community and specifically the States Parties to the Rome Statute to enforce the Court's decisions. It is all about political will. Justice Richard Goldstone, former chief prosecutor of the International Criminal Tribunals for the former Yugoslavia and Rwanda, put the ICC's dilemma bluntly: "In the case of the ICC, there is no authority with the power to enforce its decisions. It is ultimately only public opinion and the reputation of the States Parties that can lead states to comply with their international law obligations."[61] Though this remains a defining feature of the international legal system more generally, since its enforcement remains consent-based and varies depending on the "power" or "muscle" of a particular State or group of States, it is very acute in the criminal context, where lack of enforcement creates a lamentable perception of injustice for the most heinous of crimes.

Finding the political will to support international justice is challenging for all of the ICC's arrest warrants. Despite the ICC issuing arrest warrants against him in 2009 and 2010, Sudan's Al Bashir travelled freely to multiple State Parties to the Rome Statute, including South Africa, Jordan, and Uganda, without arrest.[62] South Africa's failure to arrest him during a 2015 African Union summit drew particular condemnation,[63] exposing how political solidarity and regional allegiances can override legal obligations, which States have voluntarily subscribed to by becoming party to the Rome Statute. Al Bashir remained at large even after he was ousted in a 2019

---

[58] International Criminal Court (2021b), art. 63(1).

[59] Id.

[60] Id., arts. 61, 63, 89; see Scheffer (2014).

[61] Green (2024).

[62] White (2018).

[63] Sandler Clarke (2015).

coup and detained by Sudanese authorities—not through any ICC-driven enforcement effort but as a consequence of domestic upheaval.[64] As of this writing, Sudan authorities have failed to transfer Al Bashir to The Hague to stand trial at the ICC.

Finding the political will to support an arrest warrant for Vladimir Putin is even more complex given his domestic political power and the concomitant unlikelihood that Russian political forces would ever overthrow him. More unfortunately, it is equally unlikely that the opportunity would arise where he would be arrested outside Russia. Russia is not a State Party to the Rome Statute and has made no secret of its contempt for the ICC's authority, and so the warrant can only be acted upon if Putin travels to a State Party willing to execute it pursuant to Article 89 of the Rome Statute.[65] However, this prospect is complicated by the web of political and diplomatic calculations that invariably surrounds such decisions.[66] Russia's own response to the arrest warrant was immediate and predictable: the Kremlin dismissed it as "null and void."[67]

Days after the arrest warrant was issued, Russia opened its own criminal cases against then ICC Prosecutor Karim Khan and three of the Court's judges. The United Nations described this as "deeply concerning" and called for the warrants to be withdrawn.[68] The Moscow City Court handed down prison sentences of up to 15 years for the ICC officials' role in issuing the arrest warrant for Putin. They were found guilty of "bringing a knowingly innocent person to criminal liability," "knowingly illegal detention," and most provocatively, "preparation of an attack on a representative of a foreign state for the purpose of provoking war or complicating international relations."[69] The final accusation essentially treats the legal pursuit of Putin as equivalent to an act of war.

The first major *international* litmus test of how or whether the ICC's arrest warrant would be enforced arose in 2023, when Putin was expected to attend the BRICS[70] summit in Johannesburg, South Africa. Although the warrant does not ensure surrender, it does attach a continuing legal risk to travel, summit attendance, and diplomatic engagement in States Parties.[71]

---

[64] BBC News (2019).

[65] Article 89(1) reads: "… State Parties shall, in accordance with the provisions of this Part and the procedure under their national law, comply with requests for arrest and surrender."

[66] Joldoshev (2024).

[67] Al Jazeera (2024).

[68] The list of those charged in absentia includes ICC Prosecutor Karim Khan, ICC President Piotr Hofmański, his deputies Luz del Carmen Ibáñez Carranza, Bertram Schmitt, and René Alapini-Gansou, alongside judges Tomoko Akane, Rosario Salvatore Aitala, Sergio Gerardo Ugalde Godínez, and Haykel Ben Mahfoudh. All nine were placed on Russia's international wanted list and arrested in absentia. *See* A warrant for a warrant. Moscow adds International Criminal Court leadership to wanted list for "illegal prosecution" of Russians and "provoking a war."

[69] Mediazona (2025a).

[70] BRICS is an intergovernmental organization comprising ten countries: Brazil, China, South Africa, Egypt, Ethiopia, India, Indonesia, Iran, Russia, and the United Arab Emirates.

[71] Du Plessis and Coutsoudis (2023).

For the BRICS conference, that potential risk worked. Putin's visit was ultimately cancelled following pressure by civil society and a South African court decision reaffirming South Africa's obligation to execute the ICC arrest warrant against him.[72] However, the last-minute avoidance of a diplomatic crisis did not mask the underlying lack of political willingness to support the ICC's decision. South African President Cyril Ramaphosa later stated that an attempt to arrest Putin would be seen as a declaration of war with Russia.[73]

The second major test emerged in September 2024, when President Putin visited Mongolia, a State Party to the Rome Statute. Putin's travel brought about a new diplomatic challenge. However, he never faced any serious prospect of arrest.[74] On the contrary, Mongolia offered no apologies for the welcome it extended. Soldiers on horseback and military anthems filled Genghis Khan Square as Putin arrived, the full pageantry of a state visit on display.[75] The geopolitical explanation was stark: a Mongolian Government spokesperson stated that "Mongolia imports 95% of its petroleum products and over 20% of electricity from our immediate neighbourhood, which have previously suffered interruption for technical reasons. This supply is critical to ensure our existence and that of our people."[76]

In response, the ICC's Pre-Trial Chamber II issued a formal decision on 24 October 2024 declaring Mongolia non-compliant with its obligations under the Rome Statute and referred the matter to the ICC's Assembly of States Parties.[77] However, this referral, though legally consistent with the Rome Statute, had no immediate consequences since the Assembly does not possess sanctioning powers.[78] Referring the issue to the U.N. Security Council also was not a viable option. Russia, as a permanent member of the Security Council, holds veto power and would block any attempt to escalate the matter.[79]

The ICC's case against Putin is simultaneously a landmark achievement and a demonstration of international law's limitations. On the one hand, it affirms that no leader, not even the head of a nuclear-armed "P5" state, is beyond the reach of accountability. As noted earlier, Putin does not enjoy immunity before the ICC and his official capacity is irrelevant.[80] His presence in Mongolia sparked a wave of international outrage leading to a renewed coverage of Russia's crimes in Ukraine and

---

[72] Human Rights Watch (2025); Reuters (2025).

[73] Booty and Ross (2023).

[74] Euronews (2024).

[75] Green (2024).

[76] Id.

[77] International Criminal Court (2024b), arts. 17–19.

[78] Stuart (2025).

[79] Ibid.

[80] Article 27(1) of the Rome Statute specifically states that the official capacity of the accused is irrelevant. The Statute states that it "[s]hall apply equally to all persons without any distinction based on official capacity. In particular, official capacity as a Head of State or Government, a member of a Government or parliament, an elected representative or a government official shall in no case exempt a person from criminal responsibility under this Statute, nor shall it, in and of itself, constitute a ground for reduction of sentence."

a demonstrable curtailment of his freedom of movement.[81] And while the Russian President may project confidence, advocates of international justice can draw quiet satisfaction that the Court is clearly on his mind.[82]

Yet, on the other hand the limits are also equally real and expose the ICC's structural dependence on proactive State cooperation. The 125 Member States of the ICC (as of May 2026) are legally obligated to arrest him. But as history shows, legal obligation and political reality are very different things.

There is no doubt that the ICC now finds itself in the most complex political circumstances since its inception. At a time when the international rules-based order is increasingly under strain, it is essential that States remain unwavering in their support for the ICC and uphold their treaty obligations. Without a solidified international political will, the ICC's power is stymied. The Court's jurisdictional reach may extend to the most powerful figures on the world stage, but its ability to act on that reach is effectively paralyzed when key States refuse to recognize its authority.[83] In Putin's case, the burden of enforcement rests primarily with Ukraine and Member States of the European Union, should he ever find himself on their soil.[84]

Another situation, equally contentious, under investigation at the ICC as of 2026 remained that of the State of Palestine and, in particular, actions taken by Hamas in Israel on or after 7 October 2023, as well as in Gaza, and by Israel on Palestinian territory following 7 October 2023. The ICC issued arrest warrants against three Hamas leaders, each of whom have since been killed, and against Israeli Prime Minister Benjamin Netanyahu and then Israeli Defense Minister Yoav Gallant.[85] Neither Netanyahu nor Gallant had been arrested and taken into custody at the ICC as of this writing and the international controversy over the arrest warrants against them had not abated.

International justice, however, operates over the long term. There are no statutes of limitations for atrocity crimes. History demonstrates that political and military leaders who thought themselves to be impervious to justice, eventually find themselves in the docks of international courts.[86] For example, Radovan Karadžić (the former Bosnian Serb political leader) (see Sect. 3.1.4), Ratko Mladić (the former Bosnian Serb military commander) (see Sect. 3.1.4), Charles Taylor (the former President of Liberia) (see Sect. 4.1.1), Slobodan Milošević (the former President of Serbia and former President of the Federal Republic of Yugoslavia),[87] Jean Kambanda (former Prime Minister of Rwanda),[88] and most recently, former Philippine President Rodrigo Duterte[89]—*all* found themselves before an international criminal court,

[81] Kersten (2024).

[82] Id.

[83] Stuart (2025).

[84] Chorakis (2023).

[85] See International Criminal Court (2026d).

[86] Ellis (2019).

[87] International Criminal Tribunal for the former Yugoslavia (2026).

[88] International Criminal Tribunal for Rwanda (2026).

[89] International Criminal Court (2026b).

often times years after being indicted. The same long arc of justice bends towards Vladimir Putin and the eventual prosecution of his case before the ICC.

References

Booty N, Ross W (2023) Arresting Vladimir Putin in South Africa would be 'declaration of war', says Ramaphosa. BBC News. https://www.bbc.com/news/world-africa-66238766. Accessed 29 Apr 2026

Chorakis A (2023) The ICC's arrest warrant against Putin: A grenade against peace in Ukraine? Harvard International Law Journal. https://journals.law.harvard.edu/ilj/2023/11/the-iccs-arrest-warrant-against-putin-a-grenade-against-peace-in-ukraine/. Accessed 29 Apr 2026

Du Plessis M, Coutsoudis A (2023) The Putin-South Africa arrest warrant saga: a tale of the shrinking world of an accused war criminal. EJIL:talk!. https://www.ejiltalk.org/the-putin-south-africa-arrest-warrant-saga-a-tale-of-the-shrinking-world-of-an-accused-war-criminal/. Accessed 29 Apr 2026

Ellis M (2019) The kaiser's trial: how a case that never happened helped create the international criminal justice system. Los Angeles Review of Books. https://lareviewofbooks.org/article/the-kaisers-trial-how-a-case-that-never-happened-helped-create-the-international-criminal-justice-system/. Accessed 29 Apr 2026

Euronews (2024) Mongolia declines to arrest Vladimir Putin during his visit despite ICC warrant. Euronews. https://www.euronews.com/2024/09/02/eu-calls-on-mongolia-to-arrest-putin-as-he-visits-the-icc-member-state. Accessed 29 Apr 2026

Gaeta P (2009) Does president Al Bashir enjoy immunity from arrest? J of Intl Crim Justice 7(2):315–332. https://doi.org/10.1093/jicj/mqp030

Gehani B (2023) Putin's arrest warrant, immunity and the international criminal court. Research Society of International Law. https://rsilpak.org/2023/putins-arrest-warrant-immunity-and-the-international-criminal-court/. Accessed 29 Apr 2026

Gonnella-Platts N (2025) Extending first ladies' tradition of advocacy, Melania trump focuses on Ukrainian kids. The Hill. https://thehill.com/opinion/white-house/5582489-first-lady-leadership-ukraine/. Accessed 29 Apr 2026

Green R (2024) Ukraine-Russia: Putin's visit to Mongolia defies ICC arrest warrant as the world looks on. International Bar Association. https://www.ibanet.org/putin-visit-to-mongolia-defies-icc-arrest-warrant-as-world-looks-on. Accessed 29 Apr 2026

Human Rights Watch (2025) Tajikistan: Arrest Putin. Human Rights Watch. https://www.hrw.org/news/2025/10/08/tajikistan-arrest-putin. Accessed 29 Apr 2026

International Criminal Court (2016) Report on preliminary examination activities (2016). International Criminal Court. https://www.icc-cpi.int/sites/default/files/iccdocs/otp/161114-otp-rep-PE_ENG.pdf. Accessed 29 Apr 2026

International Criminal Court (2021a) Case information sheet: Situation in Darfur, Sudan, the prosecutor v. Omar Hassan Ahmad Al Bashir, ICC-02/05–01/09. International Criminal Court. https://www.icc-cpi.int/sites/default/files/CaseInformationSheets/AlBashirEng.pdf. Accessed 8 May 2026

International Criminal Court (2021b) Rome statute of the International Criminal Court. https://www.icc-cpi.int/sites/default/files/2024-05/Rome-Statute-eng.pdf. Accessed 29 Apr 2026

International Criminal Court (2021c) Situation in Uganda in the case of the prosecutor v. Dominic Ongwen, public redacted sentence. International Criminal Court. https://www.icc-cpi.int/sites/default/files/CourtRecords/CR2021_04230.PDF. Accessed 8 May 2026

International Criminal Court (2021d) Situation in Uganda in the case of the prosecutor v. Dominic Ongwen, public redacted trial judgment. International Criminal Court. https://www.icc-cpi.int/sites/default/files/CourtRecords/CR2021_01026.PDF. Accessed 8 May 2026

International Criminal Court (2022a) Situation in Uganda in the case of the prosecutor v. Dominic Ongwen, public redacted judgment on the appeal of Mr Ongwen against the decision of Trial Chamber IX of 4 February 2021 entitled "trial judgment." International Criminal Court. https://www.icc-cpi.int/sites/default/files/CourtRecords/CR2022_07146.PDF. Accessed 8 May 2026

International Criminal Court (2022b) Summary, judgment of the appeals chamber in the prosecutor v. Dominic Ongwen, International Criminal Court. https://www.icc-cpi.int/sites/default/files/2022-12/2022-12-15-ongwen-judgment-summary-eng.pdf. Accessed 8 May 2026

International Criminal Court (2023) Situation in Ukraine: ICC judges issue arrest warrants against Vladimir Vladimirovich Putin and Maria Alekseyevna Lvova-Belova. International Criminal Court. https://www.icc-cpi.int/news/situation-ukraine-icc-judges-issue-arrest-warrants-against-vladimir-vladimirovich-putin-and. Accessed 29 Apr 2026

International Criminal Court (2024a) Situation in Uganda in the case of the prosecutor v. Dominic Ongwen, public with confidential ex parte annex I only available to the legal representatives of victims, the common legal representative of victims, the defence, and the registry and public annexes II and III. International Criminal Court. https://www.icc-cpi.int/sites/default/files/CourtRecords/0902ebd18078e195.pdf. Accessed 8 May 2026

International Criminal Court (2024b) Situation in Ukraine, public finding under article 87(7) of the Rome statute on the non-compliance by Mongolia with the request by the court to cooperate in the arrest and surrender of Vladimir Vladimirovich Putin and referral to the assembly of states parties. International Criminal Court. https://www.icc-cpi.int/sites/default/files/CourtRecords/0902ebd1809d1971.pdf. Accessed 29 Apr 2026

International Criminal Court (2025a) Situation in Darfur, Sudan, in the case of the prosecutor v. Ali Muhammad Ali Abd-al-Rahman ('Alie Kushayb'), public with annexes A, C and D, and confidential and public redacted annex B, trial judgment. https://www.icc-cpi.int/sites/default/files/CourtRecords/0902ebd180cb3b4e.pdf. Accessed 8 May 2026

International Criminal Court (2025b) Situation in Uganda in the case of the prosecutor v. Dominic Ongwen, public document, judgment on the appeal of Mr Dominic Ongwen against the decision of Trial Chamber IX of 28 February 2024 entitled "reparations order." International Criminal Court. https://www.icc-cpi.int/sites/default/files/CourtRecords/0902ebd180b2e203.pdf. Accessed 8 May 2026

International Criminal Court (2026c) International Criminal Court. https://www.icc-cpi.int/. Accessed 8 May 2026

International Criminal Court (2026a) About the court. International Criminal Court. https://www.icc-cpi.int/about/the-court. Accessed 21 May 2026

International Criminal Court (2026b) Duterte case. International Criminal Court. https://www.icc-cpi.int/philippines/duterte. Accessed 8 May 2026

International Criminal Court (2026d) State of Palestine. International Criminal Court. https://www.icc-cpi.int/palestine. Accessed 21 May 2026

International Criminal Court (2026e) Ukraine. International Criminal Court. https://www.icc-cpi.int/situations/ukraine. Accessed 29 Apr 2026

International Criminal Tribunal for Rwanda (2026) Kambanda, Jean (ICTR-97-23). International Criminal Tribunal for Rwanda. https://unictr.irmct.org/en/cases/ictr-97-23. Accessed 8 May 2026

International Criminal Tribunal for the former Yugoslavia (2026) Case information sheet: "Kosovo, Croatia & Bosnia" (IT-02-54), Slobodan Milošević. International Criminal Tribunal for the former Yugoslavia. https://www.icty.org/x/cases/slobodan_milosevic/cis/en/cis_milosevic_slobodan_en.pdf. Accessed 8 May 2026

Jackson M (2023) The ICC arrest warrants against Vladimir Putin and Maria Lvova-Belova: an outline of issues. EJIL:talk!. https://www.ejiltalk.org/the-icc-arrest-warrants-against-vladimir-putin-and-maria-lvova-belova-an-outline-of-issues/. Accessed 29 Apr 2026

Al Jazeera (2024) Russia's Putin to visit ICC member Mongolia despite arrest warrant. Al Jazeera. https://www.aljazeera.com/news/2024/8/30/russias-putin-to-visit-icc-member-mongolia-despite-arrest-warrant. Accessed 29 Apr 2026

Joldoshev J (2024) Breaking legal barriers: the ICC arrest warrant for Vladimir Putin. Federal Bar Association. https://www.fedbar.org/blog/breaking-legal-barriers-the-icc-arrest-warrant-for-vladimir-putin/. Accessed 29 Apr 2026

Kenny C (2024) Prosecutor v. Dominic Ongwen Am J of Intl Law 118(1):153–160. https://doi.org/10.1017/ajil.2023.65

Kersten M (2023) The view from Ukraine: why a new international criminal tribunal to prosecute Russian aggression is needed. Justice. Conflict. https://justiceinconflict.org/2023/01/05/the-view-from-ukraine-why-a-new-international-criminal-tribunal-to-prosecute-russian-aggression-is-needed/. Accessed 29 Apr 2026

Kersten M (2024) Silver linings: Putin visits Mongolia in defiance of ICC warrant. Justice. Conflict. https://justiceinconflict.org/2024/09/11/silver-linings-putin-visits-mongolia-in-defiance-of-icc-warrant/. Accessed 29 Apr 2026

Khan KAA (2022) Statement of ICC prosecutor, Karim A.A. Khan QC, on the situation in Ukraine: "I have been closely following recent developments in and around Ukraine with increasing concern." International Criminal Court. https://www.icc-cpi.int/news/statement-icc-prosecutor-karim-aa-khan-qc-situation-ukraine-i-have-been-closely-following. Accessed 29 Apr 2026

Leff A, Kelemen M, Maynes C (2023) The international criminal court issues an arrest warrant for Putin. NPR. https://www.npr.org/2023/03/17/1164267436/international-criminal-court-arrest-warrant-putin-ukraine-alleged-war-crimes. Accessed 29 Apr 2026

Marchuk I, Wanigasuriya A (2022) The ICC and the Russia-Ukraine war. ASIL Insights 26(4) https://asil.org/insights/volume-26-issue-4/. Accessed 29 Apr 2026

Mediazona (2025a) 15 years for a warrant: Moscow court sentences international criminal court leadership to prison in absentia for "illegal prosecution" of Vladimir Putin. Mediazona. https://en.zona.media/article/2025/12/12/ICC. Accessed 29 Apr 2026

Mediazona (2025b) A warrant for a warrant: Moscow adds International Criminal Court leadership to wanted list for "illegal prosecution" of Russians and "provoking a war." Mediazona. https://en.zona.media/article/2025/11/14/ICC. Accessed 29 Apr 2026

News BBC (2019) Omar al-Bashir: Sudan military coup topples ruler after protests. BBC News.. https://www.bbc.com/news/world-africa-47891470. Accessed 29 Apr 2026

Office of the United Nations High Commissioner for Human Rights (2026) Press statement by the independent International Commission of Inquiry on Ukraine, Palais des nations, Geneva. Office of the United Nations High Commissioner for Human Rights. https://www.ohchr.org/en/statements-and-speeches/2026/03/press-statement-independent-international-commission-inquiry. Accessed 29 Apr 2026

Parliamentarians for Global Action (2026) Ukraine and the Rome statute. Parliamentarians for Global Action. https://www.pgaction.org/ilhr/rome-statute/ukraine.html. Accessed 29 Apr 2026

Reuters (2025) Putin will not go to BRICS summit in Brazil due to ICC arrest warrant, kremlin aide says. Reuters. https://www.reuters.com/world/americas/putin-will-not-go-brics-summit-brazil-due-icc-arrest-warrant-kremlin-aide-says-2025-06-25/. Accessed 29 Apr 2026

Sandler Clarke J (2015) South Africa's failure to arrest Omar al-Bashir 'is betrayal of Mandela's ideals.' The Guardian.. https://www.theguardian.com/global-development-professionals-network/2015/jun/24/south-africas-failure-arrest-al-bashir-not-in-keeping-mandelas-ideals. Accessed 29 Apr 2026

Scheffer D (2014) Proposal for an international criminal court arrest procedures protocol. Northwestern J of Human Rights 12(3):229–252. https://scholarlycommons.law.northwestern.edu/njihr/vol12/iss3/1/

Scheffer D (2020) Reducing the funding gaps for atrocity victims. Opinio Juris. https://opiniojuris.org/2020/08/12/reducing-the-funding-gaps-for-atrocity-victims/. Accessed 8 May 2026

Scheffer DJ, Kaeb C, Babin M (2024) Social bonds: a lifeline for atrocity victims. United States Holocaust Museum Simon-Skjodt Center for the Prevention of Genocide. https://vault.ushmm.org/adaptivemedia/rendition/id_3bbec5be56edcca473841010a77da18944cfe531. Accessed 8 May 2026

Special Court for Sierra Leone (2026) AFRC: the prosecutor vs. Alex Tamba Brima, Ibrahim Bazzy Kamara and Santigie Borbor Kanu. https://rscsl.org/the-scsl/cases/afrc-the-prosecutor-vs-alex-tamba-brima-ibrahim-bazzy-kamara-and-santigie-borbor-kanu/. Accessed 8 May 2026

Stuart T (2025) The enforcement crisis of international criminal law: the case of the Putin arrest warrant. St Andrews law. Review. https://www.standrewslawreview.com/post/the-enforcement-crisis-of-international-criminal-law-the-case-of-the-putin-arrest-warrant. Accessed 29 Apr 2026

Trust Fund for Victims (2026) Trust Fund for Victims. https://www.trustfundforvictims.org/en/home. Accessed 8 May 2026

United Nations (1949) Geneva convention relative to the protection of civilian persons in time of war. United Nations Treaty Series. United Nations. Accessible via United Nations Treaty Collection, In. https://treaties.un.org/pages/showdetails.aspx?objid=0800000280158b1a. Accessed 29 Apr 2026

United Nations (2023a) International criminal court: Russia urged to withdraw arrest warrants for judges. UN News.. https://news.un.org/en/story/2023/10/1142287. Accessed 29 Apr 2026

United Nations (2023b) Russia: international criminal court issues arrest warrant for Putin. UN News. https://news.un.org/en/story/2023/03/1134732. Accessed 29 Apr 2026

United Nations (2026) Russia deportation of Ukraine children is crime against humanity: independent probe. UN News. https://news.un.org/en/story/2026/03/1167122. Accessed 29 Apr 2026

United Nations Security Council (2005) Resolution 1593 (2005), adopted by the Security Council at its 5158th meeting, on 31 March 2005. In: United Nations Digital Library. United Nations Security Council. Accessible via UNDOCS. https://digitallibrary.un.org/record/544817. Accessed 8 May 2026

White T (2018) States 'failing to seize Sudan's dictator despite genocide charge.' The Guardian. https://www.theguardian.com/global-development/2018/oct/21/omar-bashir-travels-world-despite-war-crime-arrest-warrant. Accessed 29 Apr 2026

Yale School of Public Health Humanitarian Research Lab (2023) Russia's systematic program for the re-education and adoption of Ukraine's children. Yale School of Public Health Humanitarian Research Lab. https://reliefweb.int/report/ukraine/humanitarian-research-lab-yale-school-public-health-russias-systematic-program-re-education-adoption-ukraines-children-enruuk. Accessed 29 Apr 2026

Yale School of Public Health Humanitarian Research Lab (2025a) Fact check: Russia's kidnapping and re-education of Ukraine's children. Yale School of Public Health Humanitarian Research Lab. https://medicine.yale.edu/news-article/fact-sheet-russias-kidnapping-and-re-education-of-ukraines-children/. Accessed 29 Apr 2026

Yale School of Public Health Humanitarian Research Lab (2025b) Ukraine's stolen children: inside Russia's network of re-education and militarization. Yale School of Public Health Humanitarian Research Lab. https://ysph.yale.edu/news-article/ukraines-stolen-children-inside-russias-network-of-re-education-and-militarization/. Accessed 29 Apr 2026

Chapter 6
The Creation of the Special Tribunal for the Crime of Aggression against Ukraine

6.1 Origins

The previous chapters covering the modern atrocity crimes tribunals collectively form an arc of international justice during the last three decades that had its genesis at Nuremberg in 1945 with the establishment of the International Military Tribunal (IMT) and where the crime of aggression, termed "crimes against peace," was first prosecuted. The IMT set in motion a fundamental shift in international law, moving from an exclusive emphasis on State responsibility to individual responsibility for the commission of atrocity crimes. The leaders responsible for perpetrating war crimes, crimes against humanity, and aggression would no longer enjoy impunity for their decisions and actions. In this sense, Nuremberg also served as a corrective to the international community's earlier failure to hold German Emperor Wilhelm II accountable for his role in initiating the First World War.[1] Although aggression was effectively outlawed as early as 1928, with the signing of the Kellogg-Briand Pact,[2] the IMT gave the concept concrete legal expression. It recognized the crime of aggression (crimes against peace) as the "planning, preparation, initiation or waging a war of aggression or a war in violation of international treaties, (and) agreements…".[3]

The IMT further characterized aggression as the "supreme international crime" because it contains within it the accumulation of all the atrocity crimes that would follow.[4] In the IMT's reasoning, those responsible for initiating aggression bore

[1] Article 227 of the Treaty of Versailles stated that Kaiser Wilhelm would be tried by an international court for the "supreme crime against international morality and the sanctity of treaties." It would be the first time in history that nation-states imagined the possibility of an international criminal tribunal. But in the end, it was an effort that fell short. Kaiser Wilhelm was never brought to justice. He lived out his remaining years in the Netherlands. See Schabas (2018); Ellis (2019).

[2] Yale Law School Lillian Goldman Law Library (1929); Hathaway and Shapiro (2017).

[3] International Military Tribunal (1946), p. 12.

[4] International Military Tribunal (1946), p. 25.

D. J. Scheffer and M. S. Ellis, *The Story of Modern International Justice, 1993-2025*,
https://doi.org/10.1007/978-3-032-33243-1_6

liability not only for that crime, but also for the crimes yet to come. The Nuremberg Principles soon thereafter codified this understanding, embedding the crime of aggression within the framework of international criminal law.[5] The prohibition of the crime is today recognized as a peremptory, or *jus cogens,* norm of international law.[6]

Following the fall of the Berlin Wall and end of the Cold War, the evolution of international justice accelerated. As outlined in the preceding chapters, new judicial bodies for accountability were created. Yet, despite this institutional expansion, a critical gap emerged: actual prosecutions of the crime of aggression did not occur and peace was not sustained.

Although included within the jurisdiction of the International Criminal Court (ICC), the crime of aggression remained undefined until the 2010 Review Conference in Kampala, Uganda.[7] Even then, the adoption of a definition was accompanied by significant jurisdictional limitations. The ICC may exercise jurisdiction only where both the victim State and the aggressor State are parties to the Rome Statute, unless the jurisdiction is triggered by the U.N. Security Council.[8] Moreover, State Parties to the Rome Statute have to ratify the Kampala amendments on aggression in order to fall under the ICC's jurisdiction with respect to that crime. As of this writing, 49 States Parties to the Rome Statute have ratified the amendment on aggression.[9]

Consequently, the ICC's jurisdiction over the crime of aggression is, in crucial respects, significantly more restricted than its jurisdiction over the other core crimes of genocide, crimes against humanity, and war crimes. This limitation reflects a political compromise that was necessary to secure support from key actors during the Kampala negotiations.[10]

The jurisdictional structure has created what scholars call the "impunity gap" for the crime of aggression.[11] The States most capable of waging wars of aggression are non-party States and thus remain effectively beyond the reach of this international

---

[5] International Law Commission (1950).

[6] The first Purpose stated in the UN Charter, which was adopted in 1945 at the same time as the IMT began to operate, is "to take effective collective measures for…the suppression of acts of aggression or other breaches of the peace…" (Article 1(1)). The United Nations General Assembly (UNGA) affirmed the Nuremberg Principles on December 11, 1946, in Resolution 95(1), wherein the crime of aggression is codified in Principle VI(a). In 1954, the UNGA assigned a special committee the task of preparing a report on issues relating to the crime of aggression. But because of the onset of the Cold War, it was not until twenty years later, on December 14,1974, that the UNGA adopted the Definition of Aggression in Resolution 3314 (XXIX).

[7] Following the amendments to the Rome Statute approved at the Kampala review conference of 2010, Article 8*bis*(1) of the Rome Statute reads: ""crime of aggression" means the planning, preparation, initiation or execution, by a person in a position effectively to exercise control over or to direct the political or military action of a State, of an act of aggression which, by its character, gravity and scale, constitutes a manifest violation of the Charter of the United Nations."

[8] International Criminal Court (2021), art. 15(bis).

[9] Global Campaign for Ratification and Implementation of the Kampala Amendments on the Crime of Aggression (2025).

[10] Koh and Buchwald (2015).

[11] Getgen Kestenbaum (2016); see McDougall (2024).

accountability mechanism. Russia's war against Ukraine - beginning with the annexation of Crimea in 2014 and culminating in the full-scale invasion of 2022 - exposed this gap prominently. The Russian aggression against Ukraine represented the most egregious violation of international law in Europe since the Second World War.

International condemnation of Russia's invasion of Ukraine and calls for accountability were swift and sustained. The United Nations General Assembly adopted multiple resolutions denouncing the aggression (in the years 2014, 2016, 2018, 2021, 2022, 2023, 2024, and 2025),[12] complemented by actions from the Parliamentary Assembly of the Council of Europe[13] and the Committee of Ministers.[14]

[12] United Nations General Assembly Resolution 68/262 of 27 March 2014 called upon all States to desist and refrain from actions aimed at the partial or total disruption of the national unity and territorial integrity of Ukraine including any attempts to modify Ukraine's borders through the threat or use of force or other unlawful means. United Nations General Assembly 71/205 of 19 December 2016, reaffirmed the responsibility of all States to refrain from the threat or use of force against the territorial integrity or political independence of any State and from acting in any other manner inconsistent with the purposes of the United Nations and urged the Russian Federation to immediately release Ukrainian citizens who were unlawfully detained and judged without regard for elementary standards of justice. United Nations General Assembly Resolution 73/151 of 17 December 2018, condemned the temporary occupation of the Autonomous Republic of Crimea and the city of Sevastopol, and recalled that this temporary occupation and the threat or use of force against the territorial integrity or political independence of Ukraine by the Russian Federation are in contravention of commitments made to respect the independence and sovereignty and the existing borders of Ukraine. United Nations General Assembly Resolution 76/70 of 9 December 2021, urged the Russian Federation to completely and unconditionally withdraw its military forces from Crimea and end its temporary occupation of the territory of Ukraine without delay and further stressed that the presence of Russian troops in Crimea is contrary to the national sovereignty, political independence and territorial integrity of Ukraine and undermines the security and stability of neighboring countries and the European region. United Nations General Assembly Resolution ES-11/1 of 2 March 2022, recognizing that the military operations of the Russian Federation inside the sovereign territory of Ukraine were on a scale that the international community had not seen in Europe in decades, deplored in the strongest terms the aggression by the Russian Federation against Ukraine in violation of Article 2, paragraph 4, of the Charter of the United Nations, demanded that the Russian Federation immediately cease its use of force against Ukraine and deplored the involvement of Belarus in this unlawful use of force against Ukraine. United Nations General Assembly Resolution ES-11/L.7 of 23 February 2023 emphasized the need to ensure accountability for the most serious crimes under international law committed on the territory of Ukraine through appropriate, fair and independent investigations and prosecutions at the national or international level and ensure justice for all victims and the prevention of future crimes. United Nations General Assembly Resolution 79/184 of 17 December 2024 condemned the war of aggression against Ukraine by the Russian Federation in violation of Article 2, paragraph 4, of the Charter of the United Nations, and the use of Crimea for this and to support the attempted illegal annexation of the Kherson, Zaporizhzhia, Donetsk and Luhansk oblasts.

[13] On 15 March 2022, the Parliamentary Assembly of the Council of Europe condemned the Russian Federation's aggression against Ukraine in the strongest terms, noting that the escalation of military activities as of 24 February 2022 represented a continuation of the war of aggression by the Russian Federation against Ukraine since 20 February 2014.

[14] On 16 March 2022, the Committee of Ministers decided to exclude the Russian Federation from the Council of Europe because of its aggression against Ukraine, such aggression constituting a serious violation by the Russian Federation of its obligations under Article 3 of the Statute of the Council of Europe and under international law.

These developments were accompanied by demands for a credible mechanism of accountability.[15]

Simultaneously, the International Centre for the Prosecution of the Crime of Aggression against Ukraine (ICPA) was created as a judicial hub set up under the auspices of Eurojust to enhance and coordinate national investigations into Russia's aggression. Launched in 2023, it documents evidence of the crime of aggression for future submission to legal proceedings, particularly the Special Tribunal for the Crime of Aggression against Ukraine. The efforts coordinated by the ICPA are aimed at supporting prosecutions for the crime of aggression and unite the work of prosecutors in Ukraine, Poland, Lithuania, Latvia, Estonia and Romania.[16] The ICPA is also connected to the Core International Crimes Evidence Database (CICED), which is a judicial database operated by the Joint Investigation Team (JIT) also established by Eurojust to store and preserve evidence of core international crimes, alongside the Register of Damage (RD4U).[17] The activities of the JIT are specifically focused on the collection, secure storage, and rapid exchange of information and evidence of war crimes committed by Russia, gathered during investigations on the territory of Member States, as well as operational and investigative measures. The journey has been difficult, but the international community has remained steadfast in its determination to bring Russian leaders to justice.[18]

Efforts have coalesced since Russia's full-scale invasion of Ukraine on 28 February 2022 around the creation of a Special Tribunal for the Crime of Aggression against Ukraine (STCA), aimed at holding Russia's leadership accountable for the crime of aggression in light of the fact that the International Criminal Court has no jurisdiction over Russian participation in this particular war of aggression. One of the Kampala amendments on the crime of aggression insulated nationals of any non-party State to the Rome Statute from any investigation and prosecution. Article

---

[15] The idea of establishing a special tribunal to prosecute Russia for aggression against Ukraine was first officially voiced by Ukrainian Foreign Minister Dmytro Kuleba in March 2022.

[16] European Union Agency for Criminal Justice Cooperation (2026b).

[17] European Union Agency for Criminal Justice Cooperation (2024); European Union Agency for Criminal Justice Cooperation (2026a).

[18] United Nations General Assembly Resolution 79/284 of 16 April 2025, acknowledged the contribution of the Council of Europe to the work of the core group towards the establishment of a special tribunal for the crime of aggression against Ukraine, and its willingness to examine possible options to provide expert and technical support for the establishment and, as appropriate, operation of such a special tribunal; Having regard to Statutory Resolution Res(93)28 of the Committee of Ministers on partial and enlarged agreements; Resolution of the Committee of Ministers establishing the criteria for partial and enlarged agreements of the Council of Europe. On 24 June 2025 the Committee of Ministers authorized the establishment of the Management Committee of the Special Tribunal for the Crime of Aggression against Ukraine (hereinafter "Management Committee") in the form of an enlarged partial agreement within the framework of the Council of Europe and authorized the Secretary General of the Council of Europe (hereinafter "Secretary General") to sign the Agreement between the Council of Europe and Ukraine on the Establishment of the Special Tribunal for the Crime of Aggression against Ukraine (hereinafter "Agreement") on behalf of the Council of Europe. Several international organizations have already adopted resolutions supporting the idea of a special tribunal. The list currently includes the European Parliament, the Parliamentary Assembly of the Council of Europe, the NATO Parliamentary Assembly, and the OSCE Parliamentary Assembly.

15*bis*(5) of the Rome Statute requires that, "In respect of a State that is not a party to this Statute, the Court shall not exercise its jurisdiction over the crime of aggression when committed by that State's nationals or on its territory."

A Core Group of approximately 40 countries included Ukraine, Member States of the Council of Europe,[19] and other supporting nations, as well as the European Union. The Core Group worked alongside scholars and civil society groups, including the International Bar Association, over several years following the Russian invasion of Ukraine in February 2022 to design the exact structure of the proposed tribunal.[20] These sustained efforts culminated with the foundational agreement formally establishing the STCA and signed by Ukraine and the Council of Europe on 25 June 2025 in Strasbourg, France.[21] This marked a decisive step towards closing a longstanding gap in international criminal accountability.

The STCA focuses exclusively on senior political and military leaders, targeting those responsible for planning, preparing, initiating, or executing the crime of aggression.[22] It is a *sui generis* tribunal established during an active war with jurisdiction over the crime of aggression regarding an aggressor State which has not yet been defeated. This means it faces immense political pressure to succeed.

The STCA reflects a critical conceptual distinction between the *'leadership crime'* (the decision to wage war) and the *'conduct crimes'* (atrocities committed during the war). This distinction recognizes that those who initiate aggressive war may never physically commit atrocity crimes, yet they bear ultimate responsibility for creating the conditions in which such crimes occur. The Statute of the STCA affirms that "'act of aggression' means the use of armed force by a State against the sovereignty, territorial integrity or political independence of another State, or in any other manner inconsistent with the Charter of the United Nations."[23] The Statute further underscores that official position does not shield individuals from international criminal responsibility[24]—a message with implications well beyond the Russia-Ukraine War.

---

[19] The Council of Europe is a 46-member intergovernmental organization aiming to advance human rights, democracy and the rule of law. See Council of Europe (2026).

[20] The first initiative was to establish a Special Tribunal on the basis of an agreement between Ukraine and the United Nations with the adoption of a relevant UNGA resolution. The second initiative was to establish a special tribunal based on a multilateral international agreement between a coalition of willing states and Ukraine. Ukraine would delegate its territory or passive jurisdiction to this internationalized tribunal. The third approach was establishing a special tribunal as a court operating based on Ukrainian law and Ukrainian jurisdiction (i.e., as part of the Ukrainian judicial system), with the involvement of an international element in its construction and operation (international judges and prosecutors, location in Europe, international support). The fourth and final option was to establish a special tribunal through a treaty between Ukraine and either the European Union or the Council of Europe. Ultimately, this fourth option was implemented with the Council of Europe as the treaty partner with Ukraine. Of course, Ukraine's courts would continue to undertake the investigation and prosecution of the crime of aggression since Ukraine's national criminal code includes the crime of aggression.

[21] Karsu (2025).

[22] Council of Europe (2025), art. 2(1).

[23] Id., art. 2(2).

[24] Id., art. 4.

Since accountability for perpetrators of international crimes is a *sine qua non* element of a just and lasting peace in Ukraine, the STCA sets a strong precedent for both international justice and global security.

6.1.1 Structural Constraints

Notwithstanding the advances to create an accountability mechanism for the crime of aggression, two structural characteristics remain embedded in the Statute of the STCA: trials *in absentia* and head of state immunity.

6.1.2 Trials In Absentia

The use of trials *in absentia*, from the Latin for "in the absence of," remains a contentious issue in international law, oscillating between two imperatives: (1) the demand for efficient justice and (2) the need to protect the rights of the accused. International law generally leans towards the latter.

The use of trials *in absentia* as an alternative mechanism to ensure justice for victims when the accused is not present is also reflected in the experience of international criminal tribunals. In the early years of the modern international criminal justice system as we now know it, the IMT authorized trials *in absentia*. Article 12 of the London Charter stated that the IMT "shall have the right to take proceedings... in [the accused's] absence" if the individual cannot be found or the interests of justice so require.[25]

Trials *in absentia* were prohibited before the *ad hoc* International Criminal Tribunal for the former Yugoslavia (ICTY) and the hybrid Special Court for Sierra Leone and Extraordinary Chambers in the Courts of Cambodia. However, at the ICTY its Rules of Procedure and Evidence permitted the Prosecutor to proceed with *in absentia* proceedings in order to facilitate a public presentation before the Trial Chamber of the indictment and supporting evidence regarding an indicted fugitive who has not been arrested. Rule 61 of the ICTY Rules of Procedure and Evidence provided:

> (A) If, within a reasonable time, a warrant of arrest has not been executed, and personal service of the indictment has consequently not been effected, the Judge who confirmed the indictment shall invite the Prosecutor to report on the measures taken. When the Judge is satisfied that:
>
> (i) the Registrar and the Prosecutor have taken all reasonable steps to secure the arrest of the accused, including recourse to the appropriate authorities of the State in whose territory or under whose jurisdiction and control the person to be served resides or was

[25] International Military Tribunal (1946), art. 12. The IMT only tried and convicted one person *in absentia*, namely Martin Bormann. See the judgment at Yale Law School Lillian Goldman Law Library (2026).

last known to them to be; and (Amended 18 Jan 1996, amended 12 Nov 1997) IT/32/ Rev. 50 51 8 July 2015

(ii) if the whereabouts of the accused are unknown, the Prosecutor and the Registrar have taken all reasonable steps to ascertain those whereabouts, including by seeking publication of advertisements pursuant to Rule 60, (Amended 18 Jan 1996, amended 12 Nov 1997, amended 4 Dec 1998) the Judge shall order that the indictment be submitted by the Prosecutor to the Trial Chamber of which the Judge is a member. (Amended 3 May 1995, amended 18 Jan 1996, amended 12 Nov 1997, amended 4 Dec 1998).

(B) Upon obtaining such an order the Prosecutor shall submit the indictment to the Trial Chamber in open court, together with all the evidence that was before the Judge who initially confirmed the indictment. The Prosecutor may also call before the Trial Chamber and examine any witness whose statement has been submitted to the confirming Judge. In addition, the Trial Chamber may request the Prosecutor to call any other witness whose statement has been submitted to the confirming Judge. (Amended 30 Jan 1995, amended 25 July 1997)

(C) If the Trial Chamber is satisfied on that evidence, together with such additional evidence as the Prosecutor may tender, that there are reasonable grounds for believing that the accused has committed all or any of the crimes charged in the indictment, it shall so determine. The Trial Chamber shall have the relevant parts of the indictment read out by the Prosecutor together with an account of the efforts to effect service referred to in paragraph (A) above. (Amended 12 Apr 2001).[26]

But this fell far short of an actual trial and Rule 61 was nonetheless employed twice by the ICTY for a public airing of the evidence (but no trial), the first case being against Radovan Karadžić and Ratko Mladić long before either was arrested and stood trial. That decision was made on 11 July 1996.[27] The second case was *Prosecutor v. Ivica Rajic a/k/a Victor Andric (Review of the Indictment pursuant to Rule 61 of the Rules of Procedure and Evidence)*, a decision arising from the *in absentia* proceeding reached two months later on 13 September 1996.[28]

The Statute of the *ad hoc* International Criminal Tribunal for Rwanda (ICTR) had its own Rule 61 in its Rules of Procedure and Evidence[29] for *in absentia* proceedings but, like the ICTY, did not permit *in absentia* trials, at least initially. In 2003 the ICTR Rules of Procedure and Evidence were amended to include Rule 82*bis*, which in fact permitted *in absentia* trials:

> If an accused refuses to appear before the Trial Chamber for trial, the Chamber may order that the trial proceed in the absence of the accused for so long as his refusal persists, provided that the Trial Chamber is satisfied that: (i) the accused has made his initial appearance under Rule 62; (ii) the Registrar has duly notified the accused that he is required to be present for trial; (iii) the interests of the accused are represented by counsel.[30]

Only one ICTR case, against Jean-Bosco Barayagwiza as one of the defendants in the *Media* case discussed in Chap. 2, was prosecuted under Rule 82*bis*, which had been

---

[26] See International Criminal Tribunal for the former Yugoslavia (2015).

[27] See International Criminal Tribunal for the former Yugoslavia (1996a; International Criminal Tribunal for the former Yugoslavia 1996c).

[28] International Criminal Tribunal for the former Yugoslavia (1996b).

[29] International Criminal Tribunal for Rwanda (2015).

[30] Id., p. 98.

approved by the ICTR judges solely to address his situation. Barayagwiza had been captured and arrested but had refused to leave the ICTR prison to attend the *Media* trial in the ICTR courtroom. He was tried, convicted, and sentenced *in absentia* to 35 years of imprisonment.[31] Having served its singular purpose, Rule 82*bis* was repealed by the ICTR in July 2015.

The Special Tribunal for Lebanon permitted *in absentia* trials and indeed they were held in the absence of the defendants.[32] Given that the Special Tribunal for Lebanon followed the criminal procedure law of Lebanon, which is based on the civil law tradition of the French system and permits *in absentia* trials, there was little doubt at the time that such trials would be held in the absence of the defendants if arrest could not be accomplished (which proved to be the reality for the STL).

The Rome Statute of the ICC provides that "the accused *shall* be present during the trial" (emphasis added).[33] Similar to the other modern criminal tribunals, the Rome Statute provides that if a defendant present at trial absconds or disrupts proceedings, the ICC may temporarily remove that defendant. Still, the trial may *only* continue if the defendant had initially appeared before the Court.[34] The Rome Statute does not permit reaching a final verdict without the presence of the defendant.

Under Article 61 of the Rome Statute, the Pre-Trial Chamber must convene a hearing to confirm the charges and thus determine whether the evidence suffices to proceed to trial. That hearing should occur with the accused present, but the Rome Statute explicitly authorizes the Pre-Trial Chamber to proceed *in absentia* for the confirmation hearing if, after being charged, the person either (a) "has waived [the right to be present]" or (b) "has fled or otherwise cannot be found" despite reasonable efforts.[35] In practice, if an indicted suspect remains at large, the prosecutor can seek to hold a confirmation hearing without waiting indefinitely. For example, the confirmation hearing of Joseph Kony, an indicted fugitive of the ICC since 2005, was held in 2025 despite the continuing failure to achieve his capture or surrender and actual arrest.[36]

Although common law systems generally prohibit trials *in absentia*, many civil law systems, such as those found in Lebanon and Ukraine, allow such *in absentia* trials under stringent safeguards, including:

1. *effective notification*, well-documented steps to notify the accused of the charges and trial date. This is a very high bar to meet. The accused's vague or informal knowledge of proceedings is insufficient to establish a waiver of the right to be present. For instance, the mere assumption that the accused is aware of proceedings because of widespread media coverage does not meet the required safeguard

[31] See International Criminal Tribunal for Rwanda (2007).

[32] See "Attachment: Statute of the Special Tribunal for Lebanon, art. 22 in United Nations Security Council (2007),

[33] International Criminal Court (2021), art. 63.

[34] International Criminal Court (2023), para. 42.

[35] International Criminal Court (2021), art. 61(2)(b), Massimino (2024).

[36] International Criminal Court (2024; International Criminal Court 2025a); International Criminal Court (2025b), Gureghian Hall M (2026).

standard. Moreover, the European Court of Human Rights rejected the argument that the accused had waived his right to appear simply because the accused was untraceable since any waiver must satisfy several conditions established in the case law.[37]

2. *legal representation*, by qualified defense counsel. Denying this right would render proceedings manifestly unjust. While an accused may waive his right to be present at a trial, international human rights standards require that such absence be counterbalanced by counsel appointed by the court or by the accused.
3. *right to retrial*, if the accused is apprehended at a later date. The United Nations Human Rights Council emphasizes retrial as a full trial at first instance, whereas the European Court of Human Rights permits retrial to take the form of a *de novo* appellate review, based on the facts. If any doubt exists as to whether the accused had actual knowledge of the proceedings, the court must offer an opportunity for a retrial. A retrial must be granted unless the prosecution can show the accused was: (1) properly informed of the judgment, (2) received the full decision, and (3) understood their rights, including how and where to apply for a new trial.

Beginning with the IMT at Nuremberg and decades later extending through the creation and legal proceedings of the modern atrocity crimes tribunals, there has been varied usage and prohibition of the *in absentia* procedure for prosecution of individuals charged with commission of atrocity crimes. The trend has been to balance the imperative of combating impunity with the equally fundamental obligation to ensure a fair trial. While the practice remains controversial, the variations across the tribunals reveal a shared recognition that *in absentia* proceedings can be a procedural tool long accepted in trials for some national civil law systems and innovatively employed during the confirmation stage in some of the international criminal tribunals.

6.1.3 The Special Tribunal for the Crime of Aggression against Ukraine (STCA)

The Special Tribunal for the Crime of Aggression against Ukraine (STCA) reflects in its Statute a structure similar to that of previous international courts, but with necessary adaptations. Given the likelihood that senior Russian officials will not voluntarily submit to jurisdiction, the STCA conforms with Ukrainian criminal law and includes *in absentia* proceedings, with conditions:

(1) Where, upon confirmation of the indictment under Article 25, paragraph 2, of this Statute, the accused does not appear before the Special Tribunal, the Special Tribunal may conduct proceedings in his or her absence:

> (a) when he or she has waived his or her right to be present in an unequivocal manner; or

[37] European Court of Human Rights (2026).

(b) if all reasonable steps have been taken to secure his or her appearance before the Special Tribunal and to inform the person of the charges and the consequences of his or her non-appearance before the Special Tribunal; and the interests of justice so require.

(2) When hearings are conducted in the absence of the accused, the Special Tribunal shall ensure that:

(a) the accused has been duly notified or served with, or otherwise been given notice through publication in the media or communication to his or her State of residence or nationality of:
(i) the indictment;
(ii) the date, time and place of the hearing; and
(iii) the consequences of his or her non-appearance before the Special Tribunal; and

(b) the accused has designated a defence counsel of his or her own choosing, to be remunerated either by the accused or, if the accused is proved to be indigent, by the Special Tribunal; whenever the accused refuses or fails to appoint a defence counsel, such counsel is to be assigned by the Defence Unit with a view to ensuring full representation of the interests and rights of the accused.

(3) In case of a conviction in the absence of the accused, the convicted person shall have the right to a retrial in his or her presence before the Special Tribunal or a successor mechanism, unless he or she:
(a) has waived in writing his or her right to a retrial; or
(b) accepts the judgment.[38]

The STCA Statute thus guarantees core safeguards: The accused must be represented by counsel and is entitled to request reopening of the case upon appearance, unless he or she has waived that right or accepted the original judgment.[39] Without such guarantees, any conviction *in absentia* would be highly vulnerable to legal challenge under the International Covenant on Civil and Political Rights and European Convention on Human Rights and could hinder future international cooperation with STCA investigations, including the extradition of suspects.

There is a narrow but highly significant limitation to trials *in absentia* in the STCA. Members of the "Troika" of the Russian Federation (namely the Head of State, the Head of Government, and the Minister of Foreign Affairs) cannot be tried *in absentia* by the STCA. This is by far the most contentious issue in the STCA's design. As a practical matter, it means that as long as President Vladimir Putin remains in office, he would not face arrest and trial—only the possibility of an essentially tabled indictment.

---

[38] Council of Europe (2025), art. 28.

[39] Id.

6.1.3.1 Immunities

Under customary international law, members of the Troika enjoy personal immunities from civil and criminal proceedings before foreign national courts, as affirmed in the International Court of Justice *Arrest Warrant* case (in other words, *ratione personae*).[40] It is possible that other government officials might also be protected.[41]

However, such immunities do not extend to international criminal tribunals established through appropriate legal authority—such as one created by the U.N. Security Council or by treaty as examined previously.

The central debate among States during the creation of the STCA centered on whether the STCA would meet this threshold. A number of Core Group States, particularly the Baltic countries, argued that the then proposed STCA, backed by the Council of Europe and open to broader international participation, would meet the "international" threshold and could, therefore, reject Head of State immunity. However, the powerful group of G7 nations opposed this position, concerned about the precedent that it might establish.

Ultimately, a compromise was reached, limiting but not fully abolishing personal immunity. This does not mean the STCA is toothless; rather, it shifts the strategy to a long-term initiative.[42] Under the framework, official status would ***not*** protect individuals from investigations. The STCA prosecutor would be able to prepare indictments against those in positions of authority who plan, prepare, initiate, or execute acts of aggression—namely senior political and military leaders. This would include members of the Troika and thus investigation and indictment. However, under the Statute of the STCA, an indictment against any individual of this group cannot—be confirmed by the Pre-Trial Chamber while that individual remains in office. Thus, no arrest warrant could be issued in such cases, and the Pre-Trial Judge would be required to *suspend* proceedings until the individual leaves his or her position. Then the arrest warrant could be approved for enforcement against the indicted individual.

---

[40] Higgins R, Kooijmans P, Buergenthal T (2002), para. 59. That personal immunity does not preclude an investigation when such investigation may concern a high-level foreign official was also the conclusion struck by the two special rapporteurs on immunity of State officials from foreign criminal jurisdiction. See Escobar Hernández C (2018), para. 61, stating "It therefore appears impossible to conclude that immunity from jurisdiction must be taken into consideration and applied automatically right from the start of an investigation, even when the latter may concern a foreign official;" see Kolodkin (2011), para. 151, stating "In many cases, the preliminary actions of the criminal process are unrelated to measures precluded by immunity. In that situation, consideration of the issue of immunity by a State exercising criminal jurisdiction is not necessary and cannot be deemed its obligation."

[41] At least two national courts and prosecutorial authorities have also found that defence ministers of a foreign state benefit from personal immunity. In the United Kingdom, see International Law Reports (2006); in France, see the Public Prosecutor to the Paris Court of Appeal (2008); in Belgium, see International Committee of the Red Cross (2026). If a national court were to follow this reasoning, it could hold whomever is the current defence minister at the time as covered by personal immunity regarding the STCA.

[42] E-International Relations (2026).

By contrast, the STCA Statute does not recognize functional immunity (*ratione materiae*). Article 23(4) states: "Functional immunity shall not apply before the Special Tribunal. This position might seem to contradict existing international norms where functional immunities apply to all State officials for conduct they performed in an official capacity."[43] Normally, in contrast to personal immunity, functional immunity continues; it does not cease to apply once the official leaves office.[44]

However, increasingly, States recognize an exception to functional immunity for prosecution of international crimes, and the crime of aggression is so considered.[45] According to this exception, State officials who perpetrate international crimes during their term of office could be prosecuted. Whereas the existence of this exception may have been doubtful before Nuremberg, the practice of national tribunals since the Second World War, followed by the development of a general *opinio juris*, supports the customary law status of this exception regarding functional immunity for international crimes.[46]

The exception on functional immunity should be considered to apply to all major international crimes, including the crime of aggression,[47] an issue that remains under consideration by the International Law Commission.[48]

Thus, by extending this exception for state officials responsible for the crime of aggression, the STCA reflects an important evolution in law, notwithstanding the more cautious position taken by the International Law Commission.

6.2 The STCA—The Way Forward

The establishment of the STCA pursuant to an agreement between the Council of Europe and the Government of Ukraine represents an innovative institutional model. It emerged after two years of debate as to what type of tribunal model should be

---

[43] On the categories of officials covered by functional immunity, see International Court of Justice (2008), paras. 181–200; see International Criminal Tribunal for the former Yugoslavia (1997), para. 38.

[44] The ICJ notes that immunities would not bar proceedings for a former foreign minister in "in respect of acts committed during that period of office in a private capacity," as opposed to in an official capacity. See International Court of Justice (2002), para. 61.

[45] Kreß, Frank, and Barthe (2021).

[46] Bothe (1971); see also Werle (2007), at margin no. 613 with further references in note 550; speaking for immunities in general, see Zahar and Sluiter (2008), p. 503.

[47] For an overview of national prosecutions including aggression see United Nations Preparatory Commission for the International Criminal Court (2002). For an account see Strapatsas (2010), p. 454.

[48] The International Law Commission has examined a draft article for its proposed text on "Immunity of State officials from foreign criminal jurisdiction" that would provide for an exemption on functional immunity for not only the crimes of genocide, crimes against humanity, war crimes, the crime of apartheid, torture, but also crimes of aggression, slavery, and slave trade. See United Nations General Assembly (2025); Mimran and Halfon (2026).

adopted.[49] In the end, the Tribunal will be governed by an Enlarged Partial Agreement (EPA), inviting States to join a flexible legal framework. While under Council of Europe regulations, a minimum of 16 member states is required for the EPA to enter into force, a broader participation has already ensured political legitimacy and the promise of financial sustainability. On 11 February 2026, the Estonian Parliament approved legislation to join the EPA, making Estonia the first country to do so. It is also anticipated that States beyond the Council of Europe will participate, underscoring the STCA's broad geographical and political support.[50] On 15 May 2026, 36 countries, as well as the European Union, agreed to join the EPA and thus support the operations of the STCA in The Hague.[51] The focus will now be aimed at countries in Latin America, Africa, Asia, and the Indo-Pacific to join the EPA.[52]

It was crucial to ensure that the STCA become operational without delay to safeguard its credibility and prevent political erosion or attempts to undermine or obstruct its establishment. Therefore, it was essential that the process of establishing the STCA receive sustained political and financial support as early as possible. In response to these challenges, during the meeting of the STCA Working Party in Strasbourg, Ukraine proposed an innovative approach. The STCA can be implemented in three phases: ("0") an advance team; ("1") a skeleton tribunal; and ("2") the full operational tribunal.[53]

The "advance team" will work in both Strasbourg and the Netherlands for roughly 1½ to 2 years before fully relocating to the Netherlands. The team will develop the internal rules and procedures, staffing frameworks, premises, and security requirements. The next phase will be establishing a "skeleton tribunal" in The Hague. This skeleton tribunal will recruit and appoint key personnel, such as judges, establish the registry, and set prosecutorial priorities. Most importantly, the skeleton tribunal will have legal standing and enter into a host country agreement with the Netherlands and other international organizations.[54] Once these are finalized and the EPA is complete, the work of the STCA will be able to start, including the recruitment of judges, prosecutorial staff, and defense teams.

In the final phase, the STCA will become fully operational. Indictments, the issuance of arrest warrants, and trials (likely held largely *in absentia*) will be the critical elements of this final phase of the STCA.[55]

[49] Williams and Beta (2025).

[50] Mudra, Korynevych, and Ellis (2026).

[51] Liboreiro (2026).

[52] Mudra Korynevych Yurlov and Ellis (2026).

[53] Id.

[54] Mudra Korynevych and Ellis (2026).

[55] Id.

6.3 Conclusion

The STCA is not merely a response to Russia's aggression. It represents a significant development in the architecture of international criminal justice. It reaffirms the centrality of the prohibition on the use of force as a cornerstone of the international legal order. It strengthens deterrence against future wars of aggression and demonstrates that even the most senior political and military leaders are not beyond the reach of the law. The STCA also stands as the bridge between the UN Charter's aspirational promise and the practical reality of holding accountable those who choose to violate it.[56] In doing so, the STCA seeks to close one of the most enduring gaps in international criminal accountability—and in that sense, completes a trajectory that began at Nuremberg. Finally, what transpires in the trials and jurisprudence of the STCA will greatly inform how the crime of aggression will be prosecuted, and how defense counsel will handle aggression charges, in future litigation on the crime of aggression before the International Criminal Court.

References

Bothe M (1971) Die strafrechtliche Immunität fremder Staatsorgane. Zeitschrift für ausländisches und öffentliches Recht 31:246–270. https://www.zaoerv.de/31_1971/31_1971_1_2_a_246_270.pdf. Accessed 30 Apr 2026

Council of Europe (2025) Consequences of the aggression of The Russian Federation against Ukraine: statute of the special Tribunal for the Crime of aggression against Ukraine. Council of. Europe. https://search.coe.int/cm?i=0900001680b678ca. Accessed 30 Apr 2026

Council of Europe (2026) Council of Europe. https://www.coe.int/en/web/portal/home. Accessed 30 Apr 2026

E-International Relations (2026) Interview—mark Ellis. E-International Relations. https://www.e-ir.info/2026/06/04/interview-mark-ellis/. Accessed 6 Jun 2026

Ellis M (2019) The Kaiser's trial: how a case that never happened helped create the international criminal justice system. Los Angeles Review of Books. https://lareviewofbooks.org/article/the-kaisers-trial-how-a-case-that-never-happened-helped-create-the-international-criminal-justice-system/. Accessed 30 Apr 2026

Escobar Hernández C (2018) Sixth report on immunity of state officials from foreign criminal jurisdiction. United Nations Office of Legal Affairs. https://legal.un.org/ilc/documentation/english/a_cn4_722.pdf. Accessed 30 Apr 2026

European Court of Human Rights (2026) Key theme: article 6 (criminal limb) waiver of the guarantees of a free trial. European court of. Human Rights. https://ks.echr.coe.int/documents/d/echr-ks/waiver-of-the-guarantees-of-a-fair-trial. Accessed 30 Apr 2026

European Union Agency for Criminal Justice Cooperation (2024) Core international crimes evidence database (CICED). Publications Office of the European Union. https://op.europa.eu/en/publication-detail/-/publication/f4da21d5-247e-11ef-a195-01aa75ed71a1/language-en. Accessed 30 Apr 2026

European Union Agency for Criminal Justice Cooperation (2026a) Core international crimes evidence database. European Union Agency for Criminal Justice Cooperation. https://www.eurojust.europa.eu/core-international-crimes-evidence-database. Accessed 30 Apr 2026

[56] Mudra, Korynevych, Yurlov, and Ellis (2026).

European Union Agency for Criminal Justice Cooperation (2026b) International Centre for the Prosecution of the crime of aggression against Ukraine. European Union Agency for Criminal Justice Cooperation. https://www.eurojust.europa.eu/international-centre-for-the-prosecution-of-the-crime-of-aggression-against-ukraine. Accessed 30 Apr 2026

Getgen Kestenbaum J (2016) Closing impunity gaps for the crime of aggression. Chicago J of Intl Law 17(1):51–79. https://chicagounbound.uchicago.edu/cjil/vol17/iss1/2/

Global Campaign for Ratification and Implementation of the Kampala Amendments on the Crime of Aggression (2025) Status of ratification and implementation. Global Campaign for Ratification and Implementation of the Kampala Amendments on the Crime of Aggression. https://crimeofaggression.info/the-role-of-states/status-of-ratification-and-implementation/. Accessed 8 May 2026

Gureghian Hall M (2026) Confirmation of charges in absentia at the international criminal court and the right to be present. J of Intl Crim Justice. https://doi.org/10.1093/jicj/mqag002

Hathaway OA, Shapiro SJ (2017) The internationalists: how a radical plan to outlaw war remade the world. Simon and Schuster, New York

Higgins R, Kooijmans P, Buergenthal T (2002) Joint separate opinion of judges Higgins, Kooijmans and Buergenthal. International Court of Justice. https://www.icj-cij.org/sites/default/files/case-related/121/121-20020214-JUD-01-05-EN.pdf. Accessed 30 Apr 2026

International Committee of the Red Cross (1945) Agreement for the prosecution and punishment of the major war criminals of the European axis, and charter of the International Military Tribunal, London, 8 August 1945. International Committee of the Red Cross. https://ihl-databases.icrc.org/en/ihl-treaties/nuremberg-tribunal-charter-1945. Accessed 30 Apr 2026

International Committee of the Red Cross (2026) Sharon and Yaron case, appeal court, 26 June 2002 and 10 June 2003 and Cour of cassation, 14 February 2003 and 24 September 2003. International Committee of the Red Cross. https://ihl-databases.icrc.org/en/national-practice/sharon-yaron-case-appeal-court-26-june-2002-10-june-2003-and-cour-cassation-14. Accessed 30 Apr 2026

International Court of Justice (2002) Arrest warrant of 11 April 2000 (Democratic Republic of the Congo v. Belgium), judgment International Court of Justice Accessible via ICJ Reports https://www.icj-cij.org/sites/default/files/case-related/121/121-20020214-JUD-01-00-EN.pdf. Accessed 30 Apr 2026

International Court of Justice (2008) Certain questions of mutual assistance in criminal matters (Djibouti v. France), judgment International Court of Justice Accessible via ICJ Reports https://www.icj-cij.org/sites/default/files/case-related/136/136-20080604-JUD-01-00-EN.pdf. Accessed 30 Apr 2026

International Criminal Court (2010) Amendments to the Rome statute of the international criminal court. International Criminal Court. https://asp.icc-cpi.int/sites/asp/files/asp_docs/RC2010/AMENDMENTS/CN.651.2010-ENG-CoA.pdf. Accessed 30 Apr 2026

International Criminal Court (2021) Rome statute of the international criminal court. International Criminal Court. https://www.icc-cpi.int/sites/default/files/2024-05/Rome-Statute-eng.pdf. Accessed 30 Apr 2026

International Criminal Court (2023) Situation in Uganda in the case of the prosecutor v. Joseph Kony, public decision on the prosecution's request to hold a confirmation of charges hearing in the Kony case in the suspect's absence. International Criminal Court. https://www.icc-cpi.int/sites/default/files/CourtRecords/CR2023_01729.pdf. Accessed 30 Apr 2026

International Criminal Court (2024) Situation in Uganda in the case of the prosecutor v. Joseph Kony, public decision on the criteria for holding confirmation of charges proceedings in absentia. International Criminal Court. https://www.icc-cpi.int/sites/default/files/CourtRecords/0902ebd1809dcd08.pdf. Accessed 30 May 2026

International Criminal Court (2025a) Kony case: ICC pre-trial chamber III confirms the charges of war crimes and crimes against humanity; accused still at large. International Criminal Court. https://www.icc-cpi.int/news/kony-case-icc-pre-trial-chamber-iii-confirms-charges-war-crimes-and-crimes-against-humanity. Accessed 8 May 2026

International Criminal Court (2025b) Situation in the Republic of Uganda in the case of the prosecutor v. Joseph Kony, public document, judgment on appeal of Mr Joseph Kony against the decision of Pre-Trial Chamber III of 29 October 2024 entitled "decision on the criteria for holding confirmation of charges proceedings in absentia." International Criminal Court. https://www.icc-cpi.int/sites/default/files/CourtRecords/0902ebd180badaa5.pdf. Accessed 8 May 2026

International Criminal Tribunal for Rwanda (2007) Ferdinand Nahimana, Jean-Bosco Barayagwiza, Hassan Ngeze (appellants) v. the prosecutor (respondent), case no. ICTR-99-52-A, judgement. International Criminal Tribunal for Rwanda. https://ucr.irmct.org/LegalRef/CMSDocStore/Public/English/Judgement/NotIndexable/ICTR-99-52/MSC31299R0000555179.PDF. Accessed 8 May 2026

International Criminal Tribunal for Rwanda (2015) ICTR rules of procedure and evidence. International Criminal Tribunal for Rwanda. https://unictr.irmct.org/sites/unictr.org/files/legal-library/150513-rpe-en-fr.pdf. Accessed 8 May 2026

International Criminal Tribunal for the former Yugoslavia (1996a) Evidence hearing against Radovan Karadžić and Ratko Mladić. International Criminal Tribunal for the former Yugoslavia. https://www.icty.org/en/sid/10644. Accessed 8 May 2026

International Criminal Tribunal for the former Yugoslavia (1996b) Prosecutor v. Ivica Rajic a/k/a Viktor Andric, review of the indictment pursuant to rule 61 of the rules of procedure and evidence. International Criminal Tribunal for the former Yugoslavia. https://www.icty.org/x/cases/rajic/tdec/en/60913612.htm. Accessed 8 May 2026

International Criminal Tribunal for the former Yugoslavia (1996c) Prosecutor v. Radovan Karadžić, Ratko Mladić, review of the indictments pursuant to rule 61 of the rules of procedure and evidence. International Criminal Tribunal for the former Yugoslavia. https://www.worldcourts.com/icty/eng/decisions/1996.07.11_Prosecutor_v_Karadzic_1.pdf. Accessed 8 May 2026

International Criminal Tribunal for the former Yugoslavia (2015) Rules of procedure and evidence. International Criminal Tribunal for the former Yugoslavia. https://www.icty.org/x/file/Legal%20Library/Rules_procedure_evidence/IT032Rev50_en.pdf. Accessed 8 May 2026

International Criminal Tribunal for the former Yugoslavia (1997) Prosecutor v. Blaškić, judgment on the request of the Republic of Croatia for review of the decision of Trial Chamber II of 18 July 1997. International Criminal Tribunal for the former Yugoslavia. https://www.icty.org/x/cases/blaskic/acdec/en/71029JT3.html. Accessed 30 Apr 2026

International Law Commission (1950) Principles of international law recognized in the charter of the Nürnberg tribunal and in the judgment of the tribunal. International Law Commission. https://legal.un.org/ilc/texts/instruments/english/draft_articles/7_1_1950.pdf. Accessed 8 May 2026

International Law Reports (2006) Re Mofaz. International Law Reports 128:709–712

International Military Tribunal (1946) Nuremberg judgment against major war criminals. International Military Tribunal. Accessible via Legal Tools Database. https://www.legal-tools.org/doc/45f18e/. Accessed 30 Apr 2026

Karsu Ö (2025) Council of Europe and Ukraine establish a special Tribunal for the Crime of aggression against Ukraine. American Society of International Law. https://asil.org/ilib/council-europe-and-ukraine-establish-special-tribunal-crime-aggression-against-ukraine/. Accessed 8 May 2026

Koh HH, Buchwald TF (2015) The crime of aggression: the United States perspective. American J of Intl Law 109(2):257–295. https://doi.org/10.5305/amerjintelaw.109.2.0257

Kolodkin RA (2011) Third report on immunity of state officials from foreign criminal jurisdiction. United Nations Office of Legal Affairs. https://legal.un.org/ilc/documentation/english/a_cn4_646.pdf. Accessed 30 Apr 2026

Kreß C, Frank P, Barthe C (2021) Functional immunity of foreign state officials before national courts: a legal opinion by Germany's federal public prosecutor general. J of Intl Crim Just 19(3):697–716. https://doi.org/10.1093/jicj/mqab042

Liboreiro J (2026) 'Point of no return': 36 countries join special tribunal to prosecute Vladimir Putin. Euronews. https://www.euronews.com/my-europe/2026/05/15/point-of-no-return-36-countries-join-special-tribunal-to-prosecute-vladimir-putin. Accessed 8 May 2026

Massimino IV (2024) The ICC and in-absentia proceedings: finding a response to the difficulties of executing arrest warrants. ESIL Reflections 13(9) https://esil-sedi.eu/esil-reflection-the-icc-and-in-absentia-proceedings-finding-a-response-to-the-difficulties-of-executing-arrest-warrants-2/

McDougall C (2024) Expanding the ICC's jurisdiction over the crime of aggression. J of Intl Crim Just 22(3–4):543–564. https://doi.org/10.1093/jicj/mqae042

Mimran T, Halfon E (2026) ILC draft articles on immunity of state officials: Codification or progressive development? Articles of War. https://lieber.westpoint.edu/ilc-draft-articles-immunity-state-officials-codification-progressive-development/. Accessed 22 May 2026

Mudra I, Korynevych A, Ellis M (2026) From commitment to action: the next steps in holding Russia's leaders accountable for the crime of aggression against Ukraine. Ukrainian Bar Association. https://uba.ua/eng/news/apu.rf-triunfal. Accessed 30 Apr 2026

Mudra I, Korynevych A, Yurlov M, Ellis M (2026) Ukraine and the special Tribunal for the Crime of aggression: redefining international justice. Just. Security. https://www.justsecurity.org/140365/ukraine-russia-tribunal-crime-of-aggression/. Accessed 6 Jun 2026

Public Prosecutor to the Paris Court of Appeal (2008) Case of Donald Rumsfeld: triggering contesting the decision of the Paris district prosecutor (procureur de la république) to dismiss the case, 16 November 2007. European Center for Constitutional and Human Rights. https://www.ecchr.eu/fileadmin/Juristische_Dokumente/Prosecutors_Decision_Rumsfeld_France_02_08.pdf. Accessed 30 Apr 2026

Schabas WA (2018) The trial of the kaiser. Oxford University Press, Oxford

Strapatsas N (2010) Complementarity and aggression: a ticking time bomb? In: Stahn C, van den Herik L (eds) Future perspectives on international criminal justice. T.M.C. Asser Press, the Hague

United Nations General Assembly (2025) Immunity of state officials from foreign criminal jurisdiction. United Nations. Accessible via UNDCOS. https://documents.un.org/doc/undoc/ltd/g25/076/63/pdf/g2507663.pdf. Accessed 22 May 2026

United Nations Preparatory Commission for the International Criminal Court (2002) Historical review of developments relating to aggression. United Nations Digital Library. United Nations. Accessible via UNDOCS, In. https://digitallibrary.un.org/record/461833. Accessed 30 Apr 2026

United Nations Security Council (2007) Resolution 1757 (2007), adopted by the Security Council at the 5685th meeting, on 30 May 2007. United Nations security council. In: United Nations Digital Library. United Nations. Accessible via UNDOCS. https://digitallibrary.un.org/record/600560. Accessed 8 May 2026

Werle G (2007) Völkerstrafrecht. Mohr Siebeck, Tübingen

Williams PR, Beta S (2025) Toward justice for Ukraine: designing a tribunal for the crime of aggression. PILPG Frontline Scholarship. https://papers.ssrn.com/sol3/papers.cfm?abstract_id=5901802. Accessed 6 Jun 2026

Yale Law School Lillian Goldman Law Library (1929) Kellogg-Briand pact 1928. The Avalon project. Yale Law School Lillian Goldman Law Library. Accessible via the Avalon Project, In. https://avalon.law.yale.edu/20th_century/kbpact.asp. Accessed 8 May 2026

Yale Law School Lillian Goldman Law Library (2026) Judgement: Bormann. The Avalon project. Yale Law School Lillian Goldman Law Library. Accessible via the Avalon Project, In. https://avalon.law.yale.edu/imt/judborma.asp. Accessed 30 Apr 2026

Zahar A, Sluiter G (2008) International criminal law: a critical introduction. Oxford University Press, Oxford

Chapter 7
Regional Human Rights Courts in Europe, Latin America and Africa: Enforcement of Human Rights Principles

Modern international justice rests in significant part on the foundation of the International Court of Justice and the international, ad hoc, and hybrid atrocity crimes tribunals erected since 1993. But closely associated with progress in international criminal law is the enforcement of fundamental human rights principles against governments which have a duty to protect their populations from abuse and injury (often criminal in character and massive in scope) arising from violations of those principles. Whether in the realm of international or non-international armed conflicts or deadly internal assaults on civilian populations or other repressive measures by governments, international human rights law and its companion laws at the national level can intersect with obligations arising under international criminal law.

In this chapter we focus on three regional human rights courts that are dynamic laboratories of accountability of nations and delivery of remedies for individuals and populations facing violations of international human rights law reflected in the regional human rights treaties governing such courts. The European Court of Human Rights (the "European Court"), located in Strasbourg, France, was created by the Council of Europe (which is Europe's long-standing human rights organization beginning in 1959 and becoming a permanent institution in 1998).[1] Its mandate is to enforce the European Convention for the Protection of Human Rights and Fundamental Freedoms (the "European Convention"),[2] the most adjudicated and influential human rights treaty in the world but standing, of course, under the long shadow of the Universal Declaration of Human Rights.[3] The European Court has 46 member states from the European continent—all having ratified the European Convention. During its more than 60 years of operation adjudicating hundreds of cases, the European Court of Human Rights has paved a wide highway of protection for human rights

[1] Council of Europe (2026); European Court of Human Rights (2026).

[2] European Court of Human Rights (2021b).

[3] United Nations (2026).

D. J. Scheffer and M. S. Ellis, *The Story of Modern International Justice, 1993-2025*,
https://doi.org/10.1007/978-3-032-33243-1_7

that continues to elevate international justice given the European Court's influence on human rights protection not only in Europe, but globally.

The Inter-American Court of Human Rights (the "Inter-American Court"), which sits in San José, Costa Rica, was established in 1979 to enforce the American Convention on Human Rights (the "American Convention")[4] to deliver judgments on individual cases brought by the Inter-American Commission on Human Rights (located in Washington, D.C.) or a State Party to the American Convention and lodged before any of the 21 Latin American nations that have explicitly accepted its jurisdiction generally[5] or any State Party to the American Convention that accepts jurisdiction in a specific case. The Inter-American Court of Human Rights also delivers advisory opinions (32 through July 2025) on protection of human rights regarding any of the 24 countries that are Member States of the Organization of American States.[6]

The African Court of Human and Peoples' Rights (the "African Court")[7] focuses exclusively on state responsibility and commenced its operations in 2006 to enforce the African Charter on Human and Peoples' Rights (the "African Charter"), which 54 of the 55 Members States of the African Union have ratified or acceded to.[8] A total of 34 Member States of the African Union have ratified the protocol that embraces the jurisdiction of the African Court,[9] and only eight have accepted the competence of the African Court to consider applications filed by individuals and civil society rather than by Member States.[10]

In the following pages, we highlight examples of the jurisprudence of these three regional human rights courts that exemplify, in one particular instance, the jurisdictional limitations but in other cases and more significantly the expansive protection of human rights by the courts that governments falling under their jurisdiction must honor. Though these courts do not adjudicate criminal cases, their overall influence on the advancement of international justice aimed at protecting human rights has been significant and continues to grow.

---

[4] Organization of American States (2011; 2026a).

[5] Argentina, Barbados, Bolivia, Brazil, Chile, Colombia, Costa Rica, Dominican Republic, Ecuador, El Salvador, Guatemala, Haiti, Honduras, Mexico, Nicaragua, Panama, Paraguay, Peru, Suriname, Uruguay, Venezuela.

[6] Organization of American States (2026b).

[7] African Court of Human and Peoples' Rights (2026a).

[8] Organization of African Unity (1981).

[9] Organization of African Unity (1998).

[10] African Court of Human and Peoples' Rights (2026b).

7.1 The European Court of Human Rights

7.1.1 *Bankovic and Others v. Belgium and Others (2001)*

In the case of *Bankovic and Others v. Belgium and Others*,[11] the European Court of Human Rights confirmed an important guardrail, namely the limits of territorial jurisdiction in the enforcement of human rights principles under the auspices of a regional human rights treaty, in this case the European Convention. The facts of the case arose during the Kosovo War of 1999[12] when, on 23 April 1999, a NATO aircraft fired a missile that significantly damaged Radio Televizije Srbije (RTS) media facilities (three television channels and four radio stations) in Belgrade,[13] the capital of the Federal Republic of Yugoslavia (which later shed Montenegro and became the nation of Serbia). The Federal Republic of Yugoslavia was not a member of the Council of Europe and not a State Party to the European Convention. Other targets in the Federal Republic of Yugoslavia also were hit that night. The applicants in the case lost family members in the missile attack on the RTS building, as sixteen people were killed and others were injured in the attack.[14]

The applicants charged that NATO countries like Belgium, the United Kingdom, France, and other NATO members had violated the European Convention's rights protected by Article 2 (the right to life), Article 10 (freedom of expression), and Article 13 (the right to an effective remedy). However, the respondents (NATO countries) "dispute[d] the admissibility of the case. They mainly contend[ed] that the application [of the European Convention] is incompatible *ratione personae* with the provisions of the [European] Convention because the applicants [namely, the victim families] did not fall within the jurisdiction of the respondent States within the meaning of Article 1 of the [European] Convention."[15] Article 1 of the European Convention states, "The High Contracting Parties shall secure to everyone within their jurisdiction the rights and freedoms defined in Sect. 7.1 of the [European] Convention."[16] Section 7.1 of the European Convention covers in 17 articles a wide range of rights and freedoms.[17]

The European Court determined that the use in Article 1 of "within their jurisdiction" are words that "must be considered to reflect this ordinary and essentially territorial notion of jurisdiction, other bases of jurisdiction being exceptional and requiring special justification in the particular circumstances of each case."[18] In 1999, the Federal Republic of Yugoslavia was not part of the territory of any Member

---

[11] European Court of Human Rights (2001).

[12] Encyclopædia Britannica (2025).

[13] International Criminal Tribunal for the former Yugoslavia (2000), paras. 71–79.

[14] Dragović Savić (2024).

[15] European Court of Human Rights (2001), para. 31.

[16] European Court of Human Rights (2021b), art. 1.

[17] Id., arts. 2–18.

[18] European Court of Human Rights (2001), para. 61.

State of the European Convention. It was as if the NATO strikes on Belgrade and the RTS facility were as irrelevant to the European Convention as would have been NATO strikes on North Korea. The Court stated that ratifying States of the European Convention lacked any apprehension that Article 1 covered "extra-territorial responsibility in contexts similar to the present case."[19] No violations of the European Convention thus were found with respect to the NATO Member States involved in the air strikes against Belgrade and the FRY on 23 April 1999.

But the European Court paved the way for exceptional circumstances related to the "effective control" of a State Party to trigger jurisdiction over extra-territorial acts (meaning actions executed outside the territory of Council of Europe Member States):

> 70. ….[T]he Court found that, bearing in mind the object and purpose of the [European] Convention, the responsibility of a Contracting Party was capable of being engaged when as a consequence of military action (lawful or unlawful) it exercised effective control of an area outside its national territory. The obligation to secure, in such an area, the [European] Convention rights and freedoms was found to derive from the fact of such control whether it was exercised directly, through the respondent State's armed forces, or through a subordinate local administration. The Court concluded that the acts of which the applicant complained were capable of falling within Turkish jurisdiction within the meaning of Article 1 of the [European] Convention.
>
> …
>
> In its subsequent *Cyprus v. Turkey* judgment, the Court added that since Turkey had such "effective control", its responsibility could not be confined to the acts of its own agents therein but was engaged by the acts of the local administration which survived by virtue of Turkish support. Turkey's "jurisdiction" under Article 1 was therefore considered to extend to securing the full range of substantive [European] Convention rights in northern Cyprus.
>
> 71. In sum, the case-law of the Court demonstrates that its recognition of the exercise of extra-territorial jurisdiction by a Contracting State is exceptional: it has done so when the respondent State, through the effective control of the relevant territory and its inhabitants abroad as a consequence of military occupation or through the Court in favour of establishing jurisdiction only when the territory in question was one that, but for the specific circumstances, would normally be covered by the [European] Convention.[20]

The *Bankovic* judgment was refined, but not overruled, in later decisions of the European Court (for example, *Issa and Others v. Turkey*, 2004; *Mansur Pad and Others v. Turkey*, 2007; *Al-Skeini and Others v. United Kingdom*, 2011; *Al-Jedda v. United Kingdom*, 2011).[21] There clearly has been a trend in such decisions to emphasize the conduct of parties of the European Convention when exercising military power extra-territorially and the importance of complying with the human rights standards set forth in the treaty. In *Al-Skeini*, Judge Giovanni Bonello stated with clarity the evolving character of the European Court's jurisdiction in his concurring opinion:

---

[19] Id., para. 62.

[20] Id., paras. 70–71.

[21] Mallory (2021).

> In my view, the one honest test, in all circumstances (including extra-territoriality), is the following: did it depend on the agents of the State whether the alleged violation would be committed or would not be committed? Was it within the power of the State to punish the perpetrators and to compensate the victims? If the answer is yes, self-evidently the facts fall squarely within the jurisdiction of the State. All the rest seems to me clumsy, self-serving alibi hunting, unworthy of any State that has grandiosely undertaken to secure the "universal" observance of human rights whenever and wherever it is within its power to secure them, and, may I add, of courts whose only *raison d'etre* should be to ensure that those obligations are not avoided or evaded. The [European] Court has, in the present judgment, thankfully placed a sanitary cordon between itself and some of these approaches.[22]

As reflected in its *Mansur Pad and Others v. Turkey* judgment, the European Court has been willing to emphasize personal over territorial jurisdiction when the circumstances of military operations so demand in the protection of fundamental human rights.[23]

---

[22] European Court of Human Rights (2011a), para. 16.

[23] From European Court of Human Rights (2007), paras. 52–55:

52. The Court reiterates that according to Article 1 of the Convention Contracting States must answer for any infringement of the rights and freedoms protected by the Convention committed against individuals placed under their "jurisdiction". The exercise of jurisdiction is a necessary condition for a Contracting State to be held responsible for acts or omissions imputable to it which give rise to an allegation of the infringement of rights and freedoms set forth in the Convention (see *Ilaşcu and Others v. Moldova and Russia* [GC], no. 48787/99, § 311, ECHR 2004-VII).

53. Although the words "within their jurisdiction" in Article 1 of the Convention must be understood to mean that a State's jurisdictional competence is primarily territorial (see *Bankovic and Others v. Belgium and 16 other Contracting States* (dec.) [GC], application no. 52207/99, §§ 59-61, ECHR 2001-XII, and *Cyprus v. Turkey* [GC], no. 25781/94, § 76, ECHR 2001-IV), in exceptional circumstances the acts of Contracting States which are performed outside their territory or which produce effects there ("extraterritorial act") may amount to the exercise by them of jurisdiction within the meaning of Article 1 (see *Issa and Others*, cited above, § 68). Accordingly, a State may be held accountable for violations of the Convention rights and freedoms of persons who are in the territory of another State which does not necessarily fall within the legal space of the Contracting States, but who are found to be under the former State's authority and control through its agents operating—whether lawfully or unlawfully—in the latter State (see *Issa and Others*, cited above, § 71; *Öcalan v. Turkey* [GC], no. 46221/99, § 91, ECHR 2005-IV; *Sánchez Ramirez v. France*, application no. 28780/95, Commission decision of 24 June 1996, Decisions and Reports (DR) 86, p. 155; *Reinette v. France*, no. 14009/88, Commission decision of 2 October 1989, DR 63, p. 189; and *Freda v. Italy*, no. 8916/80, Commission decision of 7 October 1980, DR 21, p. 250).

54. However, in the instant case, it was not disputed by the parties that the victims of the alleged events came within the jurisdiction of Turkey. While the applicants attached great importance to the prior establishment of the exercise by Turkey of extraterritorial jurisdiction with a view to proving their allegations on the merits, the Court considers that it is not required to determine the exact location of the impugned events, given that the Government had already admitted that the fire discharged from the helicopters had caused the killing of the applicants' relatives, who had been suspected of being terrorists (see, *a contrario*, *Issa and Others*, cited above).

55. Accordingly, the Court finds that the victims of the impugned events were within the jurisdiction of Turkey at the material time.

7.1.2 *Finogenov and Others v. Russia (2011)*[24]

Finogenov and Others v. Russia (2011) concerned acts of sheer terrorism on 23–25 October 2002 in the Dubrovka Theater of Moscow, Russia, resulting in the tragic deaths of civilian hostages in the later stages of a Russian rescue mission even though the European Court of Human Rights found that the initial tactical actions by the authorities to save the hostages were lawful in character. The judgment enforced the right to life, protected by Article 2 of the European Convention,[25] in the context of shoddy government planning and operations to save the hostages.

The rescue operation commenced three days into the terrorist hostage-taking in the Dubrovka Theater. "[T]he Russian security forces pumped an unknown narcotic gas into the main auditorium through the building's ventilations system…A few minutes later, when the terrorists controlling the explosive devices and the suicide bombers in the auditorium lost consciousness under the influence of the gas, the special squad stormed the building. Most of the suicide bombers were shot while unconscious; others tried to resist but were killed in the ensuing gunfire."[26]

But during the operation.

> a large number of hostages were affected by the gas; according to information gathered by the investigative authorities by the end of 2002, 129 hostages died; 102 died on the spot (114 according to the report of 31 December 2002), including three persons who were shot; 21 died in the course of evacuation and transportation to hospital; and six persons died in the emergency rooms of various hospitals.[27]

> Witness Scht., a doctor in an ambulance…also testified that the doctors had been unaware of the content of the gas, so they had been unable to apply any specific methods of treatment to the victims.[28]

The European Court concluded "that the use of gas during the storming [of the theater] was not in the circumstances a disproportionate measure, and, as such, did not breach Article 2 of the [European] Convention."[29]

> …[T]he gas used by the Russian security forces, while dangerous, was not supposed to kill, in contrast, for example, to bombs or air missiles…Although the gas in the present case was used against a group consisting of hostages and hostage-takers, and although the gas was dangerous and even potentially lethal, it was not used 'indiscriminately' as it left the

---

[24] European Court of Human Rights (2011c).

[25] From European Court of Human Rights (2021b), art. 2:

1. Everyone's right to life shall be protected by law. No one shall be deprived of his life intentionally save in the execution of a sentence of a court following his conviction of a crime for which this penalty is provided by law. 2. Deprivation of life shall not be regarded as inflicted in contravention of this Article when it results from the use of force which is no more than absolutely necessary: (a) in defence of any person from unlawful violence; (b) in order to effect a lawful arrest or to prevent the escape of a person lawfully detained; (c) in action lawfully taken for the purpose of quelling a riot or insurrection.

[26] European Court of Human Rights (2011b), para. 22.

[27] Id., para. 24.

[28] Id., para. 8.

[29] Id., para. 236.

> hostages a high chance of survival, which depended on the efficiency of the authorities' rescue effort. The hostages in the present case were not in the same desperate situation as all the passengers of a hijacked airplane.[30]

The European Court examined.

> whether the ensuing rescue operation was planned and implemented in compliance with the authorities' positive obligations under Article 2 of the European Convention, namely whether the authorities took all necessary precautions to minimize the effects of the gas on the hostages, to evacuate them quickly and to provide them with necessary medical assistance.[31]

The European Court concluded "that the State breached its positive obligations under Article 2 of the [European] Convention."[32] The Russian Government's original plan was "in itself flawed in many respects."[33] The plan "did not make provision for medical assistance in those [evacuating] buses."[34] "Russia also breache[d] its Article 2 obligations as a result of its shoddy investigation."[35]

The judgment in *Finogenov* demonstrated a pragmatic interpretation of the right to life under Article 2 of the European Convention that embraced the complexity and risks of dealing with terrorist hostage-taking, but also the planning and implementation of an effective operation that must not recklessly put rescued hostages' lives at risk.

7.1.3 Scoppola v. Italy (No. 3) (2012)[36]

In the case of *Scoppola v. Italy (No. 3)*, the right to vote—the central pillar of democratic societies that comprise the Council of Europe—was at issue for those individuals convicted of crimes. The Italian plaintiff, Franco Scoppola, "killed his wife and injured one of his sons" in a domestic dispute over "his children having allegedly broken his mobile phone."[37] The plaintiff was ultimately sentenced to "thirty years' imprisonment and a lifetime ban from public office" as well as a "permanent forfeiture of his right to vote," though this forfeiture "was not mentioned in the judgments against him."[38]

The question before the European Court, sitting in its Grand Chamber with all of the judges participating in the case, was whether Italy violated Article 3 of the

[30] Id., para. 232.

[31] Id., para. 237.

[32] Id., para. 266.

[33] Id., para. 252.

[34] Id., para. 250.

[35] Id., para. 282.

[36] European Court of Human Rights (2012).

[37] Id., paras. 12, 16.

[38] Id., paras. 14, 21–22.

European Convention by depriving Scoppola of his right to vote. Article 3, which was approved in Protocol 1 to the European Convention on 1 January 1975, states, "The High Contracting Parties undertake to hold free elections at reasonable intervals by secret ballot, under conditions which will ensure the free expression of the opinion of the people in the choice of the legislature."[39]

The Grand Chamber analyzed a number of sources of international law related to the right to vote from around the world and examined how each State Party of the European Convention handles voting rights for convicted criminals[40] and looked at cases dealing with the issue in Canada, Australia, and South Africa.[41] The Grand Chamber examined precedents to determine whether the disenfranchisement of Scoppola was legally permissible. The judges followed a three part test laid out in *Mathieu-Mohin and Clerfayt v. Belgium* (1987),[42] which states that "[states] have a wide margin of appreciation in this sphere, but it is for the Court to determine in the last resort whether the requirements of Protocol No. 1 (PI) have been complied with; it has to satisfy itself that the conditions do not curtail the rights in question to such an extent as to impair their very essence and deprive them of their effectiveness; that they are imposed in pursuit of a legitimate aim; and that the means employed are not disproportionate."[43]

The Grand Chamber found that Scoppola's right to vote had been taken from him[44] and examined whether the disenfranchisement was pursuant to a "legitimate aim."[45] After examining such precedents as *Hirst v. The United Kingdom (No. 2)* (2005),[46] *Frodl v. Austria* (2010),[47] and *MDU v. Italy* (2003),[48] the Grand Chamber found that disenfranchising a convict must be done with the intent of "preventing crime and enhancing civic responsibility and respect for the rule of law...[and] the proper functioning and preservation of the democratic regime."[49] The judges continued:

> 102. ....[E]ach State is free to adopt legislation in the matter in accordance with "historical development, cultural diversity and political thought within Europe, which it is for each Contracting State to mold into their own democratic vision"....In particular, with a view to securing the rights guaranteed by Article 3 of Protocol No. 1...., the Contracting States may decide either to leave it to the courts to determine the proportionality of a measure restricting convicted prisoners' voting rights, or to incorporate provisions into their laws defining the circumstances in which such a measure should be applied. In this latter case, it will be for the legislature itself to balance the competing interests in order to avoid any general, automatic and indiscriminate restriction. It will then be the role of the Court to examine whether, in

[39] Council of Europe (1975).

[40] European Court of Human Rights (2012), paras. 45–48.

[41] Id., 49–60.

[42] European Court of Human Rights (1987).

[43] Id., para. 52.

[44] European Court of Human Rights (2012), para. 89.

[45] Id., paras. 90–92.

[46] European Court of Human Rights (2005).

[47] European Court of Human Rights (2010).

[48] European Court of Human Rights (2003).

[49] European Court of Human Rights (2012), paras. 91–92.

> a given case, this result was achieved and whether the wording of the law, or the judicial decision, was in compliance with Article 3 of Protocol No. 1.[50]

Based on such criteria, the Grand Chamber determined that the disenfranchisement of the plaintiff had been undertaken pursuant to "legitimate aims." Because the disenfranchisement was not "general, automatic and [of an] indiscriminate character" or permanent, the punishment of Scoppola did not violate the proportionality test applied by the judges.[51] They further concluded, "The margin of appreciation afforded to the respondent Government [Italy] in this sphere has therefore not been overstepped."[52]

The *Scoppola* judgment demonstrated the balancing act that the European Court is prepared to perform in weighing a convicted individual's right to vote with the Contracting State's own historical, cultural, and political interests that are factored into the timing of the granting of that right. Rather than decide entirely against the convicted individual's right to vote or entirely in favor of it regardless of the country's preference to deny it (at least for some period of time), the European Court exercised a degree of deference to the country's government, under a margin of appreciation analysis, while recognizing that such deference can be qualified and of limited character.

7.1.4 *Ukraine and Netherlands v. Russia (2025)*[53]

The more than decade-long armed conflict between Ukraine and Russia, commencing in 2014 and continuing as of this writing, came under the intensive scrutiny of the Grand Chamber of the European Court in *Ukraine and Netherlands v. Russia (2025)* in the context of four inter-state applications, three dealing with the actions of Russian-backed separatists in eastern Ukraine starting in spring 2014, including the downing of Malaysian Airlines Flight 17 (MH17) in that year, and the fourth dealing with Russia's full-scale invasion of Ukraine on February 24, 2022, and its actions thereafter. All other Council of Europe Member States (26 in number) and Canada (as a non-member) intervened to express their views in an unprecedented display of affinity to the rule of law. An important caveat, however, is that Russia withdrew from the Council of Europe and the European Convention effective September 2022,[54] so the inter-state applications covered actions that the European Court could examine only up to that date.

Given the situation in Ukraine, the European Court examined both the human rights law embedded in the European Convention and international humanitarian law, an exercise which marks this judgment as particularly important for the advancement

---

[50] Id., para. 102.

[51] Id., paras. 108–109.

[52] Id., para. 110.

[53] European Court of Human Rights (2025b).

[54] See Council of Europe (2022).

of international justice in recent years. The inter-twined character of the law of war, international humanitarian law, and international human rights law increasingly characterizes modern armed conflicts because of the heightened focus on the fate of civilian populations, which are targeted and victimized in such conflicts on a regular basis. Civilians do not sacrifice their human rights during war unless under extreme circumstances tied to a lawful use of armed force that requires a specific diminution of such rights. In recent years, the focus on the fate of civilians has elevated such treaties as the European Convention in a positive way to strengthen legal protections for civilian populations during warfare.

The European Court's decisions in this lengthy case examining the unlawfulness of Russian actions against and in Ukraine since 2014 have been delivered through the prism of noncompliance with the articles of human rights protection set forth in the European Convention:

1. The European Court found that launching and then directing sustained, organized attacks—such as Russia did against Ukrainian targets—is sufficient to trigger the European Convention's protections of civilians' human rights. This ruling corrected an earlier judgment of the European Court in *Georgia v. Russia (II)* (2021)[55] holding that such human rights protections were not available during an active phase of hostilities ("chaos") which precluded effective control that would activate the European Convention. What happened in Ukraine was hardly chaotic, but part of highly planned military attacks by Russia during which Russia assumed authority and control of the civilian population.[56] Thus the Ukrainian victims fell squarely within the European Convention's protection, including Article 1's right to life, and the European Court had the jurisdiction to examine "the full spectrum of state-conducted or directed violence against civilians, closing the loophole that *Georgia v. Russia II* seemed to have created."[57]
2. The Court rejected any safe harbor for warfare exclusively guided by the law of war without any role for international human rights law. The Grand Chamber rejected a *lex specialis* rationale for knocking out human rights law during times of war. "[T]he Convention cannot be interpreted and applied in a vacuum; it should so far as possible be interpreted in harmony with other rules of international law...including international humanitarian law."[58] Indeed, "there is no circumstance in which international humanitarian law will apply to the complete exclusion of the Convention's human rights guarantees."[59] Thus in any evaluation of warfare, the European Court will examine human rights issues falling within the jurisdiction of the European Convention.
3. Nonetheless, Article 15 of the European Convention[60] permits formal derogation from the treaty's obligations during warfare. Russia never filed such a derogation

[55] European Court of Human Rights (2021a).

[56] European Court of Human Rights (2025a), para. 361.

[57] Khachatryan (2025).

[58] European Court of Human Rights (2025a), para. 427.

[59] Id., para. 428.

[60] From European Court of Human Rights (2021b), art. 15:

and thus could not avail itself of essentially a waiver from the treaty's human rights obligations, even during the Ukraine war. The fact that the right of derogation remains enforceable under the European Convention can exclude the treaty's human rights protection during warfare. But in this case the European Court was able to apply international humanitarian law to the enforcement of the right to life under Article 2 of the European Convention, marking an important step towards the consolidation of both fields of law during armed hostilities even when States refuse to do so through non-participation or their pleadings.

4. The Grand Chamber ruled that Russia guided the plans and operations of the separatists in Ukraine and thus the European Convention's rights and obligations applied to the Russian-inspired and orchestrated actions in Ukraine since 2014 and up to September 2022. The separatist operations were "completely dependent on military, political and economic support" from Russia.[61] The European Court applied Article 4 of the International Law Commission's Articles on State Responsibility to conclude that throughout the temporal period under scrutiny by the Court, the separatists would be regarded as de facto organs of Russia.[62] This decision thus blew a large hole through sometimes artificial legal distinctions between non-state groups and their sponsoring nation-states. And whether the victim experienced injury at the hands of separatists or Russian soldiers, the protections of the European Convention would be enforced against the party in actual control, namely Russia. As non-state groups are a major factor in the commission of atrocity crimes in modern armed conflicts, this is no small development.
5. The Grand Chamber was careful not to address use of force issues per se, namely to determine if there had been unlawful use of military force under the U.N. Charter. The reality, recognized by the judges, is that not all uses of military force entail violations of human rights law and not all breaches of the European Convention hang on whether the use of force has been lawful.[63]
6. One astute commentator, international lawyer Davit Khachatryan, wrote shortly after the judgment in *Ukraine and Netherlands v. Russia* was delivered that: "While Strasbourg speaks the language of state responsibility for human-rights breaches, its findings are also likely to serve as important reference points for the ICC's criminal investigations into alleged war crimes in Ukraine (situation in Ukraine) and the ICJ's proceedings (for example, the Genocide Convention case filed by Ukraine). The Grand Chamber's confirmation that Russia exercised

---

Derogation in time of emergency.

1. In time of war or other public emergency threatening the life of the nation any High Contracting Party may take measures derogating from its obligations under this Convention to the extent strictly required by the exigencies of the situation, provided that such measures are not inconsistent with its other obligations under international law.

2. No derogation from Article 2, except in respect of deaths resulting from lawful acts of war, or from Articles 3, 4 (paragraph 1) and 7 shall be made under this provision.

[61] European Court of Human Rights (2025a), paras. 363–364.

[62] Khachatryan (2025).

[63] European Court of Human Rights (2025a), para. 431.

effective control over Donbas from May 2014 feeds directly into any future reparations calculus. Anyone seeking redress for injuries or losses suffered during this period will be able to point to the [European Court of Human Rights'] judgment as authoritative evidence that Russia bore legal responsibility." Khachatryan continued,

> In the end, this judgment might well become the [European Court's] own 'Nicaragua moment,' a turning point where the Court shows it is ready to grapple with patterns of violence and proxy warfare at Europe's doorstep and to shape the law for years to come. Much like the ICJ's Nicaragua decision left a deep and lasting mark on international law by engaging with the realities of contemporary conflict, the Grand Chamber's ruling has the potential to redefine how European human rights law responds to the shifting landscape of armed conflict, occupation, and state responsibility. Many aspects of the judgment are hence sure to receive separate analysis and application by commentators, adjudicators, and policymakers alike.[64]

7.2 Inter-American Court of Human Rights

7.2.1 Barrio Altos v. Peru (2001)[65]

The facts in *Barrio Altos v. Peru (2001)* before the Inter-American Court of Human Rights were gruesome: On the night of 3 November 1991 six heavily-armed assailants killed 15 people (and injured four others) in an attack on a "pollada" (a party to collect funds in order to repair a building) in Barrios Altos, Lima, Peru. The victims were told to lie on the floor and once on the floor, the assailants fired at them indiscriminately for about two minutes. The assailants were found to be members of a special unit of the Peruvian Army known as the Colina Group, which had anti-terrorist duties. Their attack was a reprisal against alleged members of the rebel group know as Sendero Luminoso. Although the Colina Group assailants were charged four years later for the Barrios Altos massacre, the Peruvian Congress adopted an amnesty law that covered all members of the security forces and civilians who had been accused, investigated, prosecuted or convicted, or serving prison sentences, for human rights violations committed between 1980 and 1995. Although that law was struck down as a violation of constitutional guarantees and international law, including that imposed by the American Convention on Human Rights, the Peruvian Congress adopted a second amnesty law specifically covering the Barrios Altos massacre and prohibiting any judicial override.

The Inter-American Commission for Human Rights submitted the case to the Inter-American Court on 10 May 2000, claiming that Peru had violated, under the American Convention, the right to life[66] of the 15 people killed in the Barrios Altos

---

[64] Khachatryan (2025).

[65] Brugnatelli (2009).

[66] Organization of American States (2011), art. 4.

massacre and the right to humane treatment[67] of the four injured persons. As one scholarly tract describes, the Commission "requested the [Inter-American] Court to determine whether Peru, by promulgating and applying the two above-mentioned laws, and as a result of the violation of the above-mentioned rights, had violated its international obligations to respect the rights and freedoms recognized in the convention and to ensure all persons subject to its jurisdiction the free and full exercise of those rights and freedoms [Article 1 of the American Convention]. It also asked the [Inter-American] Court to establish whether Peru had breached its international obligation to adopt—in accordance with its constitutional process and the provisions of the convention—such legislative or other measures as may have been necessary to give effect to those rights or freedoms whose exercise was not already ensured by legislative or other provisions [Article 2 of the American Convention]."[68]

The legitimacy of national amnesty laws, in this case focusing on Peru's experience, came under sharp scrutiny by the Inter-American Court, with a result that cautions strongly against amnesty laws covering the most serious violations of human rights. The Inter-American Court threw out the two Peruvian amnesty laws as being inadmissible and incompatible with the Inter-American Convention.[69] "…[T]he [Inter-American] Court affirmed that Art. 1(1) [the American Convention] implies a positive procedural obligation of the State to investigate the events that produced a violation of any substantial rights enshrined in the [American Convention] and to capture, prosecute, and convict those responsible of a violation….The [Inter-American] Court also took into account Art. 2 [of the American Convention], which sets forth the obligation of the State to adapt its internal legislation in order to give effect to the rights and freedoms protected by the Convention and which implies that there is the negative obligation not to adopt and apply any law incompatible with the [American Convention]….Therefore, as Amnesty Laws 26,479 and 26,492 prevented Peru from fulfilling its obligation under Art. 1(1) [of the American Convention], the [Inter-American] Court found that their adoption and application caused a violation of Arts 1(1) and 2 in connection with Arts 4 and 5 [of the American Convention] (*Barrios Altos Case Merits* para. 42)."[70]

The Inter-American Court pronounced that it "considers that all amnesty provisions, provisions on prescription and the establishment of measures designed to eliminate responsibility are inadmissible, because they are intended to prevent the investigation and punishment of those responsible for serious human rights violations such as torture, extrajudicial, summary or arbitrary execution and forced disappearance, all of them prohibited because they violate non-derogable rights recognized by international human rights law."[71]

The Inter-American Court denied the legality of the amnesty laws, ruling that "[s]elf amnesty laws lead to the defenselessness of victims and perpetuate impunity;

---

[67] Id., art. 5.

[68] Brugnatelli (2009), para. 9.

[69] Inter-American Court of Human Rights (2001a), paras. 41–44.

[70] Brugnatelli (2009), para. 13.

[71] Inter-American Court of Human Rights (2001a), para. 41.

therefore, they are manifestly incompatible with the aims and spirit of the [American] Convention. This type of law precludes the identification of the individuals who are responsible for human rights violations, because it obstructs the investigation and access to justice and prevents the victims and their next of kin from knowing the truth and receiving the corresponding reparation."[72] The Inter-American Court declared the amnesty laws as incompatible with the American Convention and thus illegal. The Court also declared "that Peru had the duty to determine the identity of those responsible for the human rights violations referred to in the judgment, to publish the results of the investigation and to punish those responsible (*Barrios Altos Case Merits* para. 44)."[73] The Court later ruled, on 3 September 2001, that its judgment about the amnesty laws would apply to any other human rights cases in Peru.[74]

7.2.2 *Mayagna (Sumo) Awas Tin Gni Community v. Nicaragua (2001)*[75]

In one of its major holdings on the rights of indigenous peoples, the Inter-American Court ruled in *Mayagna (Sumo) Awas Tingni Community v. Nicaragua* (2001) that the property rights of the Awas Tingni Community in Nicaragua were protected by Article 21 of the American Convention.[76] The Awas Tingini Community filed an "amparo remedy" on two occasions to stave off commercial logging on their indigenous property, for which they held no real property title deed. An amparo is "a means of protection against any violation of a person's (natural or legal) constitutional rights, regardless of whether the entity causing such violation is a public authority or a private party. In essence, the amparo's purpose is the direct protection of human rights."[77]

Article 21 of the American Convention reads: "1. Everyone has the right to the use and enjoyment of his property. The law may subordinate such use and enjoyment to the interest of society. 2. No one shall be deprived of his property except upon payment of just compensation, for reasons of public utility or social interest, and in the cases and according to the forms established by law. 3. Usury and any other form of exploitation of man by man shall b[e] prohibited by law."

The Inter-American Court reviewed the drafting history of the American Convention and its expansive view of "property."[78] The treaty was designed to protect "the right to property in a sense which includes, among others, the rights of members of the indigenous communities within the framework of communal property, which

[72] Id., para. 44.

[73] Brugnatelli (2009), para. 17.

[74] Id., paras. 14–18.

[75] Grossman and Gomez Echeverri (2026).

[76] Inter-American Court of Human Rights (2001b), para. 151.

[77] Hoyos and Catalina Mancilla (2019).

[78] Inter-American Court of Human Rights (2001b), para. 146.

is also recognized by the Constitution of Nicaragua."[79] The Inter-American Court determined that "the members of the Awas Tingni Community have a communal property right to the lands they currently inhabit, without detriment to the rights of other indigenous communities."[80]

The Court ordered that Nicaragua must "a) carry out the delimitation, demarcation, and titling of the territory belonging to the Community; and b) abstain from carrying out, until that delimitation, demarcation, and titling have been done, actions that might lead the agents of the State itself, or third parties acting with its acquiescence or its tolerance, to affect the existence, value, use or enjoyment of the property located in the geographical area where the members of the Community live and carry out their activities."[81]

7.2.3 *The Miguel Castro Castro Prison v. Peru (2006)*[82]

In the year 1992, a maximum security prison east of Lima, Peru, was the scene of horrific violence against its inmates during what was supposed to be a transfer of the prisoners to another location. The inmates were accused or convicted for crimes of terrorism or treason and were allegedly members of the Sendro Luminoso. Some of them had been acquitted.[83] But the Inter-American Court found in *The Miguel Castro Castro Prison v. Peru* (2006) that "the real objective of the 'operative' was not the mentioned transfer of the inmates, but instead it was a premeditated attack, an operative designed to attack the life and integrity of the prisoners located in pavilions 1A and 4B of the Miguel Castro Castro Prison. The acts of violence were directed against said pavilions, occupied at the time of the events by inmates accused or sentenced for terrorism crimes or treason."[84] What followed was a violent and often murderous confrontation with the rioting inmates. A total of 42 inmates, including 13 from the terrorist Shining Path leadership, were killed. "The majority of the inmates that were killed presented between three and twelve bullet wounds to the head and thorax."[85] Further, "[m]any of the persons injured were maintained without medical attention for several days and the injured that were transferred to the hospital did not receive the medical attention required. These omissions caused complications in the health of some of the inmates and in others it caused their death."[86]

The Inter-American Court found violations of the right to life (Article 4) and humane treatment (Article 5) provisions of the American Convention. The victims

[79] Id., para. 148.

[80] Id., para. 153.

[81] Id.

[82] Inter-American Court of Human Rights (2006).

[83] Id., para. 197(13).

[84] Id., para. 197(16).

[85] Id., para. 197(39).

[86] Id., para. 197(47).

suffered "serious psychological and emotional suffering, constituted a psychological torture carried out in offense of all of all members of the group, with violation of Articles 5(1) and 5(2) of the American Convention, and 1, 6, and 8 of the Inter-American Convention to Prevent and Punish Torture."[87]

Finally, the Court addressed the delay in rendering justice, finding violations of Articles 8 (right to a fair trial) and 25 (right to judicial protection) of the American Convention.[88] The Court wrote in 2006, "[T]he first criminal proceeding before the ordinary justice to investigate the criminal responsibility for the violations committed was initiated approximately 13 years after they occurred. In those criminal proceedings only the deaths of the inmates that resulted from the events of the Criminal Center Castro Castro from May 6 to 10, 1992 are being investigated, and in it 13 people appear in their quality of defendants…Similarly, almost three months ago a preliminary proceeding was initiated against Aberto Fujimori Fujimori, with the same purpose of investigating said deaths."[89]

Further,

> [o]n April 20, 1996, four inmates that are also victims in this case were convicted to life in prison due to the events that took place in the Miguel Castro Castro Prison from May 6 to 9, 1992. It was not until 2004 the National Terrorism Chamber of the Supreme Court of Justice of Peru acquitted these inmates of said conviction.[90]

7.2.4 Miskito Divers v. Honduras (2021)[91]

The Inter-American Court has adjudicated cases involving business and human rights which cover critical life and death issues for workers. One landmark ruling concerned indigenous men and boys in Honduras who dive for lobsters for their livelihoods. In its 2021 judgment in *Miskito Divers v. Honduras*, the "[Inter-American] Court recalls that the instant case concerns 42 victims of the Miskito indigenous community living in the department of Gracias a Dios and their next of kin, who are divided int four groups:(a) 34 divers who suffered accidents due to deep dives which caused them decompression sickness or other diving-related ailments, 12 of whom died as a result of such accidents; (b) seven Miskito divers who died as a result of the fire aboard the "Lancaster" boat in which they were traveling, due to the explosion of a butane tank; (c) the child Licar Mendez Gutierrez, who was abandoned in a cayuco by the boat owner and whose whereabouts are unknown, and (d) their next of kin."[92] The Inter-American Court further noted that "Miskito boys begin this work when they are 14 years old, that it takes place outside of current labor legislation and that it causes

[87] Id., para. 293.

[88] Id., para. 408.

[89] Id., para. 386.

[90] Id., para. 398.

[91] Inter-American Court of Human Rights (2021).

[92] Inter-American Court of Human Rights (2021), para. 40; See Limas (2023).

occupational accidents, intoxications and disabilities in people of working age. Of the 9,000 divers involved in lobster fishing—98 percent of whom are Miskitos—97 percent have suffered some type of decompression-related syndrome and 4,200 are totally or partially disabled."[93]

The case centered on how companies engaged in the lobster diving business were violating the human rights of the divers and their next of kin and how the Government of Honduras was failing to exercise its duties under the American Convention on Human Rights. "The [Inter-American] Court finds that in line with the 'Guiding Principles on Business and Human Rights: Implementing the United Nations "Protect, Respect and Remedy" Framework' as well as in the context of the obligation to guarantee rights and the duty to adopt provisions of domestic law derived from Articles 1(1) and 2 of the American Convention, the court emphasizes that States have a duty to prevent human rights violations by private companies, and therefore must adopt legislative and other measures to prevent such violations, and to investigate, punish and provide reparation when they occur."[94]

This includes.

> adopt[ing] measures to ensure that business enterprises have: a) appropriate policies for the protection of human rights; b) due diligence processes for the identification, prevention and correction of human rights violations, as well as to ensure decent and dignified work; and c) processes that allow businesses to remedy human rights violations that result from their activities, especially when these affect people living in poverty or belonging to vulnerable groups.[95]

In this case, the Inter-American Court determined that Honduras incurred responsibility under Articles 4(1) (right to have life respected and no one should be arbitrarily deprived of his life), 5(1) (right to have physical, mental and moral integrity respected), and 19 (rights of the child) of the American Convention because the government did not enforce the regulations that it had in place with respect to diving (as well as general labor regulations).[96]

Article 26 of the American Convention states, "The States Parties undertake to adopt measures, both internally and through international cooperation, especially those of an economic and technical nature, with a view to achieving progressively, by legislation or other appropriate means, the full realization of the rights implicit in the economic, social, educational scientific, and cultural standards set forth in the Charter of the Organization of American States as amended by the Protocol of Buenos Aires."

The Inter-American Court found that Honduras violated its Article 26 duties because it did not "fulfill its obligation to guarantee the right to just, equitable and satisfactory working conditions that ensure the safety, health and hygiene of the

---

93 Inter-American Court of Human Rights (2021), para. 31.

94 Id., para. 48.

95 Id., para. 49.

96 Id., paras. 54–60.

worker, since it failed to prevent occupational accidents and guarantee the acceptability and quality of the work of the victims in this case."[97] Honduras also violated Article 26 because it "failed to comply with its obligation to provide acceptable, available and quality medical care to the victims of diving accidents, as well as its obligation to ensure access to the social security system for the survivors of such accidents particularly those who suffered a disability, in violation of the right to health and social security contained in Article 26 of the [American] Convention."[98]

The Government of Honduras and the victims arrived at a settlement of reparations in the case that included educational scholarships for the victims, their children and/or their grandchildren, housing for the divers and their families, and production and broadcasting of a television documentary.

7.2.5 *Advisory Opinion 32/25 on the Climate Emergency and Human Rights (2025)*[99]

In a truly historic testament of law bending towards the existential danger of climate change, the Inter-American Court delivered in its *Advisory Opinion AO-32/25 of May 29, 2025 on the Climate Emergency and Human Rights* a comprehensive and powerful assessment of climate change, its impact on humankind and future risks, and the legal consequences under the American Convention on Human Rights and other international treaties.[100] Its target audience in the Americas was all 34 Member States of the Organization of American States, including the United States and Canada. The advisory opinion, requested by Chile and Colombia in 2023, describes the obligations of States Parties under the American Convention and several other treaties to prevent and take measures against climate change on many levels of governance.

If one could describe a single Inter-American Court advisory opinion as a blockbuster for the ages, the advisory opinion on climate change is that document. It preceded by only two months the advisory opinion of the International Court of Justice in July 2025[101] that is discussed in Chap. 1 and followed one year after an advisory opinion on climate change by the International Tribunal on the Law of the Sea (May 21, 2024).[102] The Inter-American Court advisory opinion is by far the most impressive of these three advisory opinions at the international level, clocking in at 219 pages.[103]

---

[97] Id., para. 78.

[98] Id., para. 97.

[99] Inter-American Court of Human Rights (2025).

[100] Celorio (2025); Center for Justice and International Law (2025); Khatri U (2025); Rodríguez Orúe (2025).

[101] International Court of Justice (2025).

[102] International Tribunal for the Law of the Sea (2024); Dimitrakos (2025).

[103] Inter-American Court of Human Rights (2025).

We highlight here some of the major legal interpretations made by the Inter-American Court in its advisory opinion on climate change and human rights and liberally draw upon an excellent summary authored by Professor Rosa Celorio for the *Insights* publication of the American Society of International Law[104]:

1. There is a "climate emergency" based upon six sets of facts that confirm the gravity of the threat, the role of both State and non-state actors, the impact on humans' dignified existence and thus of their human rights in general, and the global reach of the emergency.[105]
2. States must exercise enhanced due diligence in response to the climate emergency because of their obligations arising under Article 1(1) of the American Convention. In Professor Celorio's words:

> Specifically, states are required to refrain from any actions that may limit, hinder, or impede prompt action to address climate change or condone any setbacks on climate policy, in the absence justifications.[106] States are also obligated to act affirmatively to prevent and respond to climate change and its effects. This includes a general duty to prevent severe or irreparable damage to the environment, and to prevent, supervise, and regulate activities from private actors which may violate protected rights.[107]
>
> As part of this enhanced obligation, states must formulate, implement, and monitor climate change policies and design them incorporating a human rights perspective and taking into consideration their impact on persons and groups in a situation of vulnerability. States must also ensure that their domestic legal frameworks adequately address the climate emergency.[108] States should be mindful of the climate-related content of a range of critical rights contained in the American Convention, from life, personal integrity, health, and privacy to family life, property and housing, freedom of movement, culture, and education.[109]

3. In establishing a new "right to a healthy climate," the Inter-American Court proffered a range of legal duties for states and business to perform. States are expected

[104] Celorio (2025); see also Dugal (2025); Khatri (2025); Institute for Governance and Sustainable Development (2026).

[105] From Celorio (2025):

Third, the Court confirmed that both state and non-state actors contribute to the generation of greenhouse gas emissions (see Inter-Am. Ct. H.R., Advisory Opinion 32/25 on the Climate Emergency and Human Rights, paras. 44–63). Fourth, it recognized specific regions in the Americas that are particularly vulnerable to climate change, including the Amazon and the Caribbean (Id., paras. 106–119). Fifth, the Court emphasized the human impact of climate change on dignified existence, health, food, water security, and the economic situation of individuals; all with human rights consequences (Id., paras. 89–104). Finally, it acknowledged the global scope of the problem of climate change and its connection to the triple planetary crisis, referring to both the United Nations Framework Convention on Climate Change (UNFCCC) and the Paris Agreement, as well as a range of international and regional treaties, norms, principles, and initiatives related to this problem (Id., paras. 120–144).

[106] From Id.: "See Inter-Am. Ct. H.R., Advisory Opinion 32/25 on the Climate Emergency and Human Rights, supra note 1, paras. 219–223."

[107] From Id.: "Id., para. 229."

[108] From Id.: "Id., para. 245."

[109] From Id.: "Id., paras. 393–457."

to legislate mitigation measures to limit greenhouse gas emissions[110] and, as Professor Celorio writes, to "regulate, supervise, and monitor corporate conduct and require environmental impact assessments before implementing activities which may be harmful."[111]

4. The Inter-American Court "mandated states to adopt legislative and other measures to prevent, investigate, and punish human rights violations committed by public and private enterprises.[112] The Court went farther and underscored the multiple responsibilities of business enterprises to directly address climate change and its human rights impacts, including that they take action to reduce emissions; address their contribution to the climate with adequate mitigation targets; and conduct environmental impact assessment before implementing activities which may be harmful."[113]
5. The advisory opinion recognizes nature "as a subject of rights." Professor Celorio writes: "In this sense, the [Inter-American] Court underscored the states' positive obligation to adopt measures to guarantee the protection, restoration, and regeneration of ecosystems.[114] These measures should be compatible with the best available science; recognize the value of traditional, local, and Indigenous knowledge; and be guided by the principle of non-regressivity.[115] The Court also emphasized the *jus cogens* nature of the obligation to prevent environmental damage and its extension to the preservation of our common ecosystem."[116]

Throughout its pages the advisory opinion fuses the climate emergency with fundamental human rights principles and the ravages of poverty to speak in terms of legal obligations. Given the wide-ranging and multi-faceted character of such interpretation in the context of climate change, the Inter-American Court has set the stage in its advisory opinion for States in the Western Hemisphere and by virtue of its influence and legal precedent the nations and peoples on other continents to understand this: International justice now occupies a vast integrated system of rights and obligations (of environmental, economic, and human rights character) pertaining to the foremost existential challenge humankind faces: the fate of Planet Earth in a time of accelerating climate change.

---

[110] From Id.: "The Court also established broad duties for states and private actors to mitigate and adapt to climate change, as part of the right to a healthy climate. For mitigation, states are mandated to adopt mitigation measures—including legislation—to curb greenhouse gas emissions from human activities (Inter-Am. Ct. H.R., Advisory Opinion 32/25 on the Climate Emergency and Human Rights, para. 321)."

[111] From Id.: "States must also regulate, supervise, and monitor corporate conduct and require environmental impact assessments before implementing activities which may be harmful (Id.)."

[112] From Id.: "Id., para. 345."

[113] From Id.: "Id., paras. 347, 358, 362."

[114] From Id.: "Id., para. 293."

[115] From Id.: "Id., para. 283."

[116] From Id.: "Id., paras. 291–296.

7.3 African Court of Human and Peoples' Rights

7.3.1 APDR & IHRDA v. Mali (2016)[117]

With a willingness to address controversial issues such as marriage in African cultures, the African Court of Human and Peoples' Rights delivered judgment in *APDR & IHRDA v. Mali* in 2016 that set the country of Mali on a new path towards rules of marriage that would align with international human rights law. The question before the African Court was whether the Malian Family Code of 2011 violated several provisions of international human rights instruments setting a minimum age of marriage for girls and their right of consent to marriage that had been ratified by Mali. Included among those treaties was the African Charter on Human and Peoples' Rights.[118]

The Malian Family Code "[e]titles religious ministers, alongside civil registry officials to perform marriages but that no provision of this law provides for verification of the parties' consent by the religious ministers."[119] The Malian Family Code "prescribes sanctions against any civil registry official who performs marriage without verifying the consent of the parties, but no sanctions are prescribed against defaulting religious ministers who fail to perform the verification."[120] The Malian Family Code further specifies "that consent must be given orally and in person before the civil registry official by each party but that provision was not prescribed for religious ministers; the conditions that must be fulfilled by the civil registry official to be able to celebrate a marriage without the presence of the parties are similarly not required of religious ministers."[121] A law adopted in 2009 in Mali that required elimination of traditional practices and conduct harmful to the rights of women and children in line with Articles 2(2) of the Maputo Protocol, 5(a) of Convention on the Elimination of All Forms of Discrimination Against Women ("CEDAW") and 1(3) of the African Charter on the Rights and Welfare of the Child was never "promulgated because of [a] widespread protest movement by Islamic organizations."[122]

The African Court found that the Malian Family Code violated the relevant articles of the Maputo Protocol and the African Charter on the Rights and Welfare of the Child, each of which had been ratified by Mali. The Malian Family Code "set the minimum age for contracting marriage at eighteen (18) for boys and sixteen (16) for girls, whereas Article 6(b) of the Maputo Protocol sets that age at 18 for girls."[123] The plaintiffs essentially argued that the Malian Family Code actually made underage

---

[117] African Court of Human and Peoples' Rights (2018).

[118] Organization of African Unity (1981).

[119] African Court of Human and Peoples' Rights (2018), para. 79.

[120] Id., para. 80.

[121] Id., para. 81.

[122] Id., para. 6.

[123] Id., para. 59.

marriage easier than it had been under the prior Family Code of 1962.[124] In fact, the African Court held that "the impugned law allows for special exemption for marriage as from fifteen (15) years, with the father's or mother's consent for the boy, and only the father's consent, for the girl."[125] Mali tried to argue that the original law from 2009 would have been in line with international law but that they "could not...promulgate [the law] following a 'force majeure' which affected the process"[126] and that "the established rules must not eclipse social, cultural and religious realities."[127]

The African Court responded to this defense argument of Mali by noting that the Malian Family Code "envisages the application of Islamic law...and entitles religious ministers to celebrate marriages, but does not require them to verify the free consent of the parties"[128] and "that the way in which a religious marriage takes place in Mali poses serious risks that may lead to forced marriage and perpetuate traditional practices that violate international standards which define the precise conditions regarding age of marriage and consent of the parties, for a marriage to be valid."[129] The African Court found that the Malian Family Code "violated Article 21(2) of the Maputo Protocol and Articles 3 and 4 of the Children's Charter."[130] Further, the Court found that "by adopting the Family Code and maintaining therein discriminatory practices which undermine the rights of women and children, the Respondent State [Mali] has violated its international commitments"[131] with respect to "Article 2(2) of the Maputo Protocol, Articles 1(3) and 21 of the Children's Charter and Article 5(a) of CEDAW."[132]

7.3.2 Chalula v. United Republic of Tanzania (2018)[133]

In *Chalula v. United Republic of Tanzania* (2018), the African Court addressed some of the complexities of how national courts handle cases that result in a sentence of death. The plaintiff, Ladislaus Chalula, was on death row in Tanzania for a murder that he committed in 1991. Chalula alleged violation of his rights in the course of the proceedings before domestic courts. The African Court, however, found that the Tanzania courts had not discriminated against Chalula in those proceedings. However, the African Court held that the death sentence against Chalula "constitutes

[124] Id., para. 117.
[125] Id., para. 60.
[126] Id., para. 63.
[127] Id., para. 66.
[128] Id., para. 91.
[129] Id., para. 94.
[130] Id., para. 115.
[131] Id., para. 124.
[132] Id., para. 125.
[133] African Court of Human and Peoples' Rights (2025).

a violation of the right to life, as guaranteed under Article 4 of the Charter."[134] The African Court noted that although the death penalty "was meted out on the Applicant [Chalula] in accordance with the law that denies the judicial officer's discretion on sentencing…[t]he [African] Court recalls its well-established jurisprudence that the mandatory nature of the death penalty constitutes a violation of the right to life."[135]

Because "the national courts examined the Applicant's allegation that prosecution witness no. 1 framed the Applicant for the crime in order to absolve himself of any guilt and found no evidence to support that claim,"[136] the African Court "considers that the manner in which the national courts evaluated the evidence does not disclose any manifest error requiring its intervention."[137] However, the African Court found that Tanzania needed to "annul the death sentence imposed on the Applicant and remove him from death row pending the sentencing hearing that it has previously ordered."[138] The African Court ordered Tanzania to "take all necessary measures to hold a sentencing hearing for the Applicant in a procedure that does not provide for the mandatory death penalty and upholds discretionary power of the judge."[139]

Thus, while by no means ruling on the legality of the death penalty under the law of Tanzania, the African Court determined that the death penalty in Tanzania should not be automatically imposed upon sentencing but should be subject to the discretionary authority of the judge of the trial court.

7.3.3 *Ibrahim Ben Mohamed Ben Brahim Belguith v. Republic of Tunisia (2022)*[140]

The fate of a constitutional democracy surviving in Tunisia confronted the African Court in the case of *Ibrahim Ben Mohamed Ben Brahim Belguith v. Republic of Tunisia* (2022) in which it rendered judgment in 2022. The Applicant, a member of the Parliament of Tunisia, alleged that the president of Tunisia issued a set of decrees in July, August, September, and October 2021 that severely undermined numerous powers of the Parliament and of its individual members, denied the right of appeal regarding Presidential decrees, and revoked the Constitution of Tunisia except for Chapters I and II on the grounds that those particular provisions did not contradict the Presidential order of 22 September 2021. The Applicant contended that his human rights and freedoms were jeopardized by removing them from the ambit of organic laws pursuant to Article 65 of the Constitution which, in terms of its form and procedures, provides guarantees which elevate ordinary laws to decrees.

[134] Id., para. 85.
[135] Id.
[136] Id., para. 95.
[137] Id., para. 96.
[138] Id., para. 119.
[139] Id., para. 127.
[140] African Court of Human and Peoples' Rights (2022).

According to the Applicant, "this would mean that a mere decision taken by one person, namely, the President of the Republic, constitutes a 'menace' and a grave violation of rights and freedoms, especially in the absence of any oversight or counter authority and in the absence of any imminent danger within the meaning of Article 80 of the Constitution."[141]

The African Court found that Tunisia's "restrictive measures were neither adopted in accordance with the law nor were they proportionate for the purpose for which they were adopted."[142] This arose primarily because the grant of power from the Presidential decrees at issue was too broad, because "there is nothing on record showing that the substantive conditions of an imminent danger to the nation's institutions or the security and independence of the country or the abovementioned procedural requirements were met before the President issued the decrees in question"[143] and because "the decrees in question disproportionately disrupted the work of the government including that of elected institutions such as the House of People's Representatives."[144]

Finally, the African Court found that Article 1 of the African Charter was also violated as Tunisia "has failed to operationalize its Constitutional Court to give effect to its citizens' right to be heard by enabling them to challenge the constitutionality of Presidential decrees. This has violated their right to participation in political affairs of their country directly and through their freely chosen representatives."[145]

The judgment's challenge to the executive authority in Tunisia's national government was an extraordinary exercise of judicial oversight power by the African Court and established a foundation for similar challenges to executive overreach of national constitutional constraints, where they exist, among African nations.

---

[141] Id., para. 104; from Constitute (2014), art. 80:

In the event of imminent danger threatening the nation's institutions or the security or independence of the country, and hampering the normal functioning of the state, the President of the Republic may take any measures necessitated by the exceptional circumstances, after consultation with the Head of Government and the Speaker of the Assembly of the Representatives of the People and informing the President of the Constitutional Court. The President shall announce the measures in a statement to the people.

The measures shall guarantee, as soon as possible, a return to the normal functioning of state institutions and services. The Assembly of the Representatives of the People shall be deemed to be in a state of continuous session throughout such a period. In this situation, the President of the Republic cannot dissolve the Assembly of the Representatives of the People and a motion of censure against the government cannot be presented.

Thirty days after the entry into force of these measures, and at any time thereafter, the Speaker of the Assembly of the Representatives of the People or thirty of the members thereof shall be entitled to apply to the Constitutional Court with a view to verifying whether or not the circumstances remain exceptional. The Court shall rule upon and publicly issue its decision within a period not exceeding fifteen days.

These measures cease to be in force as soon as the circumstances justifying their implementation no longer apply. The President of the Republic shall address a message to the people to this effect.

[142] African Court of Human and Peoples' Rights (2022), para. 119.

[143] Id., para. 116.

[144] Id., para. 117.

[145] Id., para. 127.

References

African Court of Human and Peoples' Rights (2018) The matter of APDF and IHRDA v. Republic of Mali, Application no. 046/2016, judgment. African Court of Human and Peoples' Rights. https://www.african-court.org/cpmt/storage/app/uploads/public/5f5/215/dbc/5f5215dbcd90b917144785.pdf. Accessed 8 May 2026

African Court of Human and Peoples' Rights (2022) The matter of Ibrahim Ben Mohamed Ben Ibrahim Belguith v. Republic of Tunisia, Application no. 017/2021, judgment. African Court of Human and Peoples' Rights. https://www.african-court.org/cpmt/storage/app/uploads/public/633/48f/dcc/63348fdcc9449943680203.pdf. Accessed 8 May 2026

African Court of Human and Peoples' Rights (2025) The matter of Ladislaus Chalula v. United Republic of Tanzania, Application no. 003/2018, judgment. African Court of Human and Peoples' Rights. https://www.african-court.org/cpmt/storage/app/uploads/public/67a/607/496/67a607496e525306962831.pdf. Accessed 8 May 2026

African Court of Human and Peoples' Rights (2026a) African Court of Human and Peoples' Rights. https://www.african-court.org/afchpr/. Accessed 8 May 2026

African Court of Human and Peoples' Rights (2026b) Basic information. African Court of Human and Peoples' Rights. https://www.african-court.org/afchpr/basic-information-2/. Accessed 8 May 2026

Brugnatelli S (2009) Barrios Altos case. In: The Max Planck encyclopedia of public international law. Max Planck Institute for Comparative Public Law and International Law. Accessible via Oxford Public International Law. https://opil.ouplaw.com/display/10.1093/law:epil/9780199231690/law-9780199231690-e1801. Accessed 8 May 2026

Celorio R (2025) Advisory opinion 32/25 on the climate emergency and human rights: the Inter-American Court of Human Rights meets the moment. ASIL Insights 29(14). https://asil.org/insights/volume-29-issue-14/. Accessed 8 May 2026

Center for Justice and International Law (2025) The Inter-American Court of Human Rights and the climate emergency: an analytical summary of advisory opinion AO-32/5. Center for Justice and International Law. https://opinion-consultiva-clima.cejil.org/wp-content/uploads/2025/08/RESUMEN-OC-ENGLISH.pdf. Accessed 8 May 2026

Constitute (2014) Tunisia's constitution of 2014. Constitute. https://www.constituteproject.org/constitution/Tunisia_2014.pdf. Accessed 8 May 2026

Council of Europe (1975) Protocol 1 to the European convention on human rights and fundamental freedoms, Paris, 20 March 1952. Organization for Security and Co-operation in Europe. https://odihr.osce.org/odihr/elections/19167. Accessed 8 May 2026

Council of Europe (2022) The Russian Federation is excluded from the Council of Europe. Council of Europe. https://www.coe.int/en/web/portal/-/the-russian-federation-is-excluded-from-the-council-of-europe. Accessed 8 May 2026

Council of Europe (2026) Council of Europe. https://www.coe.int/en/web/portal. Accessed 8 May 2026

Dimitrakos D (2025) The ITLOS advisory opinion on climate change: a brief review. ASIL Insights 29(5). https://asil.org/insights/volume-29-issue-5/. Accessed 8 May 2026

Dragović Savić B (2024) 25 years of silence about the responsibility for the death of RTS workers in the NATO bombing. ProPeace. https://www.propeace.de/en/25-years-silence-about-responsibility-death-rts-workers-nato-bombing. Accessed 8 May 2026

Dugal M (2025) Climate emergency as a human right: decoding the IACtHR's groundbreaking advisory opinion. Earth.org. https://earth.org/understanding-the-iacthrs-advisory-opinion-on-the-climate-emergency-and-human-rights-and-its-implications/. Accessed 8 May 2026

Encyclopædia Britannica (2025) Kosovo conflict. In: Encyclopædia Britannica. Encyclopædia Britannica, Inc. https://www.britannica.com/event/Kosovo-conflict. Accessed 8 May 2026

European Court of Human Rights (1987) Case of Mathieu-Monin and Clerfayt v. Belgium (application no. 9267/81), judgment. European Court of Human Rights. https://hudoc.echr.coe.int/fre?i=001-57536. Accessed 8 May 2026

European Court of Human Rights (2001) Grand chamber decision as to the admissibility of application no. 52207/99. European Court of Human Rights. https://hudoc.echr.coe.int/eng?i=001-22099. Accessed 8 May 2026
European Court of Human Rights (2003) Décision sur la recevabilité de la requête no 58540/00. European Court of Human Rights. https://hudoc.echr.coe.int/eng?i=001-44046. Accessed 8 May 2026
European Court of Human Rights (2005) Case of Hirst v. the United Kingdom (application no. 74025/01), judgment. European Court of Human Rights. https://hudoc.echr.coe.int/eng?i=001-70442. Accessed 8 May 2026
European Court of Human Rights (2007) Third section decision as to the admissibility of application no. 60167/00. European Court of Human Rights. https://hudoc.echr.coe.int/eng?i=001-81672. Accessed 8 May 2026
European Court of Human Rights (2010) Case of Frodl v. Austria (application no. 20201/04), judgment. European Court of Human Rights. https://hudoc.echr.coe.int/eng?i=001-98132. Accessed 8 May 2026
European Court of Human Rights (2011a) Case of Al-Skeni and others v. the United Kingdom (application no. 55721/07), judgment. European Court of Human Rights. https://hudoc.echr.coe.int/eng?i=001-105606. Accessed 8 May 2026
European Court of Human Rights (2011b) Case of Finogenov and others v. Russia (applications nos. 18299/03 and 27311/03), judgment. European Court of Human Rights. https://hudoc.echr.coe.int/eng?i=001-108231. Accessed 8 May 2026
European Court of Human Rights (2011c) Information note on the Court's case-law no. 147. European Court of Human Rights. https://hudoc.echr.coe.int/eng?i=002-240. Accessed 8 May 2026
European Court of Human Rights (2012) Case of Scoppola v. Italy (no. 3) (application no. 126/05), judgment. European Court of Human Rights. https://hudoc.echr.coe.int/eng?i=001-111044. Accessed 8 May 2026
European Court of Human Rights (2021a) Case of Georga v. Russia (II) (application no. 38263/08), judgment. European Court of Human Rights. https://hudoc.echr.coe.int/en?i=001-207757. Accessed 8 May 2026
European Court of Human Rights (2021b) European convention on human rights, as amended by protocols nos. 11, 14 and 15, supplemented by protocols nos. 1, 4, 6, 7, 12, 13 and 16. European Court of Human Rights. https://www.echr.coe.int/documents/d/echr/convention_ENG. Accessed 8 May 2026
European Court of Human Rights (2025a) Case of Ukraine and the Netherlands v. Russia (applications nos. 8019/16, 43800/14, 28525/20 and 11055/22), judgment. European Court of Human Rights. https://hudoc.echr.coe.int/eng?i=001-244292. Accessed 8 May 2026
European Court of Human Rights (2025b) Legal summary, Ukraine and the Netherlands v. Russia [GC]—43800/14, 8019/16, 28525/20 et al. European Court of Human Rights. https://hudoc.echr.coe.int/en?i=002-14493. Accessed 8 May 2026
European Court of Human Rights (2026) European Court of Human Rights. https://www.echr.coe.int/. Accessed 8 May 2026
Grossman CM, Gomez Echeverri J (2026) Mayagna (Sumo) Awas Tingni community v Nicaragua case. In: The Max Planck encyclopedia of public international law. Max Planck Institute for Comparative Public Law and International Law. Accessible via Oxford Public International Law. https://opil.ouplaw.com/display/10.1093/law:epil/9780199231690/law-9780199231690-e1793?p=emailAmIEiu/9sN8Jw&d=/10.1093/law:epil/9780199231690/law-9780199231690-e1793. Accessed 8 May 2026
Hoyos D, Catalina Mancilla A (2019) The Amparo: Key factor in the arbitration scene of Central America and Mexico. Kluwer Arbitration Blog. https://legalblogs.wolterskluwer.com/arbitration-blog/the-amparo-key-factor-in-the-arbitration-scene-of-central-america-and-mexico/. Accessed 8 May 2026

Institute for Governance and Sustainable Development (2026) Judicial responses to the advisory opinion from the Inter-American Court of Human Rights on the climate emergency. Institute for Governance and Sustainable Development. https://www.igsd.org/judicial-responses-to-the-advisory-opinion-from-the-inter-american-court-of-human-rights-on-the-climate-emergency/. Accessed 8 May 2026

Inter-American Court of Human Rights (2001a) Case of Barrios Altos v. Peru, judgment of March 14, 2001 (merits). Inter-American Court of Human Rights. https://www.corteidh.or.cr/docs/casos/articulos/seriec_75_ing.pdf. Accessed 8 May 2026

Inter-American Court of Human Rights (2001b) Case of the Mayagna (Sumo) Awas Tingni community v. Nicaragua, judgment of August 31, 2001 (merits, reparations and costs). Inter-American Court of Human Rights. https://oas.org/dil/XXXV_Course_IACHR_Case_Mayagna_v_Nicaragua_Luis_Toro.pdf. Accessed 8 May 2026

Inter-American Court of Human Rights (2006) Case of the Miguel Castro-Castro Prison v. Peru, judgment of November 25, 2006 (merits, reparations and costs). Inter-American Court of Human Rights. https://www.corteidh.or.cr/docs/casos/articulos/seriec_160_ing.pdf. Accessed 8 May 2026

Inter-American Court of Human Rights (2021) Case of the Miskito divers (Lemoth Morris et al.) v. Honduras, judgment of August 31, 2021. Inter-American Court of Human Rights. https://www.corteidh.or.cr/docs/casos/articulos/seriec_432_ing.pdf. Accessed 8 May 2026

Inter-American Court of Human Rights (2025) Advisory opinion AO-32/35 of May 29, 2025. Inter-American Court of Human Rights. https://www.corteidh.or.cr/docs/opiniones/seriea_32_en.pdf. Accessed 8 May 2026

International Court of Justice (2025) Obligations of states in respect of climate change, advisory opinion. International Court of Justice. https://www.icj-cij.org/sites/default/files/case-related/187/187-20250723-adv-01-00-en.pdf. Accessed 8 May 2026

International Criminal Tribunal for the former Yugoslavia (2000) Final report to the prosecutor by the committee established to review the NATO bombing campaign against the Federal Republic of Yugoslavia. International Criminal Tribunal for the former Yugoslavia. https://www.icty.org/x/file/Press/nato061300.pdf. Accessed 8 May 2026

International Tribunal for the Law of the Sea (2024) Request for an advisory opinion submitted by the commission of small island states on climate change and international law, advisory opinion. International Tribunal for the Law of the Sea. https://www.itlos.org/fileadmin/itlos/documents/cases/31/Advisory_Opinion/C31_Adv_Op_21.05.2024_orig.pdf. Accessed 8 May 2026

Khachatryan D (2025) The judgment in Ukraine and the Netherlands v. Russia: A “Nicaragua moment” for the ECTHR? Strasbourg Observers. https://strasbourgobservers.com/2025/07/23/the-judgment-in-ukraine-and-the-netherlands-v-russia-a-nicaragua-moment-for-the-ecthr/. Accessed 8 May 2026

Khatri U (2025) What a historic Inter-American Court ruling means for global climate justice. Cent Int Environ Law. https://www.ciel.org/unpacking-the-inter-american-court-ao/. Accessed 8 May 2026

Limas S (2023) Lemoth Morris et al. (Miskitos divers) v. Honduras. Loyola of Los Angeles Intl and Comp Law Rev 46(2): 24–66. https://iachr.lls.edu/sites/default/files/uploads/2022-2023%20R2s/46.2.2.Lemoth%20Morris.pdf

Mallory C (2021) A second coming of extraterritorial jurisdiction at the European Court of Human Rights? Quest Int Law. https://www.qil-qdi.org/a-second-coming-of-extraterritorial-jurisdiction-at-the-european-court-of-human-rights/. Accessed 8 May 2026

Organization of African Unity (1981) African Charter on Human and Peoples’ Rights. African Union. https://au.int/sites/default/files/treaties/36390-treaty-0011_-_african_charter_on_human_and_peoples_rights_e.pdf. Accessed 8 May 2026

Organization of African Unity (1998) Protocol to the African charter on human and peoples’ rights on the establishment of an African court on human and peoples’ rights. African Union. https://au.int/sites/default/files/treaties/36393-treaty-0019_-_protocol_to_the_african_charter_on_human_and_peoplesrights_on_the_establishment_of_an_african_court_on_human_and_peoples_rights_e.pdf. Accessed 8 May 2026

Organization of American States (2011) American convention on human rights “pact of San Jose, Costa Rica” (B-32). Organization of American States. https://www.oas.org/dil/treaties_b-32_american_convention_on_human_rights.pdf. Accessed 8 May 2026

Organization of American States (2026a) Inter-American commission on human rights. Organization of American States. https://www.oas.org/en/iachr/Default.asp. Accessed 8 May 2026

Organization of American States (2026b) Organization of American States. https://www.oas.org/en/. Accessed 8 May 2026

Rodríguez Orúe JD (2025) Inter-American Court says countries must prevent climate harms. Human Rights Watch. https://www.hrw.org/news/2025/07/07/inter-american-court-says-countries-must-prevent-climate-harms. Accessed 8 May 2026

United Nations (2026) Universal declaration of human rights. United Nations. https://www.un.org/en/about-us/universal-declaration-of-human-rights. Accessed 8 May 2026

Chapter 8
The Critical Role of Defense Counsel in the Modern Atrocity Crimes Tribunals

8.1 Nuremberg

When the Allies created the International Military Tribunal at Nuremberg (IMT) it quickly exhibited structural defects: "victor's justice" limited procedural guarantees by modern standards, broad evidentiary admissibility, no appellate review, and a pronounced asymmetry between prosecution and defense.[1] Although the IMT accepted that the accused would require counsel, it did not embrace any expansive conception of defense.[2]

Defense counsel at Nuremberg were appointed late, afforded inadequate time to prepare, denied anything approaching parity of access to the documentary record, and required to work in an atmosphere in which the very act of defending the accused could be viewed as morally suspect.[3] Affidavits and hearsay constrained confrontation rights.[4] More fundamentally, the defense faced the larger structural grievance that only the defeated were prosecuted, while Allied conduct remained beyond scrutiny.[5]

Defense at Nuremberg was conducted overwhelmingly by German lawyers, and the structure of representation was tightly controlled by the IMT rather than developed as an ordinary transnational defense bar. Each of the twenty-two defendants appearing before the IMT was either assigned or selected a German lawyer.[6]

The same pattern emerged in Tokyo at the International Military Tribunal for the Far East, which convened after World War II in Tokyo. There too, the defense encountered a tribunal born of victory, tasked with adjudicating novel crimes and

[1] Wilson (2006), pp. 31, 42–43.

[2] International Committee of the Red Cross (1945), art. 16(d).

[3] Knoops (2017), pp. 10–15.

[4] International Criminal Tribunal for the former Yugoslavia (1996), pp. 2–5.

[5] Minear (1971), pp. 3–16.

[6] Yale Law School Lillian Goldman Law Library (2008); Bass (2023), pp. 350–371.

D. J. Scheffer and M. S. Ellis, *The Story of Modern International Justice, 1993-2025*,
https://doi.org/10.1007/978-3-032-33243-1_8

modes of liability, and shadowed by the suspicion that the legal form masked rather than resolved political asymmetry.[7]

Formally, the right to defense encompassed several key guarantees, including receipt of the indictment, the opportunity to respond to the charges, legal representation, and the ability to confront and cross-examine witnesses.[8] On paper, these rights were meaningful. In practice, however, defense counsel faced severe resource disparities. While prosecution teams were staffed, funded, and supported by state apparatuses, defense counsel operated with minimal institutional backing, inadequate time to prepare, and limited access to evidence.[9]

The broader professional climate compounded these constraints. For example, in Britain, the Bar Council declared it "undesirable" for members of the English Bar to represent defendants at the IMT.[10] Although not a formal legal prohibition—the Attorney General clarified as such—the episode reflects the prevailing stigma around defense representation.[11] Similar pressures existed in the United States, although less formally expressed.[12] The atmosphere surrounding the trial repeatedly pushed toward punishment with as little adversarial dignity as possible.[13]

That tendency drew sharp criticism. U.S. Chief of Counsel (and Associate Justice of the U.S. Supreme Court) Robert Jackson himself had insisted before trial that, if the Allies wished simply to shoot German leaders as a matter of policy, they should do so openly rather than disguise the act behind a court; Harlan Fiske Stone, from a different angle, derided the proceedings as a "high-grade lynching party" when legal form seemed in danger of being overwhelmed by victor's certainty.[14] Taken together, these episodes exposed the same underlying fear: a criminal trial that distrusts defense too deeply risks becoming something closer to exemplary vengeance than law.

Although the Cold War temporarily ended any focus on international criminal justice, the easing of those geopolitical tensions with the fall of the Berlin Wall in 1989 and the collapse of the Soviet Union two years later fostered a renewed multilateralism agenda for international justice. However, the issue of defense remained both layered and uneven. It is the challenge of implementing international guarantees of fair trials that unequivocally includes the rights of defense.

---

[7] Minear (1971), pp. 3–16; Bass (2023), pp. 350–371.

[8] Encyclopædia Britannica (2026).

[9] Reinhardt and Feirabend (2018); Knoops (2017), pp. 9–15.

[10] House of Commons of the United Kingdom (1945), col. 198W.

[11] Id.

[12] Knoops (2017), pp. 9–15.

[13] Temminck Tuinstra (2009), pp. 17–19.

[14] Harris (1999), pp. 35–37; Morrison (2017), pp. xvi–xvii.

8.2 International Norms

At the universal level, the foundational text regarding fair trial rights remains Article 14 of the International Covenant on Civil and Political Rights.[15] It guarantees a fair and public hearing by a competent, independent, and impartial tribunal; the presumption of innocence; prompt and detailed notice of the nature and cause of the charge; adequate time and facilities for the preparation of the defense; the right to communicate with counsel of one's own choosing; trial without undue delay; trial in one's presence; examination of witnesses; free assistance of an interpreter where necessary; and freedom from compulsion to testify against oneself or confess guilt.[16] These guarantees are reinforced by the U.N. Basic Principles on the Role of Lawyers, which emphasize independence, confidentiality, and professional protection.[17]

Regional human-rights law provides an additional protective foundation. Article 6 of the European Convention on Human Rights enshrines the principle of protection.[18] Strasbourg jurisprudence has significantly influenced international criminal proceedings, particularly in areas such as detention, confrontation, and the admissibility of prior statements. The importance of cases such as *Ilijkov v. Bulgaria*, *Saïdi v. France*, and *Unterpertinger v. Austria* have informed the articulation of minimum standards for proceedings before international courts.[19]

The modern test for defense in international tribunals emerged when large-scale atrocities committed in the former Yugoslavia and in Rwanda in the 1990s demanded action. The creation of the International Criminal Tribunal for the former Yugoslavia (ICTY) by UN Security Council Resolution 827 (1993),[20] and of the International Criminal Tribunal for Rwanda (ICTR) by Resolution 955 (1994),[21] marked the first sustained attempt to institutionalize international criminal justice since Nuremberg.

These tribunals established a far more developed vocabulary of fair trial. Their statutes and rules guaranteed core defense rights, including a fair and public hearing, adequate time and facilities, legal assistance, and appellate review.[22] Nonetheless, the defense continued to operate within an institutional architecture more naturally aligned with the prosecution.[23] As former ICTY Judge Patricia Wald once noted, defense counsel are often seen as being "allied with their nemeses in the docks."[24]

[15] Office of the United Nations High Commissioner for Human Rights (1966), art. 14.

[16] Id.

[17] Office of the United Nations High Commissioner for Human Rights (1990), paras. 1–8, 16–22.

[18] European Court of Human Rights (2021), art. 6.

[19] European Court of Human Rights (1986), paras. 30–33; European Court of Human Rights (1993), paras. 43–44; European Court of Human Rights (2001), para. 81.

[20] United Nations Security Council (1993).

[21] United Nations Security Council (1994).

[22] Id, arts. 19–27; United Nations Security Council (1993), arts. 20–21.

[23] Fedorova (2017), pp. 204–208.

[24] Wald (2001), p. 104.

8.3 ICTY *Tadić* Case

Based in The Hague, The Netherlands, the ICTY's mandate was to prosecute those individuals most responsible for serious violations of international humanitarian law committed in the former Yugoslavia since 1991.[25] The Tribunal's first case, *Prosecutor v. Tadić*, became the crucible for modern defense rights in international criminal law. Duško Tadić, a Bosnian Serb political leader, was charged with crimes committed against Bosnian Muslims and Croats in the Prijedor region of Bosnia and Herzegovina during the war in the early 1990s.[26]

The importance of Tadić receiving a fair trial and proper defense was paramount. This sentiment was set forth in the Tribunal's Statute.[27] Justice Richard Goldstone, the Chief Prosecutor for both the ICTY and ICTR, recognized this point, noting that: "There is no question that history will judge the Tribunals for the former Yugoslavia and Rwanda on the fairness or unfairness of their proceedings. Whether there are convictions or whether there are acquittals will not be the yardstick. The measure is going to be the fairness of the proceedings."[28] In essence, a tribunal that cannot acquit where guilt has not been established beyond a reasonable doubt has ceased to function as a criminal court.[29]

Goldstone's sentiment was exactly right. International criminal tribunals derive their authority not from the gravity of the crimes they address, but from the legality of the process by which they assign individual criminal responsibility. Proof that crimes occurred is not proof that the accused committed them. That distinction is elementary in criminal law but decisive in international criminal justice, where proceedings arise amid war, political rupture, public outrage, and long-settled narratives of guilt can often translate collective atrocities into individual guilt. The defense gives the distinction practical force.

The defense, thus, does more than protect the accused against wrongful conviction. It also secures the tribunal's own claim to legality. International criminal courts are not empowered to punish because the underlying events are morally evident; they may do so only if guilt is established through fair procedures. The defense is the structure through which the tribunal is required to explain why the accused, rather than the criminal setting around him, is the lawful object of condemnation.[30]

---

[25] United Nations Security Council (1993).

[26] International Criminal Tribunal for the former Yugoslavia (1995).

[27] United Nations Security Council (1993), art. 21.

[28] Bakkum and Williams (2025).

[29] Morrison (2017), pp. xvi–xviii.

[30] Temminck Tuinstra (2010), pp. 463–464.

8.4 Equality of Arms

The principle of equality of arms lies at the core of fair trial rights. It is indispensable to the legality and legitimacy of the proceedings. Equality of arms is the duty to ensure that parties to criminal proceedings have substantially equivalent means to present their case.[31] This principle is formally endorsed by every major international tribunal.[32]

Equality of arms extends beyond financial parity, though money matters. It requires adequate time and facilities to prepare a case. International criminal trials are often vast in scale, with millions of pages of disclosure, large witness lists, extensive intercept evidence, and years of proceedings.[33] This was visible in the *Milošević* and *Karadžić* cases, where the management of self-representation intersected with the accused's ability to prepare and present a defense under enormous evidentiary pressure.[34]

In common-law settings, equality of arms more naturally requires that the defense have sufficient facilities to conduct its own investigations and present exonerating evidence on a footing that is not substantively inferior to the prosecution.[35] In more traditionally civil-law settings, the defense is expected to rely more heavily on the prosecutor or investigative judge to gather evidence, and equality of arms, therefore, does not necessarily imply proportionality of investigative resources in the same way. International criminal courts contain both assumptions at once.[36]

This was a pivotal issue during the *Tadić* trial and, subsequently, influenced the interpretation and application of the principle of equality of arms in future international criminal proceedings.[37] For instance, the ICTY jurisprudence established that equality of arms does not necessarily amount to the material equality of having the *same* financial and/or personal resources, but rather obligates the court to ensure that neither party (particularly the defense) is put at a *disadvantage* when presenting its case.[38] The ICTY Appeals Chamber affirmed that equality of arms encompasses the right to adequate time and facilities for the preparation of the defense, as outlined in Article 21(4)(b) of the ICTY Statute.[39]

Nevertheless, the defense teams at the ICTY frequently faced serious challenges due to insufficient resources. The resources available to defendants, both in preparation for and during a trial, were fundamental to the justice through due process. Low remuneration for defense lawyers and limited support for their travel and witness

---

[31] International Criminal Tribunal for the former Yugoslavia (1999b), paras. 23, 25.

[32] Human Rights Watch (2008).

[33] Rohan and Ackerman (2017), pp. 321–324.

[34] International Criminal Tribunal for the former Yugoslavia (2004), para. 19 International Criminal Tribunal for the former Yugoslavia (2010), pp. 1–6.

[35] Temminck Tuinstra (2009), pp. 466–467.

[36] Id.

[37] See Bakkum and Williams (eds) (2025).

[38] Reinhardt and Feirabend (2018).

[39] International Criminal Tribunal for the former Yugoslavia (1999a).

interviews were relevant examples. Defense investigations are unusually vulnerable in the international setting. Witnesses may be frightened, politically aligned, difficult to locate, or physically inaccessible.[40] Crime sites may be remote, altered, or under official control. Documentary evidence may be held in state archives that prosecutors enjoy better access to or greater diplomatic leverage to request.[41] A defense team unable to inspect the site, interview the witness, or obtain the order, report, logbook, or personnel file it needs is not merely inconvenienced—it is prevented from effectively representing its client.[42] In fact, the defense counsel for Mr. Tadić argued that the defense's inability to gain access to evidence and enter key villages and towns in hostile states, necessary to build the defense case, had weakened counsel's ability to represent their client effectively.[43]

These challenges were compounded by institutional design. The ICTY Statute, like its ICTR counterpart, enumerated three organs of the Court: the Chambers, the Registry, and the Office of the Prosecutor.[44] The defense was not mentioned as an organ. Defense lawyers were external practitioners, not Court employees, and accessed institutional support only through the Registry, the same body responsible for administering the tribunal as a whole.[45] They had no independent budget line, no permanent staff, and no institutional voice in the development of rules and procedures.

The same was true for the Special Court for Sierra Leone. The original Defense Office had no independent budget and had to seek resources annually through the Registry.[46] The disparity between prosecution and defense resources has been described as "gapingly glaring."[47] Similarly, at the Extraordinary Chambers in the Courts of Cambodia, the defense support structure was located within the Registry and functioned less as an independent institutional counterweight than as an administrative provider of facilities.[48] Only the Special Tribunal for Lebanon (STL) established a Defense Office as a formal organ of the tribunal, funded centrally and staffed by officials enjoying the same privileges and immunities as other tribunal personnel.[49]

For the ICTY, the practical consequences of such disparities were stark. While the Office of the Prosecutor could draw on a permanent staff of investigators, analysts, and lawyers,[50] defense teams were assembled case by case, funded through legal aid administered by the Registry, and dependent on the goodwill of registrars for

[40] Buisman and Hooper (2017), pp. 519–558.

[41] Id.

[42] Id.

[43] See Bakkum and Williams (eds) (2025).

[44] International Criminal Tribunal for the former Yugoslavia (2026a).

[45] Reinhardt and Feirabend (2018).

[46] Kennedy and Düsterhöft (2017), pp. 168–169.

[47] Temminck Tuinstra (2010), pp. 482–484.

[48] Kennedy and Düsterhöft (2017).

[49] Id.

[50] International Criminal Tribunal for the former Yugoslavia (2026b).

basic logistical support.[51] The structure clearly needed improving. The STL model provided a new baseline.

Thus, the establishment of the independent Office of Public Counsel for the Defence (OPCD) at the ICC represented a significant institutional development for defense interests. Its role is to provide defendants and counsel with essential logistical support, advice, and information.[52] The Office is independent, established under Regulation 77 of the Regulations of the Court, and reports to the Registry only for administrative matters. A key function of this office is to help safeguard the rights of the accused during the investigation's initial stages.[53]

The OPCD represented a genuine institutional advance. For the first time, the defense had a dedicated presence within the Court—an independent body mandated to provide substantial legal and logistical support to defense teams.[54] However, the OPCD's independence remained qualified, reflecting earlier structural limitations seen at the ICTY and ICTR. The OPCD sits within the Registry for administrative purposes and is not a fully autonomous organ of the ICC. However, even though the OPCD was placed within the Registry, it was "solely for administrative purposes." At the same time, the OPCD was expected to be "wholly independent."[55] This dual positioning—administratively within the Registry yet operationally independent—ensured that the OPCD was not subject to external pressure.[56]

The challenge to equality of arms extends beyond the structure of the defense office. The *Tadić* case exposed the related issue of the inadequacy of early remuneration structures.

The original ICTY 1994 Directive on the Assignment of Defence Counsel (amended several times) provided minimal remuneration for defense counsel. In the *Tadić* case, counsel received a fixed rate of $800 for the entire trial ($400 per phase), along with a daily rate of only $200. As written previously,[57] this compensation was hardly commensurate with the amount of time devoted to the case. Assigned Counsel routinely worked 12 to 14 hours a day, six days a week, undertaking both pre trial preparation and trial advocacy. Calculated based on a standard seven-and-a-half-hour workday, lead counsel's remuneration amounted to approximately $26 per hour—an amount that also had to cover basic administrative expenses. Tadić's lead counsel, Mischa Wladimiroff, waived his usual fees to comply with the ICTY's

---

[51] Reinhardt and Feirabend (2018).

[52] International Criminal Court (2026).

[53] Id.; see International Criminal Court (2024); The OPCD fulfils four key roles: 1. Representing and providing assistance to protect the rights of defence during the initial stages of proceedings; 2. Providing general legal support and assistance to Defence teams; 3. Acting as an Amicus on Defence issues; 4. Advancing submissions on behalf and/or representing individuals, not otherwise represented, on specific assignment, short or full case.

[54] International Criminal Court (2026).

[55] Fulford (2011).

[56] International Criminal Court (2026).

[57] Ellis (2003).

payment schedule.[58] However, following *Tadić*, compensation regimes at the ICTY and ICTR improved significantly.[59]

8.5 Ethics

One of the persistent challenges that plagued the early *ad hoc* tribunals was the regulation of professional ethics. The ICTY faced serious difficulties in regulating ethical standards and discipline among defense counsel, many of whom came from diverse legal and geographical backgrounds. A notable problem was the emergence of "fee-splitting" arrangements, whereby defendants appointed lawyers from the former Yugoslavia, and a portion of the lawyers' fees paid to the defendant's family.[60]

These practices prompted the development of the first modern Code of Professional Conduct for an international criminal tribunal.[61] The Code, substantially revised in 2002, sought to clarify the rights, duties and responsibilities of defense counsel, including rules governing confidentiality and conflicts of interest. It also imposed a disciplinary regime, including the creation of a Disciplinary Panel. A similar Code was introduced at the ICTR, and the ICTY code significantly influenced the development of the ICC's Code of Professional Conduct for Counsel.[62] The International Bar Association played an active role in drafting the Code of Professional Conduct.

8.6 Association of Defence Counsel

A major institutional milestone development for defense counsel was the establishment of the Association of Defence Counsel for the ICTY (ADC-ICTY).[63] Although the ICTY was created in 1993, it took nine years for ICTY to establish the ADC-ICTY (September 2002).[64] Its creation marked a significant turning point, providing defense teams with collective institutional representation for the first time and substantively improving the functioning of the defense.[65]

---

[58] Id.

[59] Id.; the fixed daily rate was also raised considerably. In the early 2000s, depending on years of experience, lead counsel at the ICTY were remunerated at rates between $80 and $110 per hour, up to a maximum of 175 hours per month. The Directive, amended in 2000, raised the fixed rate from $400 per trial stage to $2000. Experienced counsel could earn in excess of $230,000 annually.

[60] See Bakkum and Williams (eds) (2025).

[61] International Criminal Tribunal for the former Yugoslavia (2009).

[62] International Criminal Court (2011).

[63] Association of Defence Counsel Practising before the International Courts and Tribunals (2026).

[64] See Bakkum and Williams (eds) (2025).

[65] Reinhardt and Feirabend (2018).

The ICTY judges recognized a need for an association for several reasons.[66] First, it would ensure higher professional standards among defense counsel. Second, it would enable collective representation before the ICTY on issues affecting defense teams. Third, it would provide a mechanism for addressing ethical and disciplinary issues.

To support this development, the judges amended the ICTY's Rules of Procedure and Evidence, making membership in a recognized association of counsel a requirement for inclusion on the so-called Rule 45 List (list of qualified counsel), as provided for in the ICTY Rules of Procedure and Evidence.

The ADC-ICTY also produced the *Manual on Developed Practices*—a comprehensive guide to defense practice at the ICTY covering areas such as evidence, disclosure, witness protection, and courtroom procedure.[67] The manual reflected the accumulated institutional knowledge of counsel who, in many respects, developed international criminal defense practice from scratch.

The ADC-ICTY later served as a catalyst for similar developments at the ICC. Established in 2016, the International Criminal Court Bar Association (ICCBA) functions as the professional association for counsel and legal assistants appearing before the Court. Its core objectives include strengthening the independence of counsel, protecting the professional interests of its members, and advancing greater equality of arms at the ICC.[68] While the ICCBA and its predecessors have made important progress through advocacy and professional development, structural imbalances remain, and reform has been gradual.

8.7 Selection of Counsel

Another critical issue in the early international criminal tribunals concerned the assignment and selection of defense counsel. The Statutes of the ICTY and ICTR, referred to a right of the accused to communicate with "counsel of his or her own choosing."[69] However, the right to counsel of an accused's choosing was not absolute.

In practice, the ICTY and ICTR left the administrative task of selecting counsel to the Registrar, who was tasked with ensuring that appointed counsel met the necessary qualifications. Nevertheless, the accused persons had great latitude in selecting their counsel. Indeed, during the ICTY's history refusals of requests for assigned counsel were rare.[70]

The process was further governed by the Directive on the Assignment of Defence Counsel. The original 1994 Directive provided in Article 16(A), that an accused was

66 Association of Defence Counsel (2026).

67 United Nations Interregional Crime and Justice Institute, Association of Defence Counsel Practising Before the International Criminal Tribunal for the former Yugoslavia (2011).

68 Coalition for the International Criminal Court (2026).

69 United Nations Security Council (1993).

70 See Bakkum and Williams (2025).

entitled to *one* attorney as assigned counsel only, and this limitation was interpreted strictly.[71] However, the complexity and scale of the *Tadić* case exposed the inadequacy of this restriction. In that case, co-author Mark S. Ellis successfully petitioned the ICTY for the appointment of an additional international defense attorney. The then ICTY Registrar, Dorothee de Sampayo Garrido-Nijgh, reasoned that while the Directive limited representation to one counsel, it allowed discretionary use of funds to secure the additional services of defense support.

Following the *Tadić* trial, the Directive was amended in 1996 to permit the assignment of a second counsel in exceptional circumstances. By 2000, the ICTY had furthered its approach, routinely allowing the assignment of co-counsel, as well as support staff including investigators, translators, and language assistants, to address the significant evidentiary and logistical elements of complex international trials.[72] At the ICC, the Legal Aid Policy now links the number of defense lawyers to the phases up to the trial, which would then typically comprise five full-time lawyers.[73]

8.8 The Enduring Challenge

Defense counsel have not merely operated *within* international criminal law; they have shaped its development. International criminal law has developed through adversarial engagement. Defense counsel have repeatedly compelled tribunals to define the limits of culpability, clarify the evidentiary standard, and articulate procedural conditions under which criminal responsibility may lawfully be imposed.[74]

The evolution of defenses such as superior orders illustrates this dynamic. The IMT rejected any broad superior-orders defense, and later jurisprudence repeated the point with force.[75] However, the drafters of the Rome Statute chose to specify the limited conditions under which obedience to orders may matter.[76] That clarification was the product not merely of legislative drafting and input by, for example, NATO

[71] Id.

[72] International Criminal Tribunal for the Former Yugoslavia (2006); Article 16(C) of the Directive on the assignment of defence counsel provided that the Registrar may, in the interests of justice and at the request of the lead counsel, "assign a second counsel to assist with the defense [...]." The Directive clarified the distinction between lead counsel and co-counsel too: acting under the authority of the lead counsel, the co-counsel may deal with all stages of the proceedings and all matters arising out of the defense. Article 16(D) allowed the Registrar to "assign a co-counsel who does not speak either of the two working languages of the Tribunal but who speaks the native language of the suspect or accused." Finally, Article 16(E) provided for the assigning of "other persons such as legal assistants, consultants, investigators and interpreters, as required, to provide support to counsel." The article clarified that the lead counsel and the persons assisting him shall be referred to as the defense team.

[73] See Gibson (2026).

[74] Morrison (2017), pp. xvii–xviii.

[75] International Committee of the Red Cross (1945), art. 8.

[76] International Criminal Court (2021), art. 33.

countries, but of decades of defense argument about the relation between obedience, coercion, mistake, and culpability.[77]

The history of the defense in international criminal law is not a linear progression towards fairness. Rather, it reflects a persistent tension—where international accountability and justice require fairness in proceedings, which in turn is supported by resources, access, and institutional recognition for the defense.[78]

Thus, it should not come as a surprise that the contemporary legal framework of the defense is extensive but fragmented across general human-rights instruments, professional standards, regional jurisprudence, and the constitutive texts of international criminal tribunals themselves. The enduring challenge is not the articulation of norms, but their consistent and meaningful implementation.

References

Association of Defence Counsel (2026) About us. Association of Defence Counsel. https://www.adc-ict.org/about-us. Accessed 29 Apr 2026

Bakkum E, Williams P (eds) (2025) The inception of international defense: an interview with Dr. Mark S. Ellis. Public International Law and Policy Group. https://www.publicinternationallawandpolicygroup.org/lawyering-justice-blog/2025/11/26/the-inception-of-international-defense-an-interview-with-mark-s-ellis. Accessed 29 Apr 2026

Bass GJ (2023) Judgment at Tokyo: world war II on trial and the making of modern Asia. Knopf, New York

Buisman C, Hooper D (2017) Defense investigations and the collection of evidence. In: Rohan C, Zyberi G (eds) Defense perspectives on international criminal justice. Cambridge University Press, Cambridge, pp 519–558. https://www.cambridge.org/core/books/defense-perspectives-on-international-criminal-justice/defense-investigations-and-the-collection-of-evidence/2B63F09013730F20101334489A90051B

Coalition for the International Criminal Court (2026) Fair trials. Coalition for the International Criminal Court. https://www.coalitionfortheicc.org/fight/strong-icc/fair-trials. Accessed 29 Apr 2026

Ellis M (2003) The evolution of defense counsel appearing before the international criminal tribunal for the former Yugoslavia. New England Law Rev 37(4)

Encyclopædia Britannica (2026) Nuremberg trials. Encyclopædia Britannica. Encyclopædia Britannica, Inc. Available via Encyclopædia Britannica, In. https://www.britannica.com/event/Nurnberg-trials. Accessed 29 Apr 2026

European Court of Human Rights (1986) Case of Unterpertinger v. Austria (application no. 9120/80), judgment. European Court of Human Rights. https://hudoc.echr.coe.int/eng?i=001-57588. Accessed 29 Apr 2026

European Court of Human Rights (1993) Case of Saidi v. France (application no. 14647/89), judgment. European Court of Human Rights. https://hudoc.echr.coe.int/eng?i=001-57839. Accessed 29 Apr 2026

European Court of Human Rights (2001) Case of Ilijkov v. Bulgaria (application no. 33977/96), judgment. European Court of Human Rights. https://hudoc.echr.coe.int/eng?i=001-59613. Accessed 29 Apr 2026

[77] O'Reilly (2017), pp. 485–490.

[78] Kennedy and Düsterhöft (2017), pp. 137–172.

European Court of Human Rights (2021) European convention on human rights, as amended by protocols nos. 11, 14 and 15, supplemented by protocols nos. 1, 4, 6, 7, 12, 13 and 16. European Court of Human Rights. https://www.echr.coe.int/documents/d/echr/convention_ENG. Accessed 29 Apr 2026

Fedorova M (2017) The principle of equality of arms in international criminal proceedings. In: Rohan C, Zyberi G (eds) Defense perspectives on international criminal justice. Cambridge University Press, Cambridge, pp 204–234. https://www.cambridge.org/core/books/defense-perspectives-on-international-criminal-justice/principle-of-equality-of-arms-in-international-criminal-proceedings/197DF0897AB660510ED3A8DC5C506CF1

Fulford A (2011) Review committee response in relation to the OPCD interlocutor: Office of the Public Council for Defence. International Criminal Court. https://www.icc-cpi.int/sites/default/files/iccdocs/LT/OPCD/OPCDEng.pdf. Accessed 29 Apr 2026

Gibson K (2026) How do you sleep at night? Representing accused before the international courts. J of Intl Crim Just https://doi.org/10.1093/jicj/mqag021. Accessed 6 Jun 2026

Harris WR (1999) Tyranny on trial: the trial of the major German war criminals at the end of world war II, rev edn. Southern Methodist University Press, Dallas

House of Commons of the United Kingdom (1945) German war crimes trials. House of Commons of the United Kingdom. https://api.parliament.uk/historic-hansard/written-answers/1945/nov/19/german-war-crimes-trials. Accessed 29 Apr 2026

Human Rights Watch (2008) Courting history: The landmark International Criminal Court's first years. Human Rights Watch. https://www.hrw.org/report/2008/07/11/courting-history/landmark-international-criminal-courts-first-years. Accessed 29 Apr 2026

International Committee of the Red Cross (1945) Agreement for the prosecution and punishment of the major war criminals of the European axis, and charter of the International Military Tribunal, London, 8 August 1945. International Committee of the Red Cross. https://ihl-databases.icrc.org/assets/treaties/350-IHL-49-EN.pdf. Accessed 29 Apr 2026

International Criminal Court (2011) Code of professional conduct for counsel. International Criminal Court. https://www.icc-cpi.int/sites/default/files/Publications/Code-of-Professional-Conduct-for-counsel.pdf. Accessed 29 Apr 2026

International Criminal Court (2021) Rome statute of the International Criminal Court. International Criminal Court. https://www.icc-cpi.int/sites/default/files/2024-05/Rome-Statute-eng.pdf. Accessed 29 Apr 2026

International Criminal Court (2024) The office of public counsel for the defence. International Criminal Court. https://www.icc-cpi.int/sites/default/files/2024-08/2024-opcd-eng-v.4.pdf. Accessed 29 Apr 2026

International Criminal Court (2026) Defence. International Criminal Court. https://www.icc-cpi.int/about/defence. Accessed 29 Apr 2026

International Criminal Tribunal for the former Yugoslavia (1995) The prosecutor of the tribunal against Dusko Tadic a/k/a "Dule" a/k/a "Dusan," Goran Borovnica, indictment (amended). International Criminal Tribunal for the former Yugoslavia. https://www.icty.org/x/cases/tadic/ind/en/tad-2ai951214e.pdf. Accessed 29 Apr 2026

International Criminal Tribunal for the former Yugoslavia (1996) Prosecutor v. Duško Tadić a/k/a "Dule," decision on defence motion on hearsay. International Criminal Tribunal for the former Yugoslavia. https://www.legal-tools.org/doc/6c94b8. Accessed 29 Apr 2026

International Criminal Tribunal for the former Yugoslavia (1999a) Prosecutor v. Duško Tadić, judgement. International Criminal Tribunal for the former Yugoslavia. https://www.icty.org/x/cases/tadic/acjug/en/tad-aj990715e.pdf. Accessed 29 Apr 2026

International Criminal Tribunal for the former Yugoslavia (1999b) Prosecutor v. Zlatko Aleksovski, decision on prosecutor's appeal on admissibility of evidence. International Criminal Tribunal for the former Yugoslavia. https://www.icty.org/x/cases/aleksovski/acdec/en/90216EV36313.htm. Accessed 29 Apr 2026

International Criminal Tribunal for the former Yugoslavia (2004) Slobodan Milosevic v. prosecutor, decision on interlocutory appeal of the trial chamber's decision on the assignment of defense counsel. International Criminal Tribunal for the former Yugoslavia. https://www.icty.org/x/cases/slobodan_milosevic/acdec/en/041101.htm. Accessed 29 Apr 2026

International Criminal Tribunal for the former Yugoslavia (2006) Directive on the assignment of defence counsel (directive no. 1/94). International Criminal Tribunal for the former Yugoslavia. https://www.icty.org/x/file/Legal%20Library/Defence/Assignment_of_counsel_july2006.pdf. Accessed 29 Apr 2026

International Criminal Tribunal for the former Yugoslavia (2009) Code of professional conduct for counsel appearing before the International Tribunal. International Criminal Tribunal for the former Yugoslavia. https://www.icty.org/x/file/Legal%20Library/Defence/defence_code_of_conduct_july2009_en.pdf. Accessed 29 Apr 2026

International Criminal Tribunal for the former Yugoslavia (2010) Prosecutor v. Radovan Karadžić, public decision on Radovan Karadžić's appeal from decision on motion to vacate appointment of Richard Harvey. International Criminal Tribunal for the former Yugoslavia. https://www.icty.org/x/cases/karadzic/acdec/en/100212.pdf. Accessed 29 Apr 2026

International Criminal Tribunal for the former Yugoslavia (2026a) Chambers. International Criminal Tribunal for the former Yugoslavia. https://www.icty.org/en/about/chambers. Accessed 29 Apr 2026

International Criminal Tribunal for the former Yugoslavia (2026b) Office of the prosecutor. International Criminal Tribunal for the former Yugoslavia. https://www.icty.org/en/about/office-of-the-prosecutor. Accessed 29 Apr 2026

Kennedy D, Düsterhöft I (2017) The proper role for international defense counsel organizations. In: Rohan C, Zyberi G (eds) Defense perspectives on international criminal justice. Cambridge University Press, Cambridge, pp 137–172. https://www.cambridge.org/core/books/defense-perspectives-on-international-criminal-justice/proper-role-for-international-defense-counsel-organizations/FD286666EC18DD48D817A59C1D62ED05

Knoops GJA (2017) The pioneering role of defense counsel in international criminal trials. In: Rohan C, Zyberi G (eds) Defense perspectives on international criminal justice. Cambridge University Press, Cambridge, pp 7–40. https://www.cambridge.org/core/books/defense-perspectives-on-international-criminal-justice/pioneering-role-of-defense-counsel-in-international-criminal-trials/5E32A470FE18E33C3684C5D5FC4920F7

Minear RH (1971) Victors' justice: Tokyo war crimes trial. Princeton University Press, Princeton

Morrison H (2017) Foreword. In: Rohan C, Zyberi G (eds) Defense perspectives on international criminal justice. Cambridge University Press, Cambridge, pp xv–xviii. https://www.cambridge.org/core/books/defense-perspectives-on-international-criminal-justice/foreword/84298FD1826EF2AC356E0ABD6929A086

O'Reilly A (2017) Affirmative defenses in international criminal proceedings. In: Rohan C, Zyberi G (eds) Defense perspectives on international criminal justice. Cambridge University Press, Cambridge, pp 475–518. https://www.cambridge.org/core/books/defense-perspectives-on-international-criminal-justice/affirmative-defenses-in-international-criminal-proceedings/1627A2509E3F43A29BEA1FA902CAD191

Office of the United Nations High Commissioner for Human Rights (1966) International covenant on civil and political rights. Office of the United Nations High Commissioner for Human Rights. https://www.ohchr.org/en/instruments-mechanisms/instruments/international-covenant-civil-and-political-rights. Accessed 29 Apr 2026

Office of the United Nations High Commissioner for Human Rights (1990) Basic principles on the role of lawyers. Office of the United Nations High Commissioner for Human Rights. https://www.ohchr.org/en/instruments-mechanisms/instruments/basic-principles-role-lawyers. Accessed 29 Apr 2026

Reinhardt F, Feirabend L (2018) The development of the defence at the ICTY from an institutional perspective: Lessons learned with regard to counsel's qualification, remuneration and participation. International Crimes Database. https://www.internationalcrimesdatabase.org/upload/documents/20181011T154007-Reinhardt%20und%20Feirabend%20The%20Defence%20before%20the%20ICTY.pdf. Accessed 29 Apr 2026

Rohan C, Ackerman J (2017) The role of defense counsel on appeal. In: Rohan C, Zyberi G (eds) Defense perspectives on international criminal justice. Cambridge University Press, Cambridge, pp 312–346. https://www.cambridge.org/core/books/defense-perspectives-on-international-criminal-justice/role-of-defense-counsel-on-appeal/3D28B414EAD7EAEB1853E73F0DB0A602

Temminck Tuinstra J (2009) Defence counsel in international criminal law. C. Asser Press, the Hague, T.M

Temminck Tuinstra J (2010) Defending the defenders: the role of defence counsel in international criminal trials. J of Intl Crim Just 8(2):463–486. https://doi.org/10.1093/jicj/mqp085

United Nations Interregional Crime and Justice Institute, Association of Defence Counsel Practising Before the International Criminal Tribunal for the former Yugoslavia (2011) Manual on international criminal defence ADC-ICTY developed practices. https://www.icty.org/x/file/About/Reports%20and%20Publications/manual_developed_practices/ADC_ICTY_developed_practices_en.pdf. Accessed 29 Apr 2026

United Nations Security Council (1993) Resolution 827 (1993), adopted by the Security Council at its 3217th meeting, on 25 May 1993. In: United Nations Digital Library. United Nations Security Council. Accessible via UNDOCS. https://digitallibrary.un.org/record/166567. Accessed 29 Apr 2026

United Nations Security Council (1994) Resolution 955 (1994), adopted by the Security Council at its 3453rd meeting, on 8 November 1994. In: United Nations Digital Library. United Nations Security Council. Accessible via UNDOCS. https://digitallibrary.un.org/record/198038. Accessed 29 Apr 2026

Wald PM (2001) The international criminal Tribunal for the Former Yugoslavia comes of age: some observations on day-to-day dilemmas of an international court. Washington Univ J of L and Policy 5(1):87–123. https://openscholarship.wustl.edu/law_journal_law_policy/vol5/iss1/9. Accessed 6 Jun 2026

Wilson RJ (2006) A history of the role of defense counsel in international criminal and war crimes tribunals. In: Bohlander M, Boed R, Wilson RJ (eds) Defense in international criminal proceedings. Transnational Publishers, Ardsley, pp 31–66. https://doi.org/10.1163/ej.9781571053312.i-900.17

Yale Law School Lillian Goldman Law Library (2008) Defendants and defense counsel. In: The Avalon project. Yale Law School Lillian Goldman Law Library. Accessible via the Avalon Project. https://avalon.law.yale.edu/imt/defense.asp. Accessed 29 Apr 2026

Chapter 9
Conclusion: A Foundation of Justice for the Future

One could have imagined a different world. The mass atrocities unleashed during the Balkans War of the early 1990's could have been forgotten or negotiated away with amnesties by the warring parties and the major powers that managed peace talks. The genocide in Rwanda could have fallen into a legal black hole similar to how other mass killings had disappeared from the global agenda throughout history, including since World War II. The civil war in Sierra Leone, with its mutilated and murdered civilians scarring its society during the 1990's, might have been deemed far too inconsequential to merit a special hybrid court requiring the engagement of the United Nations and powerful nations to finance, build, and operate. The atrocity crimes of the Pol Pot regime in Cambodia during the late 1970's, leading to an estimated two million deaths, easily could have been swept into the dustbin of history without bothering to pursue justice and build an empire of evidence in treacherous political waters decades later.

In that altered world what one man, Hissène Habré, was responsible for inflicting upon his own people in Chad during a reign of terror in the 1980's might have become a historical footnote had not a judicial reckoning in a special court sitting in Senegal emerged many years later. The U.N. Security Council never would have referred the atrocity crimes in Darfur, Sudan, to the International Criminal Court in 2005 if the United States had decided to veto rather than abstain on the critical resolution of referral. And the institutional risks associated with the International Criminal Court charging national leaders of atrocity crimes in Africa, the Middle East, Asia, and Russia might have been threatening enough to forestall the arrest warrants that ultimately were approved. Indeed, the negotiations leading to the creation of the International Criminal Court might have derailed in any number of ways, either stalling its establishment or resulting in a far different type of court from that which exists today in The Hague.

The regional human rights courts of Europe, Latin America, and Africa might have been overwhelmed with national pressures to back off of judgments that held governments accountable for human rights abuses growing far too common on those

D. J. Scheffer and M. S. Ellis, *The Story of Modern International Justice, 1993-2025*,
https://doi.org/10.1007/978-3-032-33243-1_9

continents or to reveal the facts of climate change and the duties of governments to confront these truths. The Council of Europe may never have gathered the courage to create alongside the Government of Ukraine a new special tribunal to investigate and prosecute the crime of aggression, an outcome that would have rendered impotent, in connection with one of the most blatant and destructive wars of aggression in modern times, a key Nuremberg Principle and a foundational tenet of the United Nations Charter, each outlawing acts and wars of aggression.

The right to a fair trial and the critical importance of defense counsel in the complex litigation that arises in situations of atrocity crimes and the role of political and military leaders may never have been tested and strengthened to the degree that clearly has occurred if not for the opportunities afforded by the criminal trials in the new tribunals of the last 30 years.

The International Court of Justice may never have discovered its own jurisdiction to adjudicate cases brought by aggrieved governments which had experienced or decided on behalf of others to confront genocide, torture, military assaults or occupation in the Balkans, the Democratic Republic of the Congo, or Myanmar. The political will may never have coalesced within the U.N. General Assembly to request advisory opinions from the International Court of Justice about the legality of the threat or use of nuclear weapons or the obligations of States with respect to climate change.

Yet, all of this did not come to pass. In fact, international justice was discovered, pronounced, fortified, and expanded because courts of international or hybrid character rendered historic rulings at times of great peril in world affairs. These judicial interventions occurred during three decades of massive violence against civilian populations following the end of the Cold War, an era that also increasingly witnessed the existential challenges of climate change.

In this book we have highlighted some of the judicial interventions that should be remembered in order to understand their intrinsic importance to the pursuit of international justice and to stand in deterrence of further violations of the international law underpinning each such intervention. Cataloguing all of the contributions during the years of 1993 through 2025 in such domains of global rule of law as international humanitarian law, the law of war, international criminal law, international human rights law, international environmental law, and international law in its more general character by the courts and tribunals identified in this book would constitute a monumental feat of scholarship that we did not attempt to undertake. Those contributions are practically unfathomable in their entirety—they will be identified and enforced as courts draw upon them as precedents in future cases (international, regional, and national) during the decades that follow. But here we summarize the cases we described in this book:

At the International Court of Justice ("ICJ"), acts of genocide and the mental intent required to commit the crime of genocide as a matter of state responsibility were adjudicated for the first time in two cases that involved, first, *Bosnia and Herzegovina versus Serbia* and second, *Croatia versus Serbia* (see Sect. 2.1), years after the war in the Balkans had ended. Central to these cases was the Convention on the Prevention and Punishment of the Crime of Genocide (the "Genocide Convention").[1] The ICJ determined critical criteria that are required for a finding of genocide under the Genocide Convention and also confirmed the duty under the Genocide Convention that states have a responsibility to prevent genocide and punish those who commit the crime of genocide. Further, the ICJ took an interpretative leap in the reading of the Genocide Convention as a treaty that also prohibits states from committing the crime of genocide, a common sensical conclusion but one that required judicial confirmation to be enforced.

The ICJ essentially liberated the legal principle of *erga omnes partes* from a relatively long slumber. In three cases involving defendant nations Senegal, Myanmar, and Israel (see Sect. 2.2) and spanning from the early 2000's to the present day, the ICJ reaffirmed that a State Party to the same international treaty concerning human rights, in particular, has standing to bring any other State Party of the same treaty to the court of jurisdiction, and in these cases that court means the ICJ, for violation of the state responsibilities under that treaty. The plaintiff State Party need not have incurred any direct injury under the treaty; rather, it would act in the interest of the universal principles at stake in and protected by the treaty. The two international treaties were the Convention Against Torture and Other Cruel, Inhuman or Degrading Treatment or Punishment[2] regarding Senegal, with Belgium pleading the case, and the Genocide Convention regarding Myanmar, with The Gambia pleading the case, and Israel, with South Africa and other states parties of the Genocide Convention seeking enforcement of that treaty. The ICJ's fulsome embrace of *erga omnes partes* in recent years has expanded the vista of litigation at the ICJ for governments employing that principle to enforce the fundamental human rights enshrined in a host of international treaties.

The ICJ's *Advisory Opinion on Climate Change* in 2025[3] confirmed a wide range of obligations of States arising under treaties and customary international law, points that previously had not been so clearly and authoritatively enunciated by an international court. (see Sect. 2.4) Almost thirty years earlier the ICJ issued an advisory opinion on the legality of threat or use by a state of nuclear weapons in armed conflict.[4] That advisory opinion barely rationalized the use of a nuclear weapon in the exercise of an inherent right of individual or collective self-defense, but under conditions that are difficult to imagine could ever be satisfied. The ICJ presented States with an almost implausible set of determinations under international law that would be required of a State determining whether to threaten or use nuclear weapons. But in its self-defense against an aggressive State's attack using nuclear weapons, a State might find a slim reed of logic in the ICJ's advisory opinion for the use of nuclear weapons. For those who find even this possibility an abdication of morality by the defending State given the massive death and destructiveness of any use of a nuclear weapon, the ICJ nonetheless provided a legal shield to defend against and

[1] Office of the United Nations High Commissioner for Human Rights (1948).

[2] Office of the United Nations High Commissioner for Human Rights (1984).

[3] International Court of Justice (2025).

[4] International Court of Justice (2026).

thus possibly survive, as a population and as a civilization, an offensive nuclear attack. (see Sect. 2.5)

Among the hundreds of trial and appeals rulings that emerged from the jurisprudence of the *ad hoc* international and hybrid criminal tribunals built since 1993, we have focused on a set of judgments that reflect key advancements in the march of international criminal justice for commission of atrocity crimes over more than three decades:

- *International Criminal Tribunal for the former Yugoslavia (ICTY) and International Residual Mechanism for Criminal Tribunals (IRMCT).* The *Tadić* judgment confirmed the UN Security Council's authority to create international criminal tribunals, the range of atrocity crimes that can be prosecuted in connection with international conflicts and non-international conflicts, respectively, how to establish "overall control" of a state over an armed non-state group, the elimination of an armed conflict requirement in the prosecution of crimes against humanity, and creation of the "joint criminal enterprise" mode of liability. (see Sect. 3.1.1) In the *Furundžija* judgment, the ICTY Trial Chamber concluded that the prohibition of torture is a *jus cogens* norm of international law and it provided detailed modern definitions of the crime of torture and of rape. (see Sect. 3.1.2) In *Galic*, the ICTY Trial Chamber confirmed the crime of spreading terror among the civilian population (in this case of Sarajevo) as a war crime, and that it has long existed in customary international law. (see Sect. 3.1.3) The *Karadžić* and *Mladić* judgments in the ICTY and IRMCT affirmed various types of joint criminal enterprises and thus firmly entrenched them in international criminal law. Judgements in these two cases also strengthened important criteria, particularly for specific intent and reasonable inference, in the commission of the crime of genocide. (see Sect. 3.1.4)
- *International Criminal Tribunal for Rwanda (ICTR).* The pathbreaking *Akayesu* judgment rendered precedents in international criminal law that resonated through all subsequent cases that were prosecuted before the ICTR and often before other tribunals. In *Akayesu*, the Trial Chamber identified ethnic identity from a pragmatic and historical perspective, found that rape and sexual violence can be acts of genocide, clarified how to understand incitement to commit crimes against humanity or war crimes, and found that crimes against humanity need not be committed with discriminatory intent. (see Sect. 3.2.1) In *Nahimana, Barayagwiza, and Ngeze*, otherwise known as the *Media Case*, the ICTR Appeals Chamber imposed a strict discipline on interpreting the temporal jurisdiction of the ICTR, set forth critical guidelines for determining direct and public incitement to commit genocide, found that hate speech targeting a population on ethnic grounds or on any other discriminatory grounds can constitute "factual discrimination" and can be of equivalent gravity as other crimes against humanity and can constitute acts of persecution, and provided strong foundational reasoning for judicial notice of genocide having occurred in Rwanda. (see Sect. 3.2.2)
- *Special Court for Sierra Leone (SCSL).* In *Prosecutor v. Charles Taylor*, the Appeals Chamber affirmed that the principle of head of state immunity "does not

and cannot apply before an international criminal tribunal that has a sound international legal basis," and concluded that the Special Court for Sierra Leone qualified as such a tribunal. The Appeals Chamber cemented the governing legal standard for aiding and abetting liability with a two-prong test of required elements for *actus reus* (act) and *mens rea* (mental element), enforced a norm prohibiting the enlistment, conscription or using of children under the age of 15 years to participate actively in hostilities, and judicially established a direct nexus between the illegal exploitation of natural resources and the commission of atrocity crimes. (see Sect. 4.1.1) The judgment of the Appeals Chamber of the SCSL in *Prosecutor v. Brima, Kamara & Kanu* identified, for the first time, the practice of "forced marriage" as one of the "other inhumane acts" constituting a crime against humanity and thus set the stage years later for the Extraordinary Chambers in the Courts of Cambodia and the International Criminal Court to convict individuals of this crime against humanity. (see Sect. 4.1.2)

- *The Extraordinary Chambers in the Courts of Cambodia (ECCC).* The Extraordinary Chambers in the Courts of Cambodia experienced a larger total number of visitors over its operational life than any other modern atrocity crimes tribunal and it included civil parties in the trial framework to significant levels of participation and developed a novel reparations scheme for the victims of the atrocity crimes being adjudicated before the court. In the *Duch* case, the Supreme Court Chamber of the ECCC ruled on i) the meaning of "senior leader" and someone "most responsible" for the atrocity crimes, thus establishing the parameters of personal jurisdiction, ii) the meaning of the crime of humanity of "enslavement," iii) the determination of rape as constituting the crime against humanity of torture, iv) the *mens rea* and *actus reus* requirements of the crime against humanity of persecution, v) how the gravity of the crimes should be reflected in sentencing (in this case a life sentence), and vi) how to determine "close family members" in order to qualify as civil parties in the case. (see Sect. 4.2.1) In *Nuon Chea and Khieu Samphan*, the Supreme Court Chamber confirmed important parameters of several crimes against humanity such as murder, extermination, other inhumane acts, and persecution and fully embraced a finding of joint criminal enterprise, thus strengthening its place in international criminal law. (see Sect. 4.2.2) Finally, in its 2022 judgment in *Khieu Sampan*, which followed the death of Nuon Chea in 2019 before it could rule on his appeal of the same Trial Chamber judgment in Case 002/02, the Supreme Court Chamber of the ECCC found

    (i) that the crime against humanity of extermination can occur in a number of locations,
    (ii) that the arrest of people *en masse* does not preclude a finding of persecution on political grounds,
    (iii) that particular conduct as "other inhumane acts" need not be expressly criminalized under international law, "as this would render the concept of other inhumane acts as a residual category unnecessary,"
    (iv) that "forced sexual intercourse in the context of forced marriage, fell within the scope of crime against humanity of other inhumane acts" and that

"the victims of forced sexual intercourse comprise both female and male victims,"

(v) that "the common purpose that is the object of the planned action among several persons must be of a criminal character, in the sense that it either amounted to or involved the commission of a crime" and that the Communist Party of Kampuchea's plan for a socialist revolution in Cambodia was indeed criminal in nature,

(vi) that where the participants in a joint criminal enterprise share an agreement to commit a crime with *dolus eventualis* (foreseeing the possibility of the crime) in furtherance of the common purpose, that crime is encompassed by the common purpose and thus can be prosecuted, and

(vii) confirmed key interpretations of the crime of genocide taking into account years of jurisprudence. (see Sect. 4.2.3)

- *Special Tribunal for Lebanon (STL).* The Appeals Chamber of the Special Tribunal for Lebanon discovered a fulsome rationale for reading the Lebanese Criminal Code in the context of a modern interpretation of international terrorism, holding that Lebanese law cannot be properly interpreted without taking into account international law developments that Lebanon itself has been an active participant in, particularly with respect to commitments under international treaties, and the march of customary international law in world affairs. The Appeals Chamber proceeded, then, to define the customary international rule regarding the international crime of terrorism, with three key elements—a feat never before undertaken by a court of such origin and character in international criminal law. (see Sect. 4.3.1)
- *Extraordinary African Chambers (EAC).* The novel creation of the Extraordinary African Chambers in Senegal that prosecuted only one individual, Hissène Habré, the former president of Chad, resulted in a trial that culminated in 2017 with a conviction that created important precedents in international criminal law. The EAC applied a hybrid methodology to fuse national and international criminal law into the mandate of a court integrated into Senegal's national judiciary. Bridging both fields of law, the EAC found Habré guilty of torture and extrajudicial killings as a direct perpetrator, as a member of a joint criminal enterprise, and as a superior exercising command responsibility. The EAC thus identified several forms of liability for crimes that Habré directly ordered or participated in and for crimes committed by subordinates within the security apparatus operating under his authority. (see Sect. 4.4.1)

In Chap. 5 we examined two significant judgments of the permanent International Criminal Court ("ICC"), starting with *Prosecutor v. Dominic Ongwen.* The ICC Appeals Chamber reconfirmed the crime against humanity of forced marriage as a form of "other inhumane acts," found that forced pregnancy could be charged and adjudicated as both a crime against humanity and as a war crime, strengthened sexual and gender-based crimes by distinguishing among the crimes of forced marriage, forced pregnancy, rape, and sexual slavery, and reduced Ongwen's sentence because of his experience as a child soldier but rejected the argument of victimization as a defense to the charges against him. In a subsequent ruling in 2025, the ICC Appeals Chamber confirmed a large financial reparations order for the benefit of the victims of Ongwen's crimes against humanity and war crimes of Euro 52,490,000, marking a new phase of reckoning for international criminal justice. (see Sect. 5.1)

In *Prosecutor v. Ali Muhammad Ali Abd-At-Rahman*, the ICC Trial Chamber convicted a *Janjaweed* militia leader who operated in Darfur, Sudan, during 2003 and 2004, with commission of war crimes and crimes against humanity and sentenced him to 20 years of imprisonment. That verdict remains on appeal as of this writing. But the Trial Chamber's lengthy and comprehensive judgment addresses many important characteristics of war crimes and crimes against humanity that will resonate through future litigation before the ICC. These include how to assess whether an attack is directed at a civilian population, the power of public speech by leaders that creates the context for commission of atrocity crimes and incite perpetrators to follow through with the incendiary rhetoric, how to assess the destruction of an enemy population's property under rules of military necessity and the international law of armed conflict, how to determine rape and torture each as a crime against humanity and a war crime, and what is meant by the term "outrages upon personal dignity as a war crime," including how the humiliation of victims can be part of that meaning. (see Sect. 5.2)

The arrest warrant issued by the ICC in March 2023 against Vladimir Putin, President of the Russian Federation, for war crimes committed in connection with the Russia/Ukraine war has not yet led to trial and judgment because Putin remains an indicted fugitive. But we tell the story of how the ICC ultimately indicted Putin (as well as another Russian official, Maria Alekseyevna Lvova-Belova, Commissioner for Children's Rights in the Office of the President of the Russian Federation) for war crimes connected to the abduction of Ukrainian children to Russia and the historic importance of the Putin arrest warrant. (see Sect. 5.3) Following its indictments of Putin and Lvova-Belova, the ICC indicted four senior Russian military officials on charges of war crimes and crimes against humanity, all of whom remain at large.[5] One can best conclude at this stage "to watch this space" as the arrest warrants and future trials of atrocity crimes committed during the Russia/Ukraine War will doubtless proliferate at the ICC.

Beyond the ICC, the Russian aggression against Ukraine that began in 2014 and accelerated following the massive incursion on Ukrainian territory on 28 February 2022 led to the creation in 2025 of the Special Tribunal for the Crime of Aggression against Ukraine (STCA). This tribunal's work lies mostly ahead, as investigations, indictments, arrest warrants, and ultimately trials unfold in the years to come. As described in Chap. 6, the STCA was established by treaty between the Council of Europe and the Government of Ukraine and has jurisdiction over only one crime—aggression—which the ICC cannot prosecute in the situation of Ukraine for reasons peculiar to the amendments that activated the crime of aggression under the Rome Statute. The importance of the STCA cannot be overstated as it will likely be the first criminal tribunal of international character since the IMT at Nuremberg and its

[5] International Criminal Court (2024a, 2024b).

partner in Tokyo to investigate and prosecute senior leaders of a nation that initiated, and continued for years, a massive war of aggression against another nation. Such a prospect for accountability was barely imagined in the early post-Cold War years. (see Chap. 6)

The three prominent regional human rights courts that are described in Chap. 7 have built an impressive record in the defense of human rights and holding governments responsible for gross violations of them. They represent leaps in international justice over the last three decades. But most of their rulings rarely seize the public's attention or imagination. We thought it important essentially to alert the reader to some of the judgments emerging from these regional courts and encourage victims of human rights abuses in Europe, Latin America, and Africa to consider the value of bringing their cases before such courts.

At the European Court of Human Rights, judges from the member states of the Council of Europe found in *Bankovic and Others v. Belgium and Others* that there are limits to the territorial jurisdiction of a treaty such as the European Convention on Human Rights[6] but also presaged the findings in later cases that would trigger jurisdiction over extra-territorial acts in the use of military force. (see Sect. 7.1.1) In *Finogenov and Others v. Russia*, the European Court of Human Rights enforced the right to life in the context of deficient government planning and operations to save people who were being held hostage by terrorists. (see Sect. 7.1.2) In *Scoppola v. Italy (No. 3)*, the Grand Chamber of the European Court ruled on the balancing act required of a national legislature in determining the rules of disenfranchisement of the right to vote for convicted persons. (see Sect. 7.1.3) In *Ukraine and Netherlands v. Russia*, the European Court took the unprecedented step of drawing from all three bodies of the law of war, international humanitarian law, and international human rights law in examining Russian military operations in Ukraine since 2014, including the war of aggression that accelerated with the invasion of 28 February 2022 and up to September 2022 when Russia withdrew from the Council of Europe and the European Convention on Human Rights. The findings included the triggering of the European Convention's human rights protections when Russia launched its attacks in 2014 and thereafter, rejecting arguments that international human rights law was inapplicable during times of war, finding that Russia guided the plans and operations of the separatists in Ukraine and thus attributed responsibility to Russia for the acts of non-state groups, and setting the stage for criminal investigations by the International Criminal Court. (see Sect. 7.1.4)

The Inter-American Court of Human Rights delivered judgment in *Barrio Altos v. Peru* denying the legitimacy of Peruvian amnesty laws for members of security forces and civilians accused and convicted of human rights violations during specific periods of time and specific incidents, describing them as incompatible with the American Convention on Human Rights[7] and thus illegal, and broadening the ruling to apply to any other human rights cases in Peru. (see Sect. 7.2.1) In *Mayagna (Sumo) Awas Tingni Community v Nicaragua*, the Inter-American Court upheld the property rights

[6] European Court of Human Rights (2021).

[7] Organization of American States (2011).

of indigenous communities and the responsibility of the Government of Nicaragua to legally designate territory to the indigenous community and abstain from any actions that would undermine that process. (see Sect. 7.2.2)

In *The Miguel Castro Castro Prison v. Peru*, the Inter-American Court found violations of the right to life and of humane treatment in a horrific and deadly assault by security personnel on the inmates of a maximum security prison, followed in the aftermath by violations of the right to a fair trial and to judicial protection. (see Sect. 7.2.3) In *Miskito Divers v. Honduras*, the Inter-American Court rendered a pathbreaking ruling about how companies engaged in the lobster diving business were violating the human rights of the divers and their next of kin, and that the Government of Honduras was failing to exercise its duties under the American Convention on Human Rights. The Inter-American Court found that Honduras incurred responsibility for the right to life, the right to have physical, mental and moral integrity respected, and the rights of the child under the American Convention, as well as violating its duties to guarantee just, equitable and satisfactory working conditions, medical care, and social security benefits for the survivors of accidents. (see Sect. 7.2.4) In its historic *Advisory Opinion 32/25 on the Climate Emergency and Human Rights* (2025), the Inter-American Court authoritatively interprets binding law on the Member States of the Organization of American States that fuses the climate emergency with fundamental human rights principles and the ravages of poverty. The list of obligatory duties that the Member States must undertake is long and comprehensively set forth in the advisory opinion, which is a wake-up call to action in the face of a climate emergency that the Inter-American Court determined clearly exists under the facts. (see Sect. 7.2.5)

The African Court of Human and Peoples' Rights has had far fewer cases on its docket given its much shorter term of operations when compared with the two other regional human rights courts. But among those cases in Africa there have been impressive rulings in the protection of human rights. In *APDR & IHRDA v. Mali*, the African Court set the country of Mali on a new path towards rules of marriage that would align with international human rights law. (see Sect. 7.3.1) In *Chalula v. United Republic of Tanzania*, the African Court determined that the death penalty in Tanzania should not be automatically imposed upon sentencing but rather is subject to the discretionary authority of the trial court judge. (see Sect. 7.3.2) In *Ibrahim Ben Mohamed Ben Brahim Belguith v. Republic of Tunisia*, the African Court found that certain Presidential decrees in Tunisia were legally deficient and disproportionately disrupted the work of the government, and that Article 1 of the African Charter of Human and Peoples' Rights had been violated by failing to operationalize Tunisia's Constitutional Court to give effect to its citizens' right to be heard in challenging the constitutionality of Presidential decrees, thus violating their right to participate in political affairs of their country directly and through their freely chosen representatives. (see Sect. 7.3.3)

In all of these courts and tribunals the participation of competent defense counsel is paramount and without whom the entire endeavor to build international justice upon the bedrock of due process and fair trials would be futile. The modern atrocity crimes tribunals and regional human rights courts can credit their impressive record—including convictions, acquittals, and insistence on requiring adherence to minimum standards of professional conduct for judicial proceedings—on the critical role played by defense counsel in the pursuit of credible justice. In Chap. 8 we describe the initiatives during the last three decades that have forged a strong international defense counsel bar and the institutional bodies created within the tribunals and courts to ensure a strong defense presence in trials and other legal proceedings. The International Bar Association has played a major role in this endeavor. (see Chap. 8)

We firmly believe that despite waves of cynicism about the future of international law and international organizations that built the international order of the post-World War II era, the record of international justice during the last three decades has been remarkably productive in demonstrating the resilience and growth of the rule of law. This record is a foundation of justice for the future that individuals, civil society, governments, courts, and international organizations can stand on in their struggles to achieve peace, prevent and confront atrocity crimes, manage climate change, and protect human rights and fundamental freedoms.

References

European Court of Human Rights (2021) European convention on human rights, as amended by protocols nos. 11, 14 and 15, supplemented by protocols nos. 1, 4, 6, 7, 12, 13 and 16. European Court of Human Rights. Retrieved from https://www.echr.coe.int/documents/d/echr/convention_ENG. Accessed on May 8 2026

International Criminal Court (2024a) Situation in Ukraine: ICC judges issue arrest warrants against Sergei Ivanovich Kobylash and Viktor Nikolayevich Sokolov. International Criminal Court. Retrieved from https://www.icc-cpi.int/news/situation-ukraine-icc-judges-issue-arrest-warrants-against-sergei-ivanovich-kobylash-and. Accessed on May 8 2026

International Criminal Court (2024b) Situation in Ukraine: ICC judges issue arrest warrants against Sergei Kuzhugetovich Shoigu and Valery Vasilyevich Gerasimov. International Criminal Court. Retrieved from https://www.icc-cpi.int/news/situation-ukraine-icc-judges-issue-arrest-warrants-against-sergei-kuzhugetovich-shoigu-and. Accessed on May 8 2026

International Court of Justice (2025) Obligations of states in respect of climate change, advisory opinion. International Court of Justice. Accessible via ICJ Reports. Retrieved from https://www.icj-cij.org/sites/default/files/case-related/187/187–20250723-adv-01-00-en.pdf. Accessed on May 8 2026

International Court of Justice (2026) Legality of the threat or use of nuclear weapons. International Court of Justice. Retrieved from https://www.icj-cij.org/case/95. Accessed on May 8 2026

Office of the United Nations High Commissioner for Human Rights (1948) Convention on the Prevention and Punishment of the Crime of Genocide. Office of the United Nations High Commissioner for Human Rights. Retrieved from https://www.ohchr.org/en/instruments-mechanisms/instruments/convention-prevention-and-punishment-crime-genocide. Accessed on May 8 2026

Office of the United Nations High Commissioner for Human Rights (1984) Convention against torture and other cruel, inhuman or degrading treatment or punishment. Office of the United Nations High Commissioner for Human Rights. Retrieved from https://www.ohchr.org/en/instruments-mechanisms/instruments/convention-against-torture-and-other-cruel-inhuman-or-degrading. Accessed on May 8 2026

Organization of American States (2011) American convention on human rights "pact of San Jose, Costa Rica" (B-32). Organization of American States. Retrieved from https://www.oas.org/dil/treaties_b-32_american_convention_on_human_rights.pdf. Accessed on May 8 2026

Appendix

*Disposition of Criminal Cases Before the Modern Atrocity Crimes Tribunals (1993–2025) (*Data in the Appendix has been drawn from the web sites of the tribunals and courts and of the United Nations.)

International Criminal Tribunal for the former Yugoslavia (ICTY)

- Convictions: 93
- Acquittals: 18
- Indictments: 161
- Died before or after transfer to the ICTY: 17
- Overall budget 1993–2017: ~ $2.45 billion

International Criminal Tribunal for Rwanda (ICTR)

- Convictions: 62
- Acquittals: 14
- Indictments: 93
- Deaths before or during trial: 4
- Overall budget 1994–2015: ~ $2 billion

International Residual Mechanism for Criminal Tribunals (IRMCT)

- Convictions: 6
- Acquittals: 0
- Overall budget 2012–2026: $994,678,000

Special Court for Sierra Leone (SCSL)

- Convictions: 9
- Acquittals: 0
- Indictments: 13

D. J. Scheffer and M. S. Ellis, *The Story of Modern International Justice, 1993-2025*, https://doi.org/10.1007/978-3-032-33243-1

- Deaths before or during trial: 3
- Indicted fugitives still at large: 1 (Johnny Paul Koroma's case remains open, though he is presumed to be dead)
- Overall budget: ~ $300 million

Extraordinary Chambers in the Courts of Cambodia (ECCC) (cases 001–004)

- Convictions: 3
- Acquittals: 0
- Indictments in cases 001 and 002: 5
- Investigated in cases 003 and 004 but not indicted: 4
- Deaths during trial/appeals: 3
- Cessation of participation in trial due to cognitive condition: 1
- Total public attendance at the trial proceedings: approximately 250,000 Cambodians
- Overall budget 2006–2022: ~ $337 million

Special Tribunal for Lebanon (STL)

- Convictions: 3 (additional 2 convictions for contempt of court and obstruction of justice)
- Acquittals: 1 (additional 2 acquittals for contempt of court and obstruction of justice)
- Indictments: 5 (of primary suspects)
- Deaths before or during trial: 1
- Overall budget 2007–2023: ~ $1 billion

Extraordinary African Chambers (AFC)

- Convictions: 1
- Acquittals: 0
- Indictments: 1
- Overall budget: ~ €8.6 million

International Criminal Court (ICC) (as of July 2026)

- Convictions: 13
- Acquittals: 4
- Arrest warrants: 61
- Detained and appearing in court: 22
- Indicted fugitives at large: 32
- Number of cases: 34
- Deaths following charges: 9
- Annual budget of ICC in 2026: € 196,852,900
- Overall budget 2002–2026: ~ € 3 billion

www.ingramcontent.com/pod-product-compliance
Ingram Content Group UK Ltd.
Pitfield, Milton Keynes, MK11 3LW, UK
UKHW021521200826
14574UKWH00003BA/22
* 9 7 8 3 0 3 2 3 3 2 4 2 4 *